THE AUTHOR   SinhaRaja Tammita-Delgoda is from the old Sinhalese capital of Kandy, high in the central highlands of Sri Lanka. He made his first trip to India at the age of seventeen, when he travelled by train from northern India all the way down to the very tip of the subcontinent, only to find that the ferry home to Sri Lanka had just sunk. He is a historian who has studied the history of British India and he has published articles in various countries on both India and Sri Lanka. He has an MA in Medieval Literature and Society from York University and he completed his PhD in 1991 at King's College, London. He is also a Fellow of the Royal Asiatic Society. At present he lives in Sri Lanka.

SERIES EDITOR   Professor Denis Judd is a graduate of Oxford, a Fellow of the Royal Historical Society and Professor of History at the University of North London. He has published over 20 books including the biographies of Joseph Chamberlain, Prince Philip, George VI and Alison Uttley, historical and military subjects, stories for children and two novels. His most recent book is the highly praised *Empire: The British Imperial Experience from 1765 to the Present*. He has reviewed and written extensively in the national press and in journals, has written several radio programmes and is a regular contributor to British and overseas radio and television.

Cover illustration: detail of *The Palace at Amber* by William Simpson *c* 1861. India Office Library and Records.

Other Titles in the Series

A Traveller's History of Australia
A Traveller's History of the Caribbean
A Traveller's History of China
A Traveller's History of England
A Traveller's History of France
A Traveller's History of Greece
A Traveller's History of Ireland
A Traveller's History of Italy
A Traveller's History of Japan
A Traveller's History of London
A Traveller's History of North Africa
A Traveller's History of Paris
A Traveller's History of Russia and the USSR
A Traveller's History of Scotland
A Traveller's History of Spain
A Traveller's History of Turkey

W9-AHB-466

THE TRAVELLER'S HISTORY SERIES

'Ideal before-you-go reading' *The Daily Telegraph*

'An excellent series of brief histories' *New York Times*

'I want to compliment you . . . on the brilliantly concise
contents of your books' *Shirley Conran*

Reviews of Individual Titles

A Traveller's History of France
'Undoubtedly the best way to prepare for a trip to France is
to bone up on some history. *The Traveller's History of France*
by Robert Cole is concise and gives the essential facts in a
very readable form.' *The Independent*

A Traveller's History of China
'The author manages to get 2 million years into 300 pages.
An excellent addition to a series which is already invaluable,
whether you're travelling or not.' *The Guardian*

A Traveller's History of India
'For anyone . . . planning a trip to India, the latest in the
excellent Traveller's History series . . . provides a useful
grounding for those whose curiosity exceeds the time
available for research' *The London Evening Standard*

A Traveller's History of Japan
'It succeeds admirably in its goal of making the present
country comprehensible through a narrative of its past, with
asides on everything from bonsai to *zazen*, in a brisk, highly
readable style . . . you could easily read it on the flight over,
if you skip the movie,' *The Washington Post*

A Traveller's History of Ireland
'For independent, inquisitive travellers traversing the green
roads of Ireland, there is no better guide than *A Traveller's
History of Ireland*.' *Small Press*

A Traveller's History of India

Dedication

To many friends I made along the way and some I lost.
Remembering Tchelva, whose friendship and support sustained me
while I was writing this. For Cyril, to wish him joy and happiness in
the years ahead. For Sunder, who never helped at all at any time and
the earthy and irrepressible Sarnaik.

On the subcontinent, to Bala, who introduced me to the
sport of kings and treated me like one, and Omprakash Kejariwal,
who always treats me like a son. For Iqbal, my favourite Mughal
relic, dilettante socialist and sybarite, and Beena, always a ray of
laughter and light.

In my own country, this work is dedicated to Siran, kinsman
and true Radala, 'Father', friend and companion, to whom I owe
a very great debt.

SR.

A Traveller's History of India

SECOND EDITION

SINHARAJA TAMMITA-DELGODA

Series Editor DENIS JUDD
Line drawings JOHN HOSTE

INTERLINK BOOKS
An Imprint of Interlink Publishing Group, Inc.
NEW YORK

First American edition published 1999 by

INTERLINK BOOKS
An imprint of Interlink Publishing Group, Inc.
99 Seventh Avenue • Brooklyn, New York 11215 and
46 Crosby Street • Northampton, Massachusetts 01060

Published simultaneously in Great Britain by The Windrush Press

Text © SinhaRaja Tammita-Delgoda 1995, 1999
Preface © Denis Judd 1995, 1999

The right of SinhaRaja Tammita-Delgoda to be identified as author of
this work has been asserted by him in accordance with the Copyright
Designs and Patents Act of 1988.

Library of Congress Cataloging-in-Publication Data

Tammita-Delgoda, SinhaRaja
    A traveller's history of India / SinhaRaja Tammita-Delgoda. – 1st
American ed.
        p.   cm. – (Traveller's history)
    Includes bibliographical references and index.
    ISBN 1-56656-306-2 $2290 6084$ $\frac{1}{00}$
    1. India–History. I. Title. II. Series.
DS436.T17   1999
954–dc20   94–36800
                                                    CIP

Printed and bound in Canada

To order or request our complete catalog,
please call us at **1-800-238-LINK** or write to:
Interlink Publishing
46 Crosby Street, Northampton, MA 01060
e-mail: interpg@aol.com • website: www.interlinkbooks.com

Contents

Preface

India boasts one of the oldest, most complex and most fascinating civilisations in the world, and a history reaching back 4,000 years. The philosophies and religions that have evolved there are even more attractive and intriguing today, perhaps particularly to Westerners. Tourism to India is on the increase, especially at the package end of the market. Anyone visiting India for the first time will be bombarded with a host of experiences, impressions and images. Every Indian town, and many villages, simply pulsate with life. Everywhere there are people walking, riding, running, sitting, talking, carrying, making, mending, buying, selling, haggling or just being. In the most impoverished of settings the people, especially the women, often wear the most vivid colours imaginable – bright greens, crimsons, yellows, magentas – almost as an assertion of pride and life in the midst of want and deprivation.

But India is much more than a densely populated, bustling country. It is a sub-continent, cut off from the rest of Asia by the sea to the east and the west, and by the great mountain ranges that ring its northern frontiers. This partly accounts for the continuity of Indian custom and tradition. The Hindu religion has been the binding force of society for four millennia. Although conquerors have invaded and possessed India, they have never wholly subverted Indian tradition: the Mughals introduced Islam, which is still India's second religion, but their rule slowly and ingloriously subsided; the British imposed western standards of administration, built most of the railways and many of the roads, gave a push-start to the process of industrialisation, and left in a hurry in 1947, declaring their great task complete.

As Dr Tammita-Delgoda points out in this intelligent and lucid book, 'India . . . has preserved its link with the past which remains an ever-present memory. People still believe in the same religion, they still worship the same gods and still chant the same verses and hymns which they recited 4,000 years ago.' Yet India has also changed out of all recognition, especially during the last five hundred years. It is now a democratic republic, with a progressive constitution and an independent judiciary. It is a federation, in which a strong central government is obliged to get along with provinces in which different languages, histories and traditions are strongly entrenched. Modern technology co-exists with cow worship; a flourishing English-language press is sold in a society where illiteracy is all too common; television carries alluring advertisements while lepers beg at the main tourist sites; the glamorous actresses of the Bombay film industry become international stars while millions of their sisters toil in the fields.

The staggering, sometimes shocking, contrasts that India presents to the traveller are part of the country's enduring fascination. Many visitors return home believing that their lives have been changed as a result of their experiences in the sub-continent. Others have trouble sifting the myriad images that they have absorbed. Almost without exception, they plan some day to return.

There is much to bring them back; one of the great culinary traditions of the world; a country that can offer baking heat and deserted sandy beaches as well as the snows and sparkle of Kashmir; some of the most moving and inspiring architecture anywhere, from the formal, classical buildings of the Mughal era, to elaborate Hindu temples and the imperial splendour of Lutyens and Baker's New Delhi; a cultural richness that is always fulfilling and often astonishing; and above all a people who are warm and hospitable, courteous and helpful, aware and astute, and who can never be taken for granted.

For those who wish to immerse themselves in the 'Indian experience', this comprehensive and readable history will be invaluable.

Denis Judd

CHAPTER ONE

Introduction

India, named after the river Indus, is heir to one of the world's oldest and richest civilizations. Its history stretches back for more than 4,000 years, and alongside Egypt and Mesopotamia it is one of the very cradles of civilization – the origin of many of the ideas, philosophies and movements which have shaped the destiny of mankind. In one respect however, India is unique. The modern inheritors of ancient Egypt and Mesopotamia have completely lost touch with the civilizations that once flourished there thousands of years ago; for them the ancient world is little more than a hidden memory with traditions that are now very distant and very alien. India, however, has preserved its link with the past which remains in ever-present memory. People still believe in the same religion, they still worship the same gods and they still chant the same verses and hymns which they recited 4,000 years ago.

For the traveller, India and her history are both an inspiration and a challenge. The sheer wealth of Indian culture, its vast range and often dazzling colour, has fascinated generation after generation of visitors. At the same time they have often been bewildered by its infinite variety and complexity, its strangeness and its often horrifying contrasts. India, we must remember, is not just a country but a vast subcontinent the size of western Europe. Over the course of time it has come to accommodate many different peoples, each with their own customs and traditions, and all of them speaking their own languages. The result is a society with several different faces, composed of layer upon layer of varied social groups.

Environment

The outline of the Indian subcontinent resembles a huge triangle. Bounded in the north by the Himalayan mountain range, the peninsula narrows to a tip at Cape Comorin, its southernmost point. In the west it is washed by the Arabian Sea while to the east lies the Bay of Bengal. The dimensions of this triangle are really quite breathtaking. From north to south it measures almost 2,000 miles and it is almost the same distance from east to west. Encompassed within is an area of 1,269,346 square miles, the seventh-largest country in the world.

THE NORTH

As one would expect, both the climate and the landscape of this vast country vary from region to region. India possesses almost every imaginable kind of variety and contrast. In the north there is the world's highest mountain region – the Himalayas. Extending east and west they form a barrier of hills and mountains which separate the Indian subcontinent from the rest of Asia. In the west there are the mountains of the Karakoram range and the Hindu Kush, in the east the Arakan range. The hills to the north-east are so steep and so densely forested that for generations they have served as an effective barrier to outsiders. In the north-west, however, there are several passes through the Hindu Kush which lead directly on to the plains of the subcontinent. For centuries this has been the gateway to India. It was by this route that generations of foreign invaders from the steppes of Central Asia have entered India, to leave their mark on the destiny of the subcontinent.

On one side of this route, at an altitude of 6,000 feet, lies the fertile and picturesque Kashmir valley. Surrounded on all sides by snow-capped mountains and teeming with beautiful lakes and meadows, Kashmir is justly regarded as India's Earthly Paradise. Beloved of emperors and prime ministers, it is still one of the most beautiful places on earth and continues to attract visitors from all over the world. Most people associate India only with tremendous heat, but in Kashmir and throughout the whole Himalayan region the winters are bitterly cold with frosts, snows and icy winds.

The Himalayas are also the source of the subcontinent's greatest rivers – the Indus, the Ganges and the Brahmaputra. Together these three rivers dominate the face and form of northern India. Having fought their way through the north-western passes, one set of invaders after another then followed the course of these rivers which led them deeper and deeper into India. It was by this means that the impact of new peoples and new cultures gradually penetrated into the heart of the subcontinent.

The basins of the Indus, the Ganges and the Brahmaputra form the great plain of northern India known as the Indo-Gangetic Plain. This is a vast level expanse stretching from the Arabian Sea to the Bay of Bengal. Nearly 2,000 miles long and 150–200 miles wide, it is highly fertile and almost entirely flat – there is hardly a hill to be seen for miles. Winter here can be quite chilly and at times bracingly cold. In summer the heat becomes almost unbearable and the temperature rises to as much as 120°F. Strangely enough, rice – the commodity that everyone associates with India – does not flourish here. Instead the main crops are wheat and pulses – beans, lentils, peas.

Although the geography has remained unchanged, modern politics have changed the face of the subcontinent. Today the Indus river and the Indus river basin lie inside Pakistan. A large stretch of the Brahmaputra too lies outside India – within the state of Bangladesh. What remains is the Ganges basin, an area which comprises the present day states of Uttar Pradesh and Bihar. This is separated from the Indus valley by the arid, barren lands of Rajasthan and the great Thar Desert which today acts as the frontier between India and Pakistan.

THE DECCAN

South of the great plain is another highland zone. This consists of two parallel chains of hills – the Vindhyas in the north and the Satpura mountains in the south – which run across the face of central India. Although they are nowhere near as impressive as the Himalayas and only rise to a few thousand feet, they have tended to act as a dividing line between northern India and the rest of the subcontinent. Beyond these hills lie the Deccan, a great plateau which stretches for almost the entire length of the peninsula. Known simply as 'the south', the Deccan has always been a rather parched and barren area. Although the higher parts of the plateau can be quite cool at night, the climate is usually very dry. Despite the numerous efforts which have been made to conquer it, the Deccan has always remained quite separate from northern India. Anyone visiting it today will find that it has evolved a very distinctive culture of its own.

The Deccan plateau is flanked by chains of hills, the western and eastern Ghats, which run down either side. Rising to a height of 3,000 feet, they take the form of a series of gigantic steps climbing abruptly from the plains, hence their name Ghat or 'step'. On either side of the plateau the Ghats fall away to coastal plains where typically tropical conditions prevail. Although the temperature never rises as high as in the north, the climate of the coastal and low-lying regions is continually hot and humid. The rainfall in these areas is very high and not surprisingly the landscape everywhere is very lush and green, as well as being intensely fertile. These areas, such as Bengal on the east coast and Tamil Nadu and Kerala in the far south, are the great rice-growing regions of India. Their tropical climate also encourages the growing of spices – pepper, nutmeg, cardamom – in search of which western merchants journeyed thousands of miles to the east.

Museum of Peoples

One in seven of the world's population now lives in India. Next to China, India's population (844 million in 1991) is the second largest in the world, almost as many as that of Africa and South America combined. As with everything else in India, there is a great deal of diversity in this huge total. So many different peoples have come to India at different times that India has become a veritable museum of races. This is something which is all too apparent to anyone who spends any length of time in the subcontinent. Visit certain parts of north India and you will see people with fair hair and sometimes very fair skin, with brown or even green eyes, tall and heavily built with sharp features. In the north-east, however, many of the inhabitants have distinctly Mongolian features, with rounder faces and very high cheekbones. South Indians, by contrast, tend to be much darker in complexion, with black eyes and black hair. Many of them often have rather broader features than their compatriots in the north and tend to be more slightly built.

LANGUAGE

Another sign of this tremendous variety is the extraordinary number of languages spoken throughout India. Today there are officially 15 national languages. These are: Assamese, Bengali, Gujarati, Hindi, Kannada, Kashmiri, Malayali, Marathi, Oriya, Punjabi, Sanskrit, Sindhi, Tamil, Telugu, Urdu.

In practice English is the sixteenth national language, although it is not officially recognized as such. It is widely spoken in every part of the country and often serves as a lingua franca which is understood by north and south Indians alike. Officially Hindi may be the national language of India but in practice its use is confined mainly to the north. For example, a Hindi speaker visiting a southern state like Tamil Nadu will find he has to speak English if he wants to make himself understood.

The Linguistic Survey of India (1903–28), a monumental work compiled by a British official, Sir George Grierson, listed 225 main languages and dialects. However, this vast and seemingly impossibly dense mass can be reduced to two main linguistic families – the Indo-Aryan and the Dravidian. The Indo-Aryan group of languages came with the Aryan tribes who invaded India during the second millennium BC. One of these dialects acquired a special status by becoming the language of religion and it achieved a literary form. This language was Sanskrit and it is from this source that most of the languages of north India are derived.

As new waves of fresh peoples swept into India the old dialects began to break down. In their place appeared new languages which were produced by the fusion between the old, locally spoken dialects, the new foreign tongues and the inheritance of classical Sanskrit. The most important of these languages was Hindi, which today is the most widely spoken language in northern India. Hindi is indebted to Sanskrit for its script, its grammar and its vocabulary. In the same way the other great languages of northern India – Punjabi, Kashmiri, Gujarati and Marathi in the west and Bengali in the east – are all regional offshoots and

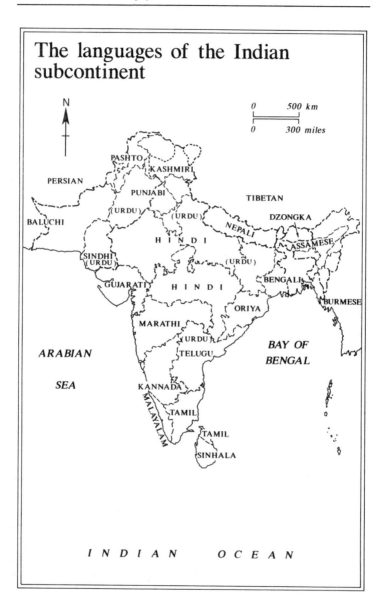

The languages of the Indian subcontinent

descendants of Sanskrit. The coming of the Muslims in the twelfth century introduced another foreign language – Persian. This led to the rise of the last of the modern Indian languages, Urdu. Unlike the others, however, it had no link with Sanskrit; its roots lay in Persian and Arabic and it was forged by the fusion of these influences with the spoken Hindi of the north.

As for the other great linguistic family, the Dravidian languages were spoken by the group of peoples who inhabited most of southern India. Unlike the Aryan dialects, this linguistic group cannot be dated with any real certainty for there is no way of knowing when the Dravidians really arrived in India. What we do know is that there are four major Dravidian languages – Tamil, Telugu, Kannada and Malayali. Of these Tamil is the oldest and the most highly developed; it was the first language to develop a literature of its own, and in its spoken form it is thought to be even older than Sanskrit.

Birthplace of Religions

Next to the physical environment, probably the most important influence on the Indian map is religion. More perhaps than any other country in the world, India's culture and society has been moulded by religion. Even today it remains the single most important influence in Indian life.

India is the home of at least seven major religions – Hinduism, Jainism, Buddhism, Islam, Sikhism, Christianity and Zoroastrianism. The traditional religion is Hinduism which dates back to at least 1500 BC if not earlier. It is still the religion of the vast majority of Indians – nearly 82 per cent of the population are Hindus of one sort or another. Next is Islam, which was brought to India from the twelfth century onwards by a series of conquerors from central Asia. For the next 600 years India was dominated by a number of Muslim dynasties who established themselves in almost every part of the subcontinent. As a result India has the second-largest Muslim population in the world. In 1991, for example, there were more than 92 million Muslims in India – 11 per cent of the total population.

India is also the birthplace of Jainism, Buddhism and Sikhism, all of which sprang up as reformist offshoots of Hinduism. Although they number only a tiny fraction of the population, the Sikhs are probably the most visible minority in the whole of India. Both Buddhism and Jainism have declined in importance since ancient times but there are still several million Buddhists and Jains in India. Buddhism, however, has spread right across south-east Asia and today is one of the world's major religions.

Christianity in India dates back to AD 52, when the apostle St Thomas is said to have landed on the western coast. Here in the area around Kerala he established a few churches and converted a number of the local inhabitants. Although written proof for this story is lacking, there is evidence of Christians in Kerala from the sixth century. They were known as Syrian Christians after the rites which they followed and today they form the oldest Christian community in India. The advent of Europeans from the sixteenth century onwards saw the beginnings of sustained missionary activity, heralding a new wave of conversions, and as a result Christians have become a small but growing minority. In 1971, for example, there were over 14 million Christians, by 1991 this total had increased to over 21 million.

The most interesting foreign religions to take root in India are Zoroastrianism and Judaism. Zoroastrianism entered India between AD 700–800, after the Arab conquest of Iran. Muslim persecution forced numbers of Persians to flee their homeland and some of them took refuge in India. They established themselves on the north-western coast where they became known as Parsees – the 'Persians'. Although they are not very numerous in comparison to other religious minorities, over the years the Parsees have become a very wealthy and highly influential community. Indira Gandhi's husband, Feroze Gandhi, and the rather better-known rock star Freddie Mercury were both Parsees. Judaism has never been very widespread but it has old roots. It was introduced by Jewish traders from the Middle East, who by the thirteenth century had established several small settlements along the western coast of India. Their numbers however have always remained very small and in recent times emigration to Israel has reduced the Jewish population to a fraction of its former size.

The World's Largest Democracy

Today India is the world's largest parliamentary democracy. It is organized in the form of a federal republic consisting of twenty-five states. Many of these states however are much more than mere provinces; a combination of several factors such as race, language, history and environment has meant that in many cases they are almost separate nations. Indeed, some of them have had a far longer history as self-governing entities.

THE STATES

The northernmost state is the breathtakingly beautiful Kashmir high up in the Himalayas. The overwhelming majority of its population are Muslims, nearly all of whom speak the local language, Kashmiri. Bordering on Kashmir are the vast wheat-growing plains of the Punjab, the most agriculturally prosperous and productive region in India.

The Indian Parliament building in New Delhi

Before Independence this area consisted of a complex mosaic of Muslims, Sikhs and Hindus. After Independence, however, the Punjab was divided into two separate provinces. East Punjab where Sikhs and Hindus were in the majority became part of India, while West Punjab which was predominantly Muslim became part of Pakistan. Today the region controlled by the Indians consists of two states, Punjab and Haryana. Of these, Punjab is predominantly Sikh while next-door Haryana is mostly Hindu. However, the language which is commonly spoken throughout the whole region is Punjabi and there is a distinct Punjab cultural identity which characterizes both communities.

To the south-west of the Punjab lies the sprawling desert state of Rajasthan. Renowned as the cradle of Hindu chivalry and culture, it is the homeland of the Rajputs, the great warrior race of India. Full of age-old traditions and breathtaking hilltop castles, Rajasthan still has a very special atmosphere of its own. Indeed, it often seems to belong more to some long-lost medieval era than to any part of modern India.

The area known as the Gangetic Plain is occupied by Uttar Pradesh and Bihar. This is the cultural heartland of India and it has been the home of some of the subcontinent's most powerful civilizations. Called Hindustan ('land of the Hindus'), it is the ancient centre of Hinduism and contains some of its holiest cities; it also contains the historic capital of Delhi which for centuries has been the focus of the whole area. It is a reflection of the continuing importance of the region that its principal language, Hindi, has been declared India's national language. Today about one-fifth of India's total population live in these two states and it is significant that since Independence nearly all her prime ministers have been elected from Uttar Pradesh constituencies.

Further east, as the Ganges nears its mouth in the Bay of Bengal, the wheat fields disappear and the landscape becomes luxuriantly tropical. This area forms the state of West Bengal, the land of the Bengalis. Together with the province of East Bengal, it once formed part of a united Bengali state. After Independence, however, East Bengal separated from India for good to become first part of Pakistan, and then in 1971 the new nation of Bangladesh. Bengal is the home of a thriving intellectual and artistic culture which is probably the most vibrant in the whole of India. Based on the Bengali language, this tradition has produced a long line of distinguished literary, religious and political figures. The centre of this zone is the enormous sprawling city of Calcutta, the one-time imperial capital of British India.

The hilly territories to the north-east of Bengal are home to a very different group of peoples. These areas are inhabited by a number of tribes of mixed origins and varied cultures. Some are Muslim, some are Hindu and some are Christian, and all of them speak their own tribal dialects. The largest state in this area is the tea-growing state of Assam which is also home to India's oil industry. The Assamese speak their own language – of Tibetan-Burmese origin – and in appearance most of them are quite different to the Bengalis.

Western India is separated from the northern plains by a stretch of deserts and hills and looks outwards on to the Arabian Sea. The indented coastline of Gujarat provides many excellent harbours and throughout the centuries Gujaratis have been renowned for their business and commercial skills. Although the Gujaratis themselves are a mixture of Hindus, Muslims and Jains, as a community they have been deeply influenced by the philosophy of Jainism, which holds life in all its forms to be sacred and inviolable. Many Gujarati businesses are based in Bombay, the colossal city which is India's foremost port and the centre of her film industry. Bombay is also the capital of the Marathi-speaking state of Maharashtra, which forms a large part of peninsular India and is the homeland of a predominantly Hindu people, the Marathas, who for the last 300 years have dominated the life of western and central India.

The four southern states of the peninsula – Karnataka, Andhra Pradesh, Kerala and Tamil Nadu – often seem to belong to a very different world. Clothes, for example, are much looser, the food is far more highly spiced, and women seem to enjoy a much greater degree of freedom. Names too are naturally quite different, indeed, many of them can hardly be pronounced by most northerners. As any visitor will observe, southern India is inhabited by people with a distinct ethnic and cultural make-up, speaking languages which are quite unlike those in the north. Probably the oldest cultural tradition of all belongs to the Tamils, who inhabit the state of Tamil Nadu in the southern tip of the subcontinent. Next to theirs the oldest culture is probably that of the

Malayalis, who people the picturesque state of Kerala, also in the deep south. Bordering both, Karnataka runs up the western coast of India. Here the official language is Kannada, while to the east, in Andhra Pradesh, yet another language, Telugu, is spoken throughout the state.

Seldom is so much diversity and variety contained within the borders of one country. Walk across a state boundary in India and one is apt to feel that one has wandered into a different world. The street signs are unfamiliar, everyone is speaking another language, and even the people themselves seem completely different. The effect can be quite disorientating, but this is one of the reasons why India remains such a fascinating country. Unlike the ruins of ancient Greece, Egypt and even China, the monuments of India are not dead archaeological exhibits, carefully preserved for the benefit of tourists and visitors. They are alive and vital, the focus of a living culture which is still part of a continuing human tradition. This above all is what gives India its special character, a character so unique that to most outsiders India still seems to belong to a world of its own.

CHAPTER TWO

The Indus Valley Civilization,
Prehistory to 1500 BC

The prehistory of India, like that of Europe and America, can be charted by a series of Ice Ages, whose glaciers left their mark on the shape and the appearance of the country. The first known signs of human life in India can be dated from the period following the second Ice Age (400,000–200,000 BC). Although there are no human remains, large numbers of crude stone tools have been discovered throughout north-western India, especially in the Punjab region, in the Soan river valley, now in Pakistan. At about the same time there are also traces of another prehistoric stone industry in southern India and throughout the Deccan. The men of this culture, known to archaeologists as the Madras Industry, made their tools by striking off the flakes from a large pebble and using the actual core of the stone. This technique was very different to their counterparts in the north, who relied only on the flakes themselves. In all probability the men of the Madras culture were a more advanced species of man, with a much greater command over their environment.

Thus for the first and the longest era in Indian history, the Palaeolithic or Old Stone Age, when man everywhere was undergoing a sort of learning process, the subcontinent was inhabited by two distinct cultures occupying very separate regions. However, we know very little about these early cultures and can only assume that Palaeolithic man in India lived in much the same way as primitive man in other parts of the world. A nomadic hunter and food gatherer, he lived and moved about in small groups, constantly in fear of his fellow animals and the powers of nature.

After the long hiatus of the Palaeolithic period came the Mesolithic Age, the Middle Stone Age. Man learned to tame the dog, he started to make implements not only from stone but out of bone and flint as well, and he began making his own pottery. In India the traces of this stage can be found principally in the Narmada river valley, which runs through central India between the Vindhya and Satpura mountains. The Mesolithic passed into the Neolithic or the New Stone Age, at which point man began to master his surroundings. The old nomadic ways were gradually abandoned in favour of a more settled agricultural life-style. Man began to grow food crops, to tame domestic animals and to make polished stone implements and pottery which were well in advance of the Palaeolithic period. At this point our knowledge of India starts to become rather more substantial and precise, something which can be identified, described and dated.

Between 9000 and 5000 BC India's western neighbours, Mesopotamia, Egypt and Persia, had already begun to lay the foundations of civilization. Eastwards the process was slower, and Neolithic culture seems to have come to India only after 4000 BC. Its first signs in South Asia have been found on the north-west frontier, in the hills of Baluchistan. Modern excavations here have discovered a series of little agricultural villages which appear to date from 3712–3688 BC. These Baluchi villagers built houses of mud-brick, made their own pottery and used stone and bone implements. They also bred their own livestock and raised sheep, goats and cattle. There appear to have been several village communities in the region, for a number of sites have been discovered. From about 3000 BC similar settlements began to appear in many parts of the subcontinent, especially in the area around the Indus river valley. There followed a gradual process of evolution which culminated in the rise of a new and sophisticated urban culture – the Indus Valley civilization.

The beginnings of Indian civilization

Named after the great River Indus around which it began, the Indus Valley civilization is the first real landmark in the history of the subcontinent. Although its origins still remain rather vague, it is thought to date from around 2500 BC and to have lasted for almost 1,000 years. It was based on the two great cities of Harappa and Mohenjo-Daro.

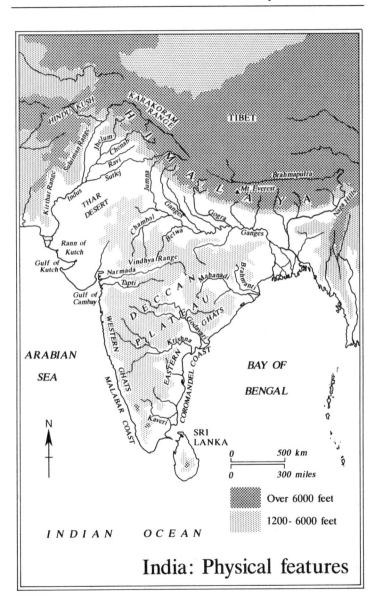

India: Physical features

Harappa, in the north, stands on the left bank of the River Ravi, in what is now the Pakistani part of Punjab, almost 100 miles south-west of the beautiful old city of Lahore. Mohenjo-Daro to the south also lies in Pakistan, on the right bank of the Indus itself, 250 miles from its mouth. It is located in the heart of Sind province, about 200 miles north of Karachi, Pakistan's business and commercial capital. These two cities, almost 400 miles apart, are thought to be the twin poles of a civilization which dates alongside the earliest-known civilizations of Egypt and Mesopotamia. In size, however, there is no comparison, for it completely overshadows its other rivals. Twice the size of the Old Kingdom of Egypt, the Indus culture extended over a huge area, far larger than any other ancient civilization. According to today's estimates it covered just under one and a half million square miles, an area considerably larger than modern Pakistan. This vast area includes almost seventy excavated sites of varying size and status. Kalibangan, for example, on the border of India and Pakistan, is almost as large as either Harappa or Mohenjo-Daro and it is built on almost exactly the same plan. There are also several other smaller towns, such as Kot Dij, Amri and Chanhu-Daro, which also share the same basic layout and could well have been provincial capitals. In addition there are a host of villages, hamlets and other minor sites, which all seem to share the same material culture.

The discovery of these cities has completely transformed our understanding of ancient India. It revealed an entirely new chapter in her history, one which extended her roots back into the past for almost another 1,000 years. It is extraordinary to realize that before 1920 this vital episode in India's past was almost completely unknown. It was discovered purely by accident in 1856 by two English engineers, John and William Brunton, who were then engaged in building a railway line from Karachi to Lahore. Whilst looking for ballast for their railway, they heard of numbers of huge shapeless mounds which were supposed to be the ruins of an ancient city built entirely of brick. This city turned out to be Harappa, which they pillaged mercilessly to provide the support for their railway.

This news came to the ears of Sir Alexander Cunningham, a British general and amateur archaeologist, later to become Director-General of the Archaeological Survey of North India. Cunningham visited the site several times while the railway work was in progress and obtained various antiquities from the workmen. He soon realized that these pieces were completely outside the span of recorded history and he began to suspect the existence of a much older India, a far more ancient civilization than was known at the time. However, he failed in his attempts to decipher the inscriptions and the seals which he had picked up; thus their true significance was not to be realized for another seventy years. Indeed it was not until 1921, when the then Director-General of Archaeology, Sir John Marshall, initiated the first systematic excavations at Harappa, that these sites began to be fully revealed to the outside world.

EXCAVATIONS AND DISCOVERIES

The remains at Harappa have been so extensively quarried that today there is very little to be seen. The first excavations however, revealed traces of a huge city, almost three miles in circumference. A year later an even more exciting discovery was made some 400 miles further south, along the Indus at a place which became known as Mohenjo-Daro (Mound of the Dead). Here an archaeologist excavating an ancient Buddhist temple (stupa) unearthed traces of an older and much more important site beneath it. Unlike Harappa, Mohenjo-Daro was almost completely untouched. Today it is a spectacular sight and its colossal remains give us a graphic idea of the nature of this extraordinary culture.

The picture which emerges is of a very rich, sophisticated and highly complex society, centred around these great metropolitan cities. At its greatest extent Mohenjo-Daro is thought to have had about 35,000 inhabitants; the same would have been true for Harappa. The environment in which these cities grew up, though, was very different to what it is today. The area around Mohenjo-Daro, for example, is now a near desert, with a rainfall of less than six inches a year; in summer the temperature rises to 120°, while in winter it falls so low that there are sharp frosts. In the third millennium, however, the landscape was heavily forested, rich in vegetation and teeming with all kinds of animal life. The arts and crafts of the Indus culture all depict a variety of wild animals – rhinoceros, tiger, water buffalo and elephant – none of which could have existed in the conditions which prevail today. In addition, the huge quantities of burnt brick from which these cities were constructed suggests that an enormous quantity of firewood must also have been required to burn so many million bricks.

It is more than possible that both Mohenjo-Daro and Harappa were built at around the same time, for both cities appear to have been laid down to a common ground plan. To begin with, each city was situated by the side of a river and each possessed a well-fortified citadel on its western edge. In both cases this citadel was built on a raised platform of mud-brick so that it towered above the rest of the city. At Mohenjo-Daro, for example, the whole site is dominated by a massive embankment which rises dramatically to a height of almost 50 feet. Encircled by massive defensive walls with rectangular towers and great gateways, the citadel encompassed all the main public buildings; on its summit are the remains of many imposing structures. Below lay the streets, shops and houses of the town proper. The most eye-catching of these is the Great Bath. Surrounded by a paved courtyard, this is an oblong bathing pool 39 feet long, 23 feet wide and some 8 feet deep. The pool itself is lined with beautifully finished brickwork and is still quite watertight. Bordering on it are several verandahs which open on to a number of small rooms and galleries. Like the later Hindus, the Indus peoples had a strong belief in the purifying effect of water, and archaeologists believe that the bath served a religious or ritual purpose.

A CAREFULLY PLANNED AND ORDERED WORLD

Although erosion has made it more and more difficult to identify the outer boundaries, both cities are thought to have been three miles in circumference and to have covered almost a whole square mile in area. No stone has been found in either city and all the buildings were built from standardized burnt bricks. Unlike many modern Indian cities the layout seems to have been very carefully planned. The street plan in both cases was almost exactly the same; based on a grid-iron pattern, it was remarkable for its order and regularity. All the streets ran from north to south and from east to west, neatly dividing the city into large blocks of roughly equal size. Within these blocks lay the many different neighbourhoods, which were reached by small lanes running at right angles to the main roads. Although they were unpaved, the main streets themselves were all unerringly straight and very broad, in many places as much as 30 feet wide.

The houses, like everything else in the Indus culture, were made of sun-dried or well-fired brick. Their size varied according to the wealth and social position of their owners. They ranged from two-roomed tenements, through houses with courtyards and several rooms, to palatial mansions with several courtyards and several dozen rooms. The houses of the well-to-do, however, all followed more or less the same plan. Entered from the street by way of a side alley, they were all based on a square courtyard around which were grouped rooms of varying sizes. Nearly all the bigger houses had two or more storeys, linked by narrow stairways leading up to a flat roof. The roof itself was normally covered by a waterproof layer of bamboo and rush matting, which was then coated with mud and earth. The floors were usually paved and there were traces of hearths and fireplaces in many of the rooms. Inside there was wide use of mud-plastering on the walls and the ceilings, although there seems to have been very little in the way of decoration or ornamentation. This impression was continued on the outside for there were no windows at all facing the street. From here it must have been a rather grim and forbidding sight, a seemingly endless view of row upon row of blank brick walls.

One of the most interesting features of these houses was their carefully planned bathrooms, with well-built brick floors and elaborate drainage systems. The bath was taken, as it still is in many parts of India, by pouring water over the body from a large jar. Pottery drainpipes ran along the floor taking the dirty water out into the street drains, which then flowed into sewers under the main streets leading finally to covered soak pits; all of these drains were covered for their entire length by large brick slabs. It is an elaborate and extremely efficient system which has no parallel anywhere else in the ancient world, with the exception of Rome which is so much later in origin. Not until modern times has India produced a city with a comparable system of town planning and drainage.

The Great Bath at Mohenjo-Daro

At the other end of the scale are a series of workmen's quarters, the remains of which have been found at both Harappa and Mohenjo-Daro. Like the houses of the rich these dwellings also exhibit a very careful degree of organization. They are almost identically planned at each site and they are all carefully arranged around a common well. At Mohenjo-Daro we find a group of cottages arranged in two parallel rows, with a narrow lane on one side and a street on the other. Each cottage was a single-storeyed building which measured 20 by 12 feet, a tiny space which was divided into two rooms, one twice the size of the other. At Harappa, too, there is a double row of cottages which are also arranged in much the same way: although they tend to be almost twice as large, they are all planned on the same principle of two main rooms, one much larger than the other. Beyond these orderly rows was a circular working floor, carefully made of baked brick. In the centre was a massive wooden mortar sunk in the ground, in which grain must have been pounded with heavy pestles. The worn bricks near the centre show where these barefooted workers, or maybe slaves, must have stood as they pounded the grain for hours on end. Behind this stands the remains of a great granary, some 200 feet long and 150 feet wide, in which the huge surpluses of wheat and barley were stored. Down the centre of the granary ran a great aisle, on each side of which were raised huge storage blocks.

Not far from here were the metal-workers' furnaces. It seems as if a particular group of occupations, with their living and working quarters, has been confined entirely to one area. The impression it leaves us with is quite extraordinary – the first completely planned industrial development in Western Asia. It suggests a system of local government which is so highly organized and so totally efficient that it almost seems to border on regimentation.

Apart from the great granary at Harappa, most of the great public buildings have been found at Mohenjo-Daro, for the extensive plundering of Harappan bricks over the last century has made it very difficult to identify any clear remains. Excavations at Mohenjo-Daro, however, have yielded a much clearer picture. The largest building measures 230 by 78 feet and is thought to have been the remains of a royal palace. This consisted of a number of rooms arranged around what appears to have been a cloistered courtyard. Not too far from this are the remains of yet another great granary, 150 feet long and 75 feet wide. Indeed, many of the largest and best-preserved buildings seem to have been the granaries. Set amidst the main royal or municipal buildings, they appear to have been the economic focus of the city, the equivalent of state treasuries, where the surplus needed to feed the population was stored. Complete with air ducts to keep the floors dry, loading platform and a planned approach for the wagons, they stand as a monument to the architectural skill of the Indus Valley peoples.

Despite the number of structures which have been unearthed, nothing resembling a temple or a place of worship has been found so far. However, this is probably because the most suitable place for it has not been excavated. This spot is still occupied by a sacred Buddhist temple of the second century AD, which as yet it has not been possible to move.

The water supply, as with everything else in the Indus cities, was extremely well organized. Each city was supplied by a number of excellently constructed wells lined with brick. Many of the large houses had their own wells but there were also a number of public ones across the city. Many of the well-heads were littered with the shards of mass-produced little clay cups. This recalls a practice which still persists in Hindu custom today, the ritual taboo against drinking from the same cup. After it had been used each cup was smashed and then thrown away.

What seems particularly curious about these cities is that there is an almost total absence of large-scale works of art or public monuments of any kind. As we have already noticed, there is hardly any decoration at all either inside or outside the houses, nor is there any trace of the squares, arenas or public meeting places one would normally associate with a great city. For all its imposing size, the architecture everywhere seems to be uniformly functional, plain and utilitarian. It is an image which recurs over and over again. The blank brick walls of the houses, the unadorned architecture of even the citadel buildings, the monotonous regularity of the streets, it all seems to go together.

TRADE AND COMMERCE

The elaborate social structure and the high standard of living implied by these remains was founded on a thriving agricultural economy, backed up by a highly developed system of trade and commerce. The rise of Mohenjo-Daro and Harappa saw the small-scale farming societies of the Baluchi villages replaced by a culture which possessed sophisticated irrigation and farming techniques. The size of the granaries suggests that the people of the Harappan civilization farmed their lands with the same efficiency which they applied to everything else and that huge surpluses were generated. The main crops were wheat and barley, although others such as field peas, dates, mustard seeds and sesame were also grown.

The Indus civilization enjoyed a thriving trade by land and sea not only with the rest of the subcontinent but also with the countries of the Nile, the Tigris and the Euphrates. Recent discoveries show that there was a particularly brisk and long-running trade with the Mesopotamian kingdom of Sumer. One of the most important industries was the manufacture of textiles, especially wool and cotton. The process of spinning cotton into yarn and weaving it into cloth was first developed by the Indus people, who began making use of it around 2000 BC. This discovery ranks amongst India's greatest gifts to the world, and the spinning and weaving of cotton has remained one of its premier industries well into the modern age. Although we do not possess much in the way of direct evidence, cotton must surely have formed a major part of the trade with Mesopotamia. The huge granaries beside the river at Harappa suggest that grain too was exported in large quantities, to Mesopotamia and elsewhere. Other items included pottery vases and luxury items like semi-precious stones, ivory combs, pearls and precious woods.

The various stones and metals in everyday use throughout the Indus Valley area give us a fairly full picture of the trade which it enjoyed with its neighbours. Some of the semi-precious stones, for example, such as turquoise and lapis lazuli, must have come from either Persia or Afghanistan. Afghanistan may also have been a source for much of the silver which has been found, though Persia seems a more likely choice. Both gold and silver were sent from Persia, which also supplied lead and tin. Southwards, in what is now Gujarat, there was a thriving trade in chank shells, which were used for decorative purposes like inlaying ornaments. Semi-precious stones like onyx and chalcedony too were imported in order to make beads. The copper and lead used by the Harappan smiths were brought from the regions which lay to the east of the Indus, probably from Rajputana. From Kashmir and the Himalayas came cedar woods, which were probably floated down the rivers, and from beyond the mountains, from as far away as Tibet, came jade.

All this traffic must have involved a numerous and well-organized merchant class with a highly developed trading system. Society, it seems, was organized into several specialized craft groups – potters, metal-workers, builders, brick-makers, bead-makers – all living and working in their own self-contained communities. The weights and measures used, no matter where they have been found, all appear to have belonged to the same uniform system. Made out of very carefully cut cubes of banded grey chert, a sort of flinty rock, they were graded into a very curious system, quite unlike anything else known in the ancient world. These weights proceeded in a series which doubled until it reached 64 – 1, 2, 4, 8, 16, 32, 64. It then went up to 160, from where it used multiples of 16 – 160 (16 × 10), 320 (16 × 20), 640 (16 × 40), 1600 (16 × 100), 3200 (16 × 200), 8000 (16 × 500). It is certainly a very unusual system, but what is even more unusual is the way that it was preserved and enforced from first to last throughout the entire Indus area, from the great cities down to the smallest villages.

We can assume that the transport system was just as highly organized and that there was a well-developed network of caravans trading along recognized routes, with the provision of regular halting places and defended outposts in the outlying areas. The camel, the ass, the bull and the water buffalo were all well known and they were widely used for carrying and hauling goods. The commonest form of transport was the oxcart, and a great number of little clay models of two- and four-wheeled carts have been found. One has only to leave the big cities and travel the country roads to see that this is still one of India's commonest forms of transport. The amount of river traffic must also have been very considerable. Unfortunately we have nothing in the way of direct evidence for the use of boats, and only two representations exist today. One is a rough drawing scratched on a fragment of pottery; the other a rather more careful engraving, showing a ship with a very high prow and stern, a mast, a furled sail and a square cabin amidships.

ART AND CULTURE

Despite this extensive picture of their trade and the impressive but rather dull physical remains of their cities, we still know very little about the Indus people themselves. The main reason is that even today the script of the Indus civilization remains a complete mystery to us. The Indus script has a total of 400 characters and consists mainly of pictures, which denote a symbol or idea of some kind. Its appearance is very stiff and precise, rather like the hieroglyphic script of Egypt. It consists of a series of brief inscriptions, never more than twenty symbols and usually no more than ten. The most striking feature of this script is that it remains almost unchanged for the whole of its history. Normally as a language and its writing develop there is a tendency to reduce the number of characters; the Indus script, however, saw no development at all and stayed exactly the same for almost 1,000 years.

Over the years many attempts have been made by many different scholars to decipher these Indus symbols. All such efforts have failed completely and the script still remains a total mystery. The text does not resemble any other known language; nor has it been possible to make any sort of connection between the pictures and the writing itself. The most frustrating factor is the total lack of any kind of public inscriptions, such as a business document, a historical record or a literary composition, which would serve to provide a parallel source of reference. Until a bilingual inscription is found and the script is eventually read by this means, it seems unlikely that we will be able to learn very much about the life and thought of the Indus people.

In the absence of a written record we have to rely on the material remains, on artefacts like pottery, jewellery, tools, sculpture and the seals themselves, in order to piece our picture together. The large amount of jewellery which has been unearthed suggests that the Indus people, especially the womenfolk, were very fond of ornaments of all kinds. They adorned themselves with a great variety of necklaces, ear-rings, girdles, amulets, brooches and beads made from semi-precious stones, which were a particular favourite. Many of these pieces were made from gold and silver, though silver seems to have been more commonly used. There were also a number of household vessels – bowls, dishes, cups, saucers and vases of various kinds – made from copper, silver, bronze and of course clay. As for pottery, the majority of this tended to be very plain; it was mostly mass-produced ware intended for purely functional purposes. However, we do have some examples of decorated pottery, known as black on red ware because the designs were painted in black on a red background. One type was decorated with geometric patterns, the commonest form of which was a very distinctive circle motif repeated several times on the same piece. The other type, which seems to have been far less popular, depicted animal and plant designs. There were also a few examples of what is called polychrome ware, a multi-coloured design which was painted in several colours – blue, red, green and yellow. This, however, tended to be very much rarer than the others.

The use of metal was well understood by the Harappan smiths, and both copper and bronze were widely used to make tools and weapons. However, the Indus people did not abandon the use of stone and continued to make stone tools in great numbers. Although their workmanship was competent enough, there is no disguising the fact that much of it was actually very primitive. Indeed, compared to Mesopotamia the technology of the Harappan civilization seems quite backward, far more appropriate for a culture in the earliest stages of metal-working than an advanced civilization in its prime. The blades of their knives and their spears were of the simplest flat type and were easily bent, while their axe-heads still had to be lashed to their handles. Unlike the Mesopotamians, they do not seem to have had the skill to devise ribs in the middle to give their knives and spears extra strength, nor do they seem to have known how to make axe-heads with holes for the shafts.

Despite their massive fortifications, it is also unlikely that they were a very warlike people for there are no signs of any swords, shields or body armour. The spears, daggers, arrowheads, slings and axes which have been unearthed are all very weak and inefficient and cannot be compared with the excellent tools which have been found. Indeed they often appear to resemble tools far more than weapons. The gift of the Harappans was for making things which would work and which would do the job asked of them; beyond this they did not choose to go. They may have understood complex technological processes, but for all this their output remained essentially sterile.

One of the most endearing qualities of this strange and rather mysterious people was their great love for making toys. In this area the Harappans appear to have excelled themselves. Using baked clay they produced models of men and women at work, animals and beautiful little oxcarts, or ekka carts as they are called – a small covered trap drawn by oxen, with a roof and a curtain perched on four poles above the frame. The animal figures are very lifelike: especially charming are the cattle that waggle their heads on a string, monkeys that slide down a rope and tiny squirrels which act as pinheads. Unfortunately very little has survived in the way of larger sculptures, barely a dozen pieces from

Mohenjo-Daro and two or three from Harappa. Most of these are mutilated or fragmented in one way or another; they are not very large and all of them are well under life-size. The most striking figure is that of a bronze dancing girl from Mohenjo-Daro. This shows a naked girl, adorned with necklaces and bangles, her hair dressed in a very complicated style, standing in a provocative manner, one arm on her hip and with one lanky leg half bent. This thin, pert, almost boyish figure is a very unusual piece, quite outside the normal traditions of Indian sculpture. Not only is it quite different from the voluptuous maidens who came to characterize later Hindu art, it also has none of the gravity or seriousness which is usually found in so much ancient sculpture. What it does suggest is that citizens of Mohenjo-Daro enjoyed themselves with far more gusto and abandon than we would otherwise suppose.

From what is left of these sculptures we can gather that the men of Mohenjo-Daro and Harappa wore robes which left one shoulder bare and that many of them wore beards. The garments of the upper classes were often richly patterned and both men and women wore their hair long. The richer women in particular had a taste for dressing their hair in a very intricate manner. We have only to look at the complicated styles favoured by the dancing girl and some of the other female terracotta figures to guess at the elaborate fashions of the day. Pigtails too seem to have been very popular. We also know that they loved jewellery, especially heavy bangles, large necklaces and ear-rings.

THE INDUS SEALS

More than anything else, it is perhaps their seal engravings which tell us the most about the civilization of the Indus people. As many as 2,000 of these terracotta figures have been discovered. Ranging in size from three-quarters of an inch to one and a half inches square, they depict scenes representing real or mythical animals in profile – bulls, buffaloes, tigers, elephants, rams and rhinoceroses. Carved with great sureness of touch, they exhibit a degree of beauty and vitality which is quite unknown in many of the other Harappan artefacts. They are quite free of the stifling uniformity which characterizes so many other aspects of Harappan culture and they have a spirit which is very much their own.

A seal from the Indus Valley civilization

As such they tell us much more than the rows and rows of impressive but faceless ruins.

Our picture of the religion and the beliefs of the Harappan people, as with so much else, has to be pieced together from many different fragments. The Indus peoples worshipped not one but many gods. The most important of these was the Mother Goddess. This cult, which seems to have been common to all ancient civilizations, believed in the female as the source of all creation. The woman was seen as the origin of life, the fount of fertility from which everything – man, animals, trees and plants – sprang. In addition to a number of clay figures and statues there are also several seals, all depicting a female goddess. Even today such goddesses are common in Hinduism and many wayside shrines in the countryside are still littered with such figures.

Several of the seals also portray a male god, horned and three faced. This god is shown with his legs drawn into his body like a yogi and he is naked except for his bangles and necklaces. On the largest of the seals he is surrounded by four wild animals – an elephant, a tiger, a rhino and a buffalo – with a couple of deer by the throne at his feet. Although this figure has not been clearly identified, he is thought to be the forerunner of Shiva, one of the great gods of Hinduism, the god of three faces and Pasupati – lord of beasts. Animals, as we can see, played a large part in the religion of the Indus peoples. The bull in particular seems to have been worshipped as a sacred figure, something which has since become one of the most powerful elements in Hindu thought. One of the unforgettable pictures of India is the sight of the living descendants of this sacred bull picking their way through the chaos of teeming streets and markets, ignoring the onrushing cars and buses, untouched and quite unperturbed, as if lost in contemplation of this distant and half-forgotten link with a remote past.

Several seals also show a tree being worshipped by an array of figures. This tree was the pipal tree, the sacred fig tree, which is still regarded by the Hindus as a holy tree. The Indus peoples also practised a form of phallic worship, for there are many images of male and female sexual organs, which suggests the existence of another fertility cult. Here again we come across another unbroken link with the past, for the lingam or phallic symbol is still worshipped all over India as the emblem of the God Shiva.

Continuity, Uniformity and Stagnation

What can we say about this huge civilization, whose ruins suggest so much but tell us so little? How was it governed? Who was it governed by? What sort of society was it and who were its citizens? They are all weighty and important questions but unfortunately we cannot answer them with the substance they deserve, for we still do not have the evidence. The key to Mohenjo-Daro and Harappa remains lost in the recesses of its impenetrable script; until it is found we have to rely on inference and informed guesswork, half fact maybe but more than half fiction.

The most striking feature of this culture is its intense conservatism and its absolute uniformity. It is a conservatism which borders on stagnation – everywhere one looks one is confronted by a picture which has hardly changed over the course of a millennium. At Mohenjo-Daro, for example, there are nine phases of rebuilding in the city's history. Excavations have revealed that, despite being interrupted by disastrous flooding, the new houses continued to be built on exactly the same sites for generation after generation, and that the street plan had remained the same for nigh on 1,000 years. This stifling continuity is echoed in the preservation of the script, the system of weights and measures and the same curiously primitive technology for century after century. Nowhere does there seem to have been any real development or advance, certainly no capacity for change.

Curious though it may seem, the amazing efficiency which we see everywhere is all part of a much wider stagnation. Near-total uniformity seems to have prevailed in every walk of life. As we can see from the layout of the cities almost everything was established and standardized on the same pattern. The same production techniques were employed in every part of the Harappan civilization to produce tools of the same type, pots with a similar capacity and bricks of a regular size. The extent of this uniformity suggests a strong centralized regime which possessed the overriding power and authority to be able to control almost every detail of daily life. The sheer size and scale of the ruins suggest enormous wealth and a great deal of all-round prosperity. This was a society which could even afford to provide for the needs of its poorest and most lowly elements, even the workers or slaves. In many cases they were far better housed than the average Indian labourer is today. The prosperity of this world rested on its stability: order was far more important than change. Society was very clearly stratified into separate layers, each with own function and place. On the citadel lived the ruling élite, below them in the main town lived the mass of the population, while the poor lived in a series of barrack line tenements. So many things – the overwhelming uniformity, the lack of development, the absence of decoration or any kind of art – suggest the stifling influence of an unchanging tradition, enforced perhaps by the power of religion, with the result that every detail of life remained intact for centuries. In all probability Harappa and Mohenjo-Daro were governed by generation after generation of priest-kings, a priestly elect ruling over a mass of merchants, artisans, servants, labourers and slaves.

An Indus Valley vase

Archaeologists think that the decline of the Harappan civilization was the result of a series of important changes in the environment. Around 1700 BC the Indus River seems to have changed course, causing a series of disastrous floods. Widespread and long-lasting flooding signalled the end of the finely balanced agricultural system which the Harappans had relied on for their prosperity. The area around Mohenjo-Daro became a marshy lake and every year the city dwellers were forced to raise their homes higher and higher. As the floodwaters rose the carefully ordered world of the Harappans began to collapse. By 1650 BC there are signs of chaos everywhere. Buildings crumbled and fell apart, streets became uneven and pavements were torn up. The new buildings which were put up were cramped and shoddy; rooms became smaller and housed many more people as residential areas turned into slums. Order was replaced by panic, fear and an impending sense of doom.

By 1500 BC the Indus Valley civilization had completely disintegrated. The great towns and cities were now ruins, inhabited by small communities of squatters living in crude and primitive conditions amongst the rubble.

CHAPTER THREE

The coming of the Aryans, 1500–334 BC

The next chapter in the story of India begins with the advent of barbarian invaders from the north. They were made up of a number of tribes who called themselves the Arya, or Aryans as they are known to us today. After the long stagnation of the Harappan period, their arrival was like a gale of change. They brought with them new ideas, new technology, new gods and a new language. This period, which begins around 1500 BC, is one of the most important epochs in Indian history. It is the source of many of the essential characteristics of Indian civilization; the roots of India's religion, its philosophy, its literature and its customs all derive from this period.

The Aryans were a group of nomadic tribes who had originally inhabited the steppes of Central Asia, in particular the region between the Caspian Sea and the Black Sea. In appearance they were tall, fair-haired and fair-skinned, with clear-cut features, and they spoke a group of languages which have become known as Indo-European. They lived the life of nomads and herdsmen, roaming the steppes of central and southern Russia with their flocks of cattle, sheep and goats, moving from pasture to pasture as the seasons changed. Despite this simple way of life they were not technologically backward, indeed in certain respects they were more advanced than many of the more sophisticated cultures of the East. They had already tamed the horse, which they harnessed to a revolutionary new development, a chariot with spoked wheels. At this time the best form of transport known to man was still the slow, lumbering ass-drawn wagon with its four solid wheels. This new type of chariot was far in advance of anything the ancient world had yet seen.

Around 2000 BC these tribes were driven from their homeland in Southern Russia. We do not know what brought this about, possibly plague or famine, or some natural disaster like a prolonged drought or frost. It may even have been the pressure of other peoples inhabiting an even more remote corner of the world. Whatever it was, it had momentous consequences for the history of both Europe and Asia. From the Russian steppes the Aryans moved in every direction, driving their herds before them and conquering the local peoples they encountered. Some tribes invaded Europe, to become the ancestors of the Greeks, the Latins, the Celts and the Teutons; others invaded Asia, whose ancient civilization crumbled before them. The Hittites were the first Indo-European tribe to settle down, establishing themselves in Anatolia (in what is now Turkey); from there they launched themselves on the fabled civilization of Sumer, bringing an end to the ancient cultures of Mesopotamia. Another group of tribes journeyed even further east, across Asia to Iran, where they appear to have remained for a time. About 1500 BC they began moving east again and advanced across the subcontinent's great north-western barrier, the mountains of the Hindu Kush, into India.

Sanskrit

Our knowledge of these early peoples comes not from archaeology or history but from the study of languages. It is a story which goes back for over 200 years, to 1783 and the arrival in India of an Englishman, Sir William Jones (1746–94), to take up his position as a judge in the High Court of the British East India Company. Throughout his life, Jones's greatest passion had been the study of oriental languages (he had already mastered Arabic and Persian), and on his arrival in India he turned to the ancient and then almost forgotten language of Sanskrit. In the course of these ground-breaking studies, he discovered that Sanskrit shared many characteristics with Greek, Latin, German and other western languages. This led him to conclude that all these different tongues were branches of the same family.

During the course of the next century Jones's theory was taken up and developed by other western scholars, foremost amongst them the

Sanskritist and Professor of Comparative Philology at Oxford, Friedrich Max Müller (1823–1900). By analysing all the languages and comparing their shared characteristics, Müller was able to construct a picture of their original homeland and the routes by which they subsequently reached their respective destinations. It is entirely due to the efforts of these scholars and others like them that today we have some knowledge of the origin of the Aryans, who they were and where they came from.

THE VEDAS

Unlike the peoples of the Indus Valley, the Aryans left nothing behind them in the way of concrete remains. As a result there is very little that archaeology can tell us about them. However, they have left a very vivid picture in their literature. This consisted of a number of religious verses, known as the Vedas, and two great epic poems, the *Mahabharata* and the *Ramayana*. These poems were carefully handed down by word of mouth from generation to generation, and only centuries later actually put down in writing. The word Veda itself means knowledge and the Vedas were a collection of hymns, poems, prayers and instructions. They are so sacred that even minor changes have not been permitted, for fear of what might happen if the magic words were even slightly altered. Thus the Vedas have been preserved almost unchanged for nearly 3,000 years.

The earliest and most important of the Vedas is the Rig Veda ('Rich in knowledge'), which was compiled some time between 1500 and 1000 BC. It is the oldest religious text in the world and contains 1,028 hymns to various Aryan gods. Between 900 and 760 other Vedas were added – the Sama Veda, the Yajur Veda and the Atharva Veda, which contain instructions for performing prayers, sacrifices and other rituals. The Vedas, however, became increasingly more obscure, and some time after 1000 BC two other texts, the Brahmanas and the Upanishads, were added as commentaries. The Brahmanas were an explanation of the Vedic hymns, while the Upanishads were philosophical musings and commentaries based on the Vedas. Last of all and much later were the Sutras, a collection of legal and ritual treatises which acted as manuals of the rites accompanying the Vedic prayers.

The Rig Veda is followed by the great epic poems, the *Ramayana* and the *Mahabharata*. Both poems were formulated around 400 BC, although the *Ramayana* is thought to be the older of the two. The *Mahabharata* is a huge compendium of sub-stories, myths, legends and religious treatises; along with the *Ramayana* it acts as a virtual encyclopedia of Hindu social and religious ethics. Together with the Vedas these works form a collection of literature which make up the basis of Hinduism, its religion and its philosophy. In the absence of any other kind of evidence it provides us with a vital glimpse of the past, of the world in which the Aryans lived and what they believed in. Together they show us how the Aryans gradually adapted themselves to their environment and began to blend in with it, in the process changing the beliefs and the society which they had brought with them.

Vedic India

Although the Rig Veda cannot be precisely dated, as such it reflects the life of the period. It tells us that the Aryans settled in the Land of the Seven Rivers (Sapta Sindhava), consisting of the Punjab and the area round the Indus river. This was more or less the same area which had been inhabited by the Indus Valley peoples. The Ganges as yet was barely known to the Aryans, which suggests that it was a very long time before they began to move further east, into the heart of India.

Unlike the peoples of the Indus civilization, the Aryans did not build any large cities, did not bake bricks or construct any large buildings. They did not carve any seals, nor did they have any knowledge of the art of writing. They were a primitive people, whose world was the sky and the open spaces. Their dwellings were made not from stone but from bamboo, wood and mud, which is why no trace of them has survived. They lived as they had lived on the Russian steppes, as tribal nomads tending their herds and their flocks.

For the Aryans warfare seems to have been almost a way of life, and the Rig Veda tells us that they made war ceaselessly, not only on their enemies but also against each other. Many of their hymns talk of the long war which they waged against the Dasas, the inhabitants of the land. The Dasas it seems were well settled and dwelt in fortified places, called 'pur', and were rich in cattle. There is no disguising the contempt which the Aryans felt for these peoples, whom they described as dark, snub-nosed and bull-lipped, with alien habits and strange, uncouth speech. In the Vedas it is said that Indra, the Aryan war god, destroyed these forts in their hundreds, enslaving their inhabitants. Although it is no longer thought that the Aryans themselves brought about the end of the great Indus cities, it seems likely that they did destroy the remnants of the culture that survived. The wretched Dasas who were enslaved by the Aryans may indeed have been the survivors of the once-proud Harappan civilization.

The Aryan warriors fought from light, two-horsed chariots. These were driven by a charioteer who had two armed warriors standing beside him. Their weapons were the spear, the axe and the bow. In common with many of the other cultures of the East, the Aryans had a great love for the bow, which was their favourite weapon. In the Vedic poems the twang of the bowstring is described as the sweetest sound a warrior could hear.

The Aryans were divided into tribes, each ruled by its own king or raja. The raja was advised by a council of elders, the 'sabha' or the 'samiti', while at his side stood the 'purohita', the chief priest, whose sacrifices ensured the prosperity of the tribe in peace and its victory in war. The foremost Aryan tribe, for it seems to have been the one most frequently mentioned in the Vedas, was the Bharata. This legacy is still preserved in the constitution of India, which has adopted Bharat as its official Sanskrit name. The Vedas and the Epics are written in Sanskrit, the tongue spoken by the Aryans when they first came to India, and which gradually developed into a written language. In due course it became the great literary language of the subcontinent.

The word 'Arya' itself means 'noble' or 'high born'. It tells us a great deal about how the Aryans saw themselves – as a noble or chosen people. Their world originally consisted of three classes or *varnas*, the priests, the nobility and the *vis*, the common people or ordinary tribesmen. However, by the time of the Rig Veda Aryan society had become divided into four classes. The most exalted position was occupied by the priests or Brahmins, for it was they who knew the Vedic texts and performed the sacred rites. Then came the Kshatriyas, the warrior class, who made up the kings and the rulers. Third were

How a Vedic village may have looked

the Vaishyas, the cultivators, who were the merchants, the traders and the artisans. The fourth class was made up of the newly conquered and enslaved peoples, the descendants of the Dasas. These were the sudras, the serfs, who performed all the menial tasks and whose duty was to serve the other classes. These four classes represent the origins of the Hindu caste system.

The tribe lived in large family groups, animals and humans all sharing the same roof. The family hearth was regarded as especially sacred and a fire was always kept burning there. The head of the family was the father, who was the dominant figure in every household. The son, as is still the case all over India, was valued above all else. One of the most frequent prayers made in the Vedas was for manly, heroic (*vira*) sons, for it was the son who looked after the herds and whose deeds in battle brought glory to his father and his tribe. He alone could perform the sacrifice which was required before the soul of his dead father could rest in peace.

As with all nomadic peoples, their most valued possessions were their herds which provided them with their food, their transport and their clothing. The Aryans kept flocks of goats and sheep, which gave them their wool, but their most precious commodity was their herds of cattle. Yoked oxen hauled their wagons and their carts, while the cow supplied them with milk, curds and ghi (clarified butter). Beef too was freely eaten, for the taboos against the killing of cattle which are still so powerful today do not seem to have been as strong in early Aryan times. Cattle were the most important source of wealth and served as a sort of currency. The farmer prayed for an increase in cattle, the warrior expected cattle as booty and the priest was rewarded for his services with cattle. The horse was almost as important, and the Aryans delighted in its beauty and speed. 'His mane is golden, his feet are bronze. He is swift as thought' (Rig Veda I. 163). The horse was used for both war and sport, drawing the chariots of men and goods in wartime, at other times being used for chariot racing, the Aryans' greatest passion.

The Aryans of the Rig Veda were a wild and turbulent people. While war and chariot-racing were their favourite pastimes, they delighted in wine and gambling. 'Soma', an intoxicating mixture, was frequently drunk at sacrifices, whilst 'sura' was taken on normal occasions. Avid gamblers, they were willing to stake everything on the fall of the dice. One of the most famous of all Indian legends is the episode in the *Mahabharata* where the virtuous Pandava prince Yudhishthira stakes all he owns on a game of dice. In the course of the game he gambles away everything that belongs to him and his brothers, their possessions, their thrones and finally even his own wife. One of the best-known Vedic hymns, the 'Gamester's Lament', is a poem which warns against the dangers of *gambling*:

> Her mother hates me; my wife repels me –
> a man in trouble finds no one to pity him,
> They say, 'I've no more use for a gambler,
> than for a worn-out horse put up for sale.'
> (Rig Veda X. 34)

The Aryans also had a great love of music and song. All their hymns were recited in the form of musical chants, which revealed a highly developed knowledge of tone, pitch and sound. These chants were accompanied by lutes, drums, flutes and cymbals. Since then song and dance have become an essential part of religious worship in India: no Hindu ceremony today would be complete without its musicians and dancers.

Although a comparatively simple people the Aryans were technically very skilled; they were especially proficient in the art of metal-working, where they were far superior to the Harappans. Gold was the metal most frequently mentioned in the Rig Veda and both men and women wore anklets, necklaces and earrings. The most common metal was bronze (*ayas*), which was used until it was replaced around 1000 BC by the discovery of iron. The Rig Veda mentions the existence of several types of craftsmen: smiths, jewellers, potters, weavers, carpenters and chariot-makers. All these professions were referred to with considerable respect and it seems that the status of the craftsman was now much higher than it had been in Harappan times.

ARYAN RELIGION

The Aryans brought with them a new pantheon of gods and a new set of religious beliefs. A people of the sky and the open spaces, their beliefs revolved around the power of nature.

> The goddess Light has looked abroad
> with her eyes, everywhere drawing near.
> She has put all her glories on.
>
> The immortal goddess now has filled
> wide space, its depths and heights. Her
> radiance drives out the dark.
>
> Approaching, the goddess has expelled her sister
> Dawn. Now darkness also disappears.
>
> (Rig Veda X.127)

When they made their appearance in the Punjab the Aryans were guided by Dyaus, the Heavenly Father (called Zeus by the Greeks), who was the Universal God of the Aryans. In common with their Iranian brethren they also worshipped two gods descended from Dyaus, Varuna and Mitra, sons of the sky. The fire god Agni was their most intimate friend and protector, usually addressed as 'Brother' in the Vedic hymns. Agni was also the sun 'Surya', who like the Greek god Helios drove across the sky in a flaming chariot. The Vedic poets exhausted their genius in praise of Soma, god of the intoxicating drink made from the soma plant. In contrast to Agni, 'Soma' was liquid fire, the source of Vedic mysticism, and it was offered up at sacrifices to the gods. Mortals too have a presence in this early period, in Vivasat, a saintly priest, and his sons Yama and Manu. Yama was the first mortal to die and pass into the underworld, where he became the host. His messenger was Death and those who were about to die were escorted to his abode by his helpers. Manu was the first man, the ancestor of the Aryans.

In time Varuna became the king of the gods, overshadowing Dyaus, presiding over the cosmic order, 'Rta', by which the world was governed. The divine judge of Aryan India, Varuna was a very pure and holy figure, supposedly omnipotent and omniscient. It was to him that those who strayed from the path of virtue addressed their appeals. At some point in this early period a profound change took place in this pantheon and a new deity Indra, the war god, emerged. In the imagination of the Vedic sages Indra was the personification of the south-western monsoon, the storm god. Cast in the image of an Aryan battle leader, he rode across the skies in his chariot, armed with the thunderbolt (*vajra*) as he brought rain to the parched earth. In his train rode the young warrior band of the Maruts, the storm wind.

Unlike Varuna, who was an older, wiser figure, Indra was a youthful, vigorous hero; given to bragging, drinking and eating huge quantities, his tremendous energy and strength overcame all obstacles. He was the first great leader of the Aryan conquest; heaven and earth are said to have quaked in terror at his birth. His father was Trvastre, the morose, grudging keeper of the heavenly soma. Indra, scarce born, drinks the soma which is given to him, but greedy for more he overpowers his father and hurls him down.

> Who made your mother a widow?
> Who wished to kill you when you were
> lying still or moving?
> What God helped you when you grabbed your
> father by the foot and crushed him?
>
> (Rig Veda I. 18)

It was Indra who defeated the demon Vritra, whose limbless body enveloped the whole world, keeping it in a state of lifelessness and perpetual darkness. Indra destroyed Vritra with his thunderbolt, releasing the sun and the waters, thus bringing life to the earth.

> Let me proclaim the valiant deeds of Indra,
> the first he did, the wielder of the thunder,
> when he slew the dragon and let loose the waters,
> and pierced the bellies of the mountains.
>
> (Rig Veda I. 32)

The Aryans did not build temples, rather sacrificial hearths where they made offerings to the gods. They believed that gods as well as men were all part of the cosmic order, Rta, in which the world followed its regular course and day followed night, season followed season. Only when everyone behaved properly would the universe function in accordance with Rta. This was the point of sacrifice, to placate the gods and preserve the true order. In this context great stress came to be laid on the rituals observed during the sacrifice itself, which had to be precise as this was the only way of approaching the gods. Herein lay the importance of the priest, for it was his duty to conduct the rituals and to act as the intermediary between man and the gods. The importance of sacrifice turned even the cooking of food into a ritual. The first thing cooked every morning was usually a small round of unleavened bread which was always left for the gods. This ritual is still repeated every day in many parts of India; every morning there are other rituals which are observed before breakfast and every evening before the lamps are lit.

The World of the Epics

By the end of the Rig Vedic period the Aryan conquest had begun to take on a much more settled character. The Aryans had also begun moving further eastwards, deeper into the heart of India. Our knowledge of this period is obtained from the two great epic poems, the *Mahabharata* and the *Ramayana*, which reveal that the Aryans had now moved much further into the subcontinent for they had a far wider knowledge of it than before. The world spoken of by the Aryan poets now seemed to embrace much of northern India, extending as far as the Himalayas in the north and the Vindhyas in the south, and bounded on either side by the Arabian Sea and the Bay of Bengal. At its heart was the fertile country between the Yamuna and the Ganges rivers, called by the poets 'Aryavarta', the land of the Aryans.

THE *MAHABHARATA*

The *Mahabharata*, the 'Great Epic of the War of the Descendants of Bharata', was composed by the sage (*rishi*) Vyasa. Originally a poem of 24,000 *slokas* or verses, there have been many additions over the centuries. As it stands today, it is a huge work of about 100,000 verses, about eight times the size of the Greek epics, the *Iliad* and the *Odyssey*, put together.

The poem tells of a famous struggle between two sets of cousins, the Kauravas, the 100 sons of King Dhritharasthra, and the Pandavas, the five sons of Pandu. Dhritharasthra was born blind so his younger brother Pandu ascended the throne of Hastinapura (supposed to have been thirty miles north east of Delhi). However, while out hunting Pandu mortally wounded a holy man, whose dying curse forced him to abdicate. Thus Dhritharasthra became king in his place. Upon Pandu's death his five young sons were brought back to the court, where they were educated alongside their cousins. Yudhishthira, the eldest, was made the heir apparent but this was bitterly resented by the Kauravas. Led by Duryodhana, the eldest of Dhritharasthra's sons, they plotted to destroy the Pandavas. After foiling a number of plots against their lives, the Pandavas fled the country and travelled from one court to another as soldiers of fortune. At the court of the king of the Panchalas, Arjuna, the second son, won the hand of the beautiful princess Draupadi. However, to avoid strife he shared her with his brothers and she became the wife of all five Pandavas.

Hearing of their renown, the blind Dhritharasthra recalled the Pandavas to Hastinapura. He divided the kingdom between his own sons and the five brothers who built a new capital for themselves at Indraprastha (Delhi). However, the Kauravas were not content with this settlement, especially Duryodhana who was consumed by hatred and jealousy. Determined to cheat the Pandavas of their patrimony, he challenged Yudhishthira to a great gambling match, in which Yudhishthira lost not only all his possessions but his kingdom as well. He then wagered the possessions of all his brothers and their kingdoms too. Finally he was left with nothing else but his beloved wife Draupadi; nevertheless he wagered her too, only to lose yet again. Draupadi was dragged before the assembled crowd and humiliated. In revenge Bhima, the third of the Pandavas, swore that one day he would wipe out the stain of her disgrace by drinking the blood of the Kauravas. Finally a compromise was reached and it was agreed that the Pandavas would go into exile for thirteen years, whereupon their kingdom would be restored to them.

After thirteen years the Pandavas returned to reclaim their inheritance, but their demands were refused and both sides prepared for war, summoning their allies from all over India. Battle was joined on the plain of Kurukshetra. For eighteen days a furious struggle raged as the Aryan nations fought each other to the death. This great battle marks the peak of Aryan chivalry, and it is characterized by deeds of high courage and nobility along with acts of violent savagery.

> Then the violent Bhima, remembering the acts of family hostility committed by the Kauravas, leapt down from his chariot on to the ground, fixing his eye eagerly on Duhshasana.
>
> Drawing his sharp sword with its excellent blade, and treading upon the throat of the writhing man, he cut open his heart as he lay on the ground, and drank his warm blood. Then, having quaffed and quaffed again, he looked up and spoke these words in his excessive fury:
>
> 'Better than mother's milk, or honey with ghee, better than well prepared mead, better than a draught of heavenly water, or milk, or curd, or the finest buttermilk, today I consider this draught of the blood of my enemy better than all these!'
>
> With these words he rushed forward once more, bounding on in exhilaration after his drink; and those who saw him then, they too fell down, confounded with fear.
>
> (*Mahabharata* 8.61.5–8)

At the end of the battle hardly anybody was left alive, only the Pandavas and their ally, the god Krishna, remained. Thus Yudhishthira was crowned king and the Pandavas reclaimed their inheritance.

The core of both the *Mahabharatha* and the *Ramayana* gives us a picture of society in the centuries before 500 BC. The Aryan tribes were now settling down to become farmers, developing cities and becoming attached to the land. What had formerly been tribal groups were now becoming territorial kingdoms. At the same time the horizons of the Aryan world were also beginning to expand and their poets were beginning to look beyond the frontiers of north India. This is the theme of the *Ramayana*.

THE *RAMAYANA*

The *Ramayana*, the 'Story of Rama', was composed around about the same time as the *Mahabharata*, although it is thought to be slightly older. It is a much shorter poem and today it numbers some 25,000 verses. Although it too has been swollen by later additions, most of it is thought to have been the work of one man, the poet Valmiki. The poem is composed of seven books, the first and last of which are later additions, but the rest are all believed to have been written by Valmiki.

The *Ramayana* is set somewhat further to the east than the *Mahabharata*, in eastern Uttar Pradesh. It is a story of courtly intrigue, heroic renunciation, fierce battles, and the triumph of good over evil. Its hero is Rama, prince of Ayodhya, the eldest son of the king of Kosala, who marries Sita, princess of Videha. Although Rama was the rightful heir to the throne of Kosala, he was passed over and banished by his father in favour of the son of a younger wife. Rama, Sita and his brother Lakshmana took refuge in the forests, where they dwelt as hermits. Sita however, was kidnapped by Ravana, the demon king of Lanka (Sri Lanka), who carried her off in his flying machine. Desperate with grief the brothers searched far and wide but to no avail. They were helped at last by the monkey god Hanuman, and it was he who finally discovered Sita, a prisoner in the palace of Ravana. With the aid of a great army of monkeys, a causeway of stones was built across the sea to Lanka and the brothers laid siege to Ravana's island fortress. After a ferocious battle, Rama and Lakshmana finally triumphed and Ravana and all his demons were slain.

> And in joy the monkeys
> roared a cheer of triumph
> and proclaimed the victory of Rama,
> and his slaying of Ravana.
>
> In the sky there sounded
> the lovely drums of the gods,
> and there blew a pleasant wind
> bearing a heavenly fragrance.
>
> A rain of flowers fell
> from heaven upon earth,
> flowers rare and lovely
> bestrewing Rama's chariot.
>
> (*Ramayana* VI, 108)

However, Sita's innocence was still doubted and Rama, in accordance with Sacred Law, had no option but to repudiate her. To prove her purity Sita threw herself on a funeral pyre, but she was saved by the fire god Agni who refused to accept her sacrifice. Her innocence proven beyond all doubt, Sita was reunited with her beloved husband. Together, Rama, Sita and Lakshmana returned to Kosala where Rama was restored to his rightful heritage. Today the return of Rama and Sita to Ayodhya is celebrated all over India by the festival of Divali, the Festival of Light. Everywhere the streets and houses are illuminated with the flickering glow of oil lamps, lit to mark the beginning of the new. To commemorate the passing of darkness, new clothes are worn, gifts are exchanged and everywhere the houses are thrown open in welcome.

In the course of time the *Ramayana* has come to enjoy immense religious authority. The favourite story of millions, it is regarded with almost the same reverence which is accorded to the New Testament. Today Ayodhya is revered as a sacred shrine by millions of Hindus who regard it as the birthplace of Lord Rama and the scene of his final cremation. For many of them Rama is the ideal Hindu man, the perfect son, the perfect brother and the perfect husband. At his side is the devoted Sita, the very image of the perfect Hindu woman, and the monkey god Hanuman, the faithful servant who is always in the right place at the right time. Together their adventures have been the inspiration for much of India's finest sculpture and painting, not to mention some of its greatest literature.

By the end of the epic period it is clear that Aryan society had made the transition from the simple, tribal world portrayed in the Rig Veda. Both poems reveal a people long settled in the country, with a highly developed culture and an elaborate code of conduct. The language too had changed; Sanskrit, previously a flexible, spoken tongue, had now become a complex and highly developed language.

The Beginnings of Hinduism

In religion, too, there were many deep-seated changes. Although the old Vedic gods, such as Indra and Varuna, were still mentioned, they were now far less prominent than before, superseded by the great gods of Hinduism, Brahma, the creator of the universe, Shiva and Vishnu. With them came a whole host of other minor deities such as Hanuman, the Monkey God, and Ganesha, the Elephant God, all with different personalities of their own. Alongside these new gods came new beliefs, heralding the birth of Hinduism as we know it.

One of the main elements in Hinduism was its belief in the existence of a universal spirit (*ishwara*). This spirit had several different aspects which were represented by a number of gods who appeared in a variety of guises. Shiva, for example, was a god of many moods and many faces. In one aspect, as Shiva the Destroyer, he was the incarnation of death and time; in another aspect he was known as Shiva Nataraj, the graceful god of the Dance. His best-known incarnation was as the high god of fertility; in the form of an erect phallus – the linga – he was revered by his followers as the symbol of creative power.

Vishnu too had many different incarnations, the most celebrated of which were Rama and Krishna, the friend and ally of the Pandavas. Vishnu was the embodiment of mercy and goodness and he preserved the balance between order and disorder in the universe, hence his title Vishnu the Preserver. To many Hindus he was also the source of the universe: according to Hindu mythology, as Vishnu lay dreaming a lotus flower emerged from his navel revealing Brahma, the god who actually created the universe.

The idea of reincarnation featured very strongly in Hinduism. It was thought that the human soul (*Jiva*) was everlasting and in a perpetual state of development. After death the soul was born again on earth in a new form; its purpose was to better itself, to become one with the universal spirit (*ishwara*). Rebirth was governed by the doctrine of Karma, the law of moral consequences. Karma governed the relationship between one's actions in one incarnation and one's station in the next. Merit was rewarded but sin had to be atoned for, thus the merit and the sins of the past life were visited on the next. According to karma we are what we are because of what we were and what we did. It followed from this that everyone's position was the result of past actions in a previous birth. This belief formed the basis of the caste system, the cornerstone of Hinduism, which first began to appear during this period.

Over the course of time the four *varnas* of the Rig Veda had become clear-cut castes, which had broken up into a number of subcastes. Each group had its own carefully defined function and the barriers between them were now quite rigidly established. Beneath all the other castes were the Untouchables, who did the work considered unclean by other Hindus, such as the killing of animals and the cleaning of latrines. Contact with them was regarded as pollution and they were forced to live apart from everybody else, not allowed to enter Hindu temples or even to draw water from the village well. Caste is still an important part of Indian society. By the beginning of the twentieth century these original castes had developed into more than 2,000 separate groups, each with its own different identity and function. The Untouchables however still remained at the bottom of the ladder.

Mahajanapadas

The sixth century BC marks the beginning of some kind of certainty in Indian history. We know that by then there were sixteen major states in northern India, called Mahajanapadas or 'great states'. The most powerful were the kingdoms of Magadha and Kosala. Magadha dominated the Eastern Gangetic plain, what is now known as Bihar and Orissa, while Kosala, further to the west, occupied the Aryan heartland

and contained the epic capital of Ayodhya. By 540 BC Magadha, which controlled the Ganges valley, had become the wealthiest and most powerful kingdom in north India. Under Bimbisara (r.543–491) and Ajatashatru (491–61) Magadha conquered the neighbouring kingdoms of Kashi and Kosala and began building up a strong administration. Its capital at Rajagriha ('The King's House') was strengthened and the foundations were laid for the city of Pataliputra, alongside the Ganges. After a series of mediocre kings, Magadha became vastly more powerful in the fourth century under the rule of the Nanda dynasty. It attained its peak during the reign of Mahapadma Nanda (362–34), when its glory was known throughout the whole of northern India.

The Rise of Buddhism and Jainism

The sixth century saw the rise of new schools of thought and the development of new attitudes to religion. The old religion of the Vedas had lost much of its appeal and there was a prevailing disaffection with the Vedic view of the world. The stifling rigidity of its social order was felt to be quite inadequate for the changing social conditions. Men began to seek new answers and explanations, and this need threw up many new philosophies. These developments culminated in the birth of two new religions, Buddhism and Jainism.

BUDDHISM

Buddhism, one of the world's great religions, is named after the title, the Buddha or 'Englightened One', bestowed on its founder, Siddhartha Gautama (c.563–483 BC). A member of the Kshatriya or warrior caste, Siddhartha was the son of the ruler of a small kingdom in the Nepalese foothills. He was raised in the city of Kapilavastu, growing up in a sheltered atmosphere of luxury and ease. It was foretold that because of his concern for human suffering, Siddhartha would one day renounce the world. Hearing this his father, the king, gave strict instructions to ensure that he would be shielded from any kind of contact with pain or suffering. Nevertheless even the King could not shield his son completely and Siddhartha gradually became aware of the sorrow and suffering in the world around him. He was so shocked that at the age of twenty-nine he renounced the palace, his beautiful wife and his young child. Dressed as a hermit he set out in search of spiritual truth. He wandered for six years, seeking wisdom and the secret of sorrow. However, despite all his asceticism and self-denial Siddhartha failed to achieve his goal and he finally gave up these practices as futile. Instead he resolved to meditate until the truth came to him and he sat in meditation under the Bodhi tree at Bodhgaya, near Benares. After forty-nine days enlightenment finally dawned and the meaning of sorrow became clear to him. Arising, he went to the Deer Park near Sarnath, six miles north of Benares, where he preached his first sermon.

The heart of the Buddha's message concerned the nature of sorrow. According to his teachings, 'The Four Noble Truths', sorrow was the cause of all the evil and suffering in the world. Sorrow and suffering arose from desire, and in order to overcome suffering man first had to conquer his own desire. To guide him in his mastery of suffering, the Buddha advocated that man should follow the 'Eightfold Path'. This was a code of conduct of eight precepts, based on the principles of right thinking and right behaviour. If properly followed it promised to purify the spirit and overcome the pain of suffering. For the next fifty years the Buddha travelled throughout northern India, teaching and converting princes and peasants alike. The simplicity of his teachings attracted many followers and Buddhism rapidly acquired great popularity. The main reason for this was that the Buddha's message provided an equal way of life for everyone, there were no priests and there was no caste. Before he died at the age of eighty, the Buddha was virtually a god in the eyes of his disciples, yet as he lay dying his last message to his followers was, 'You must be your own lamps, be your own refuges.' Thus he urged them not to look to him but to work out their own salvation.

After the Buddha's death both Bodhgaya and Sarnath flourished as important religious centres and numerous shrines, temples and monasteries were created. The ruins of many of these buildings are still in evidence today and they attract numbers of pilgrims from all over the Buddhist world. For most pilgrims the focus of their visit is Bodhgaya where a sapling of the original Bodhi tree is still preserved. In comparison Sarnath, the scene of the Buddha's first sermon, is a rather quiet little place. It is noted for its museum which is built in the form of a Buddhist monastery and houses one of the richest collections of Buddhist carving and sculpture in India. Although the site itself is not as spectacular as Bodhgaya, the ruins are pervaded by a calm, gentle atmosphere which is uniquely their own.

JAINISM

A close contemporary of the Buddha was Vardhamana Mahavira (540–468 BC). He was the founder of Jainism, the other great religious movement of this period. Like the Buddha, Mahavira, whose name means 'Great Hero', was born a Kshatriya prince. At the age of thirty, he too abandoned a luxurious life and became a wandering monk. For the next twelve years Mahavira wandered through the Ganges valley in search of salvation. Unlike the Buddha, he advocated total self-denial and self-discipline as the surest path to salvation, even to the point of starvation. He believed that all living things – humans, animals, plants – had living souls and he taught that all life was sacred. His most important doctrine was the idea of 'ahimsa' or non-violence.

> Earth and water, fire and wind,
> Grass trees and plants and all creatures that move,
> Born of the egg, born of the womb,
> Born of dung, born of liquids.
>
> These are the classes of living beings.
> Know that they all seek happiness.
> In hurting them men hurt themselves
> And will be born again among them.
> (Sutrakrtanga, *Book of Sermons* 1,1–9)

Mahavira spent thirty years preaching his doctrines, finally dying at the age of seventy-two. Called Jina, the 'conqueror', because of his conquest of human passion, his followers are called Jains after his example. Unlike Buddhism, Jainism did not die out in India and there are still several million Jains living there. As a result of Mahavira's teachings, all Jains are strict vegetarians who refuse even to practise farming for fear of destroying living things. Many of them are well-to-do merchants and businessmen, renowned for their works of charity and their protection of animals of all sorts. In Old Delhi, for instance, there is a Jain hospital just for birds.

Both Jainism and Buddhism represent very similar ideas, especially in their opposition to violence and their attitude to caste. Although neither Buddha nor Mahavira saw themselves as breaking with Aryan tradition – only offering a new way to liberation – their teachings were to cause something of a social revolution and they had a profound influence on Indian society.

CHAPTER FOUR

The Mauryas:
The First Indian Empire,
330–184 BC

Alexander the Great

After centuries of obscurity, doubt and conjecture, India comes into the full light of recorded history with the invasion of Alexander the Great, king of Macedon. In 330 BC Alexander finally overthrew Darius III, the last of the Persian emperors, and set out to conquer the whole of his vast empire. At that time the Persian empire stretched from the Indus to the Mediterranean. At its heart was Egypt, Asia Minor and the Iranian plateau; in the north it bordered on the steppes of Central Asia and in the east it included the Indus valley and western Punjab. In the sixth century, when Persian military power was at its height, Darius I had invaded north-west India and subjected the region to Persian rule. The Gandharan region, as it became known, became one of the twenty provinces of the Persian empire. According to the Greek historian, Herodotus, India was the richest province in the Persian empire paying no less than 360 talents of gold dust in tribute every year.

Having made himself master of the Mediterranean world and the greater part of the Persian empire, Alexander set out for India. He fought his way across the fearsome passes of the Hindu Kush and in 326 reached the Indus river. Crossing the river with his army, he moved on to the plains of the Punjab. Although he was welcomed by the ruler of Taxila, the capital of the Gandhara region (near Islamabad the capital of Pakistan), elsewhere Alexander met with fierce resistance. At the Hydaspes river (now the Jhelum) he was confronted by the army of the Indian rajah Porus, with 50,000 troops and 200 war elephants, India's natural tank corps. The Macedonian cavalry overcame their terror of these elephants by charging around their flanks, while flaming Greek arrows drove them to panic and trample Porus' infantry underfoot. A crushing defeat was inflicted on the Indian king and, wounded in nine places, he was brought before Alexander in chains. Porus was a tall, handsome man and tradition has it that Alexander was very taken with his proud, upright bearing, despite the fact that he could barely stand for his wounds. So he asked the captive how he expected to be treated. Ignoring the pain and the humiliation of his position, Porus drew himself up and replied proudly 'Like a king.' His answer made such an impression on Alexander that he freed Porus of his chains and restored him to his kingdom.

Following his victory, Alexander continued to advance east across the Punjab, subduing new enemies as he went. He had heard of the wealth and splendour of the kingdom of Magadha, in the distant heartland of north India, and was keen to press on and conquer new worlds. However, by the time he reached his fifth great river, the Hyphasis (Beas), his troops had become weary of the endless fighting. Here they mutinied, refusing to advance any further into unknown lands against unknown opponents. Homesick and exhausted, they forced Alexander to leave India and turn back towards the West. India, so often the victim of foreign invasions, became the only country in the ancient world to bring the world conqueror to a halt.

Alexander left behind him several Greek colonies in Afghanistan and north-western India. After his death these passed into the hands of Seleucus Nicator, one of his generals. Seleucus, however, became involved in a long-drawn-out power struggle for the rest of Alexander's inheritance and it was several years before he was able to devote his attention to India. The receding tide of Greek power led to a period of confusion and uncertainty in northern India as various rulers tried to make capital of the vacuum that Alexander had left behind.

The Rise of the Mauryas

These unsettled circumstances saw the rise to power of a young adventurer, Chandragupta Maurya, who overthrew the reigning king of Magadha and seized his capital, Pataliputra. Chandragupta founded a dynasty which was to weld the diverse cultures of India into an empire lasting almost 140 years. The Mauryas, as they were called, were India's first imperial dynasty, rulers of an empire which embraced nearly the whole of the subcontinent. No Indian dynasty before them had enjoyed so much power, and it is doubtful whether any regime since has been able to exercise such complete and effective control over so much of this vast country.

CHANDRAGUPTA

Chandragupta is a somewhat unusual figure, for unlike most Indian rulers he did not inherit his power but came from a rather humble background. Nevertheless he seems to have risen very far very fast, for he was barely twenty-five when he succeeded to the throne of Magadha. In this he was aided by his brilliant and unscrupulous Brahmin adviser, Kautilya. Kautilya is supposed to have been the author of the *Arthashastra*, India's classic text on the art of politics and government (see p. 62–6). As tradition has it, it was he who supervised the young man's early development and guided him in his rise to power.

Once he had secured his position, Chandragupta subdued the area around the Ganges valley. From here he moved to the north-west, where he came into conflict with the Greek states. Chandragupta, or Sandracottus as the Greeks called him, soon overthrew the remnants of Greek power and by 305 had added western India and the Indus valley to his rapidly growing empire. By this time Seleucus Nicator had established himself as the master of western Asia and he turned eastwards once more in an attempt to recover the lost Greek provinces. This time, however, the Greeks were defeated and forced to retreat. Seleucus ceded his provinces in Afghanistan and gave one of his daughters in marriage to the Mauryan court.

The first real emperor of India, Chandragupta reigned from his capital at Pataliputra (the modern city of Patna) for twenty-three years (324–301 BC). His victories had made him master of virtually the whole of north India, and his power extended from Afghanistan and the mountains of the Hindu Kush in the far west, right across the Indus and the Ganges to the Bay of Bengal in the east. It is thanks to the extensive diplomatic contacts which Chandragupta maintained with Seleucus that we have our first clear picture of Indian history. This is found in the record of the Greek diplomat Megasthenes, who resided at Pataliputra for many years as Seleucus' ambassador to the Mauryan court. Megasthenes had great respect for Chandragupta, admiring him for his great energy and tireless capacity for hard work. According to Megasthenes, Chandragupta would remain in court the whole day attending to public business and the administration of justice. Even when he was having his hair combed and dressed there was no respite, for then he would be giving audiences to his ambassadors. Chandragupta, he tells us, dwelt in great luxury amid conditions of almost unbelievable beauty and splendour, far surpassing anything the Persian empire had to offer. His life, however, was not happy, for he lived in constant fear of assassination, a recurring danger to Indian kings throughout the ages. All his food was tasted in his presence and he never slept in the same bed twice. An elaborate network of spies and informers kept him constantly aware of whatever was happening throughout his realm, while enemies of the state were inclined to disappear without trace.

According to Jain tradition, Chandragupta finally wearied of the opulence of his surroundings and abdicated in order to become a Jain monk. He retired to the great Jain monastery at Sravana Belgola in Mysore, where he fasted to death. However, considering the difficulty he had making himself king and building up his empire, it does seem rather unlikely that he would have given up so easily. Whatever the truth, he was succeeded in 301 by his son Bindusara.

BINDUSARA

Bindusara reigned for thirty-two years (301–269 BC) but we know surprisingly little about him. By all accounts he was a man of many interests and wide-ranging tastes. He is best remembered for his curious request to the Greek king of Syria, Antiochus I, to whom he wrote asking for some Greek wine, some figs and a Greek philosopher. Antiochus sent him the wine and the figs, but replied politely that Greek philosophers, however, could not be exported so easily.

Bindusara seems to have been a man of many parts, for like his father he was also a gifted soldier and administrator. Not only did he keep the empire intact, but extended Mauryan rule deep into the Deccan, as far south as Mysore. Early Tamil poets of the south speak with awe of the Mauryan chariots, their white pennons glittering in the sun as they thundered across the land. At Bindusara's death in 269, almost the entire subcontinent had been brought under Mauryan power. Only the state of Kalinga on the east coast (now Orissa) remained more or less independent.

Asoka

Bindura's son Asoka, one of the most famous figures in Indian history and one of the great names of all ages, ruled unchallenged for thirty-seven years (269–232) over the greatest empire India had ever seen. His personality casts a huge shadow across the Indian scene. However, this reputation is not founded on the size of his empire or the extent of his power. With Asoka, whose name means 'The Sorrowless One', his greatness lies in his character as a man, the ideals for which he stood and the principles by which he governed.

For many centuries Asoka remained almost completely unknown to Indian historians. He was occasionally mentioned in the genealogies of Mauryan kings but nothing more was known about him other than the length of his reign. A considerable amount of material had been collected in the Buddhist chronicles but all this had disappeared with the decline of Buddhism in India. All that remained were a series of inscriptions carved on massive rocks and pillars throughout the subcontinent. The language in which they had been engraved was so ancient that it could no longer be read; men could only wonder at the identity of this king whose power had been so great that his monuments covered the length and breadth of the subcontinent.

In 1837 James Prinsep, an oriental scholar working in the British Mint at Calcutta, managed to decipher the script. However, although the text was now known, the identity of the ruler still remained a mystery, for he was referred to not by his name but only by his titles, such as 'Devanampiya Piyadassi', 'The Beloved of the Gods, of Gracious Mien', a title which was not mentioned in any of the lists of Indian

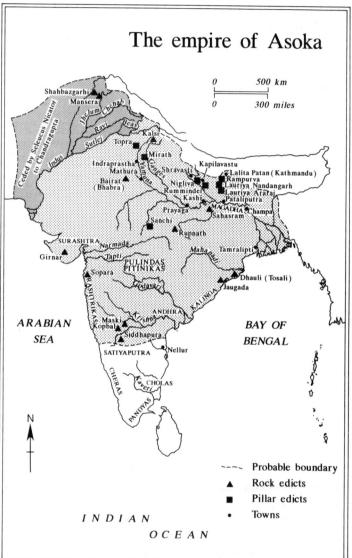

The empire of Asoka

0 — 500 km

0 — 300 miles

Shahbazgarhi
Mansera

Ceded by Seleucus Nicator to Chandragupta

Indus
Jhelum
Chenab
Ravi
Beas
Sutlej

Kalsi
Topra
Mirath
Indraprastha
Mathura
Ganges
Yamuna
Shravasti
Kapilavastu
Lalita Patan (Kathmandu)
Rampurva
Nigliva
Lauriya Nandangarh
Lauriya Araraj
Bairat (Bhabra)
Rummindei
Kashi
Pataliputra
Prayaga
MAGADHA
Champa
Sanchi
Sahasram
Rupnath
Narmada
SURASHTRA
Girnar
Tapti
PULINDAS
PITINIKAS
Godavari
Mahanadi
Tamralipti
Dhauli (Tosali)
Jaugada
Sopara
RASHTRIKAS
KALINGA
ANDHRA
Krishna
Maski
Kopbal
Siddhapura
Nellur
SATIYAPUTRA
CHERAS
Kaveri
CHOLAS
PANDYAS

ARABIAN SEA

BAY OF BENGAL

N

- - - Probable boundary
▲ Rock edicts
■ Pillar edicts
• Towns

INDIAN OCEAN

kings. It was only in the late nineteenth century, after a careful study of the Buddhist chronicles of Sri Lanka had yielded further evidence, that the bearer of these titles began to be identified with the figure of Asoka. Even then it was not until 1915, with the discovery of an inscription referring to 'Devanampiya Asoka', that this identification was finally proved and Asoka established as a real historical figure.

Asoka's greatest monuments are the edicts which he had carved on great rocks and polished pillars of sandstone throughout his empire. On his orders some 5,000 words were engraved on at least eighteen rocks and thirty pillars, although today only ten pillars remain standing in good condition. The finest of these edict columns stands near the Nepali border, at Lauriya Nandangarh in Bihar state. A solid shaft of brightly polished sandstone, it rises 32 feet into the air; at its pinnacle is a seated lion, the emblem of imperial power. Carved on the shaft itself are seven of Asoka's edicts. These edicts, which rank as India's oldest surviving historical documents, are official proclamations by Asoka to his people, declaring his ideals and the principles by which he would rule. They tell us a great deal about Asoka the man, his character and his own unique philosophy.

Little is known about the early years of Asoka's reign, which were devoted to consolidating his power and building up his empire. By all accounts, he seems to have been just as ruthlessly efficient as either his grandfather or his father. In 261, the eighth year of his reign, he decided to invade Kalinga, the last of the independent states on the Bay of Bengal. The campaign was successful and Kalinga was conquered, but only after a terrible and bloody war. According to one rock edict, 150,000 people were taken captive and 100,000 killed, many more dying of sickness and starvation. Asoka was sickened by the carnage and he was horrified by the suffering and the misery which he had caused. Stricken with remorse, he underwent a complete change of heart; he renounced the path he had previously followed and abandoned the traditional policy of war and conquest. Shortly afterwards he was converted to Buddhism.

Inspired by its teachings, Asoka embraced the Buddhist philosophy of Dharma, 'Righteousness' or moral law. Instead of the rule of force, he adopted the rule of Dharma, as the key to public action. Henceforth, he declared, conquest by Dharma, 'moral conquest', would be the most important aim of all:

> For this is my principle:
> To protect through Dharma,
> To administer affairs according to Dharma,
> To please the people with Dharma,
> To guard the empire with Dharma.
>
> (1st Pillar Edict)

This was to be the new ethos of his government and for the rest of his reign Asoka devoted himself to promoting the rule of 'moral law'.

THE RULE OF DHARMA

One of the most important elements in Asoka's philosophy was the Buddha's doctrine of 'ahimsa', of non-violence towards all living things. Asoka recognised the great moral and physical suffering caused by war. Thus he resolved that in future he would do his best to adhere to the law of Dharma and refrain from using force. As one edict declared, 'If anyone does him wrong, the Beloved of the Gods must bear all that can be borne.' Should he have to use force as a final resort, he determined to temper it with as much mercy and compassion as possible. In the cause of 'ahimsa' Asoka forbade the slaughter of animals, and it was one of his proudest boasts that he had greatly reduced the eating of meat throughout India. He himself gave up hunting, the traditional sport of kings, in its stead substituting the custom of going on pilgrimages to Buddhist holy places.

Asoka's government laid great emphasis on the value of toleration, which he regarded as one of the most important ideals of Dharma. Despite his adherence to Buddhism he did not see himself as the champion of any particular creed or sect; on the contrary, he declared that all religions were worthy of respect. His edicts called for his subjects to follow his example and recognize the importance of toleration and mutual respect as a way of life.

> On each occasion one should honour another man's sect,
> For by doing so one increases the influence of one's own sect,
> And benefits that of the other man;

While by doing otherwise one diminishes the influence of one's own sect and harms the other man's.

(12th Rock Edict)

Asoka regarded himself as the father and servant of his people, entrusted with their welfare and happiness. This was the third element of his philosophy:

All men are my children . . . just as I desire for my children that they may obtain every kind of welfare and happiness both in this and the next world, so I desire for all men.

In this cause he relaxed the harsh laws of Chandragupta's time, built roads, created hospitals and rest-houses, had wells dug and groves of shade trees planted all over the subcontinent. In order to further his ideals he created a special class of officials, the dharma-mahamattas or overseers of the law. They were responsible directly to him and it was their duty to investigate the government of the provinces and to see that the needs of the people were attended to. The welfare of the king, he declared, rested on the moral and physical well-being of his subjects. Thus it was his duty to labour night and day on their behalf. Like his grandfather Chandragupta, Asoka was tireless in his pursuit of public business, which he dealt with at all hours and in all places.

At all times, whether I am eating, or am in the women's apartments, or in my inner apartments, or at the cattleshed, or in my gardens . . . In hard work and the dispatch of public business alone I find no satisfaction. For I consider I must promote the welfare of the whole world, and hard work and the dispatch of business are the means of doing so.

(6th Rock Edict)

Yet for all his idealism Asoka remained a very practical man, and he was careful not to tamper with the main institutions of Mauryan power. For all his remorse over the conquest of Kalinga, he continued to govern it as an essential part of his empire. He retained the enormous network of spies which his predecessors had maintained and there is no sign that he made any effort to reduce the huge Mauryan standing army. He did little to relax the criminal laws and he continued to maintain the death penalty, only granting a stay of execution to allow the condemned man to put his affairs in order and prepare himself. Asoka, it seems, was well aware of what was needed to rule an empire. He was only too conscious that his contained a great mixture of races, with very different beliefs, customs and attitudes. As with other great men throughout history, he realized that force alone could not hope to maintain an empire for long. With this in mind he tried to establish the rule of Dharma as a new imperial creed which he hoped would bind everyone together in a common allegiance.

Asoka's conversion to the teachings of the Buddha had momentous consequences for the future of Buddhism. Thanks to his patronage it ceased to be a simple Indian sect and began its career as a world religion. Between 250 and 240 Asoka held the first Great Council of the Buddhist clergy at Pataliputra. Here for the first time the teachings of the Buddha were gathered together and codified. He then sent out missionaries to every part of India and to the countries beyond. Among them were his son and daughter Mahinda and Sanghamitta, who carried the word of the Buddha to Sri Lanka. As a result of his efforts Buddhism spread far beyond the frontiers of India, to survive abroad as one of the world's great religions long after it died out in the subcontinent.

Mauryan Government

By the middle of Asoka's reign Mauryan rule stretched from the foothills of the Himalayas to Mysore in the south, and from Bangladesh to the heart of Afghanistan. It is sobering to think that this empire included almost the whole of the modern nations of India, Pakistan, Bangladesh and Afghanistan. One writ in the same language ran for the length and breadth of the subcontinent, a degree of unity unparalleled anywhere until the rise of the Roman empire two centuries later. Only the Dravidian kingdoms of Kerala, Chola and Pandya in the far south of the peninsula remained independent.

To his subjects Asoka was the first true universal emperor of India, the 'chakravartin', the representative of divine knowledge and authority. The empire he ruled over rested on the foundations which had been established by his grandfather. Chandragupta had placed great reliance on the teachings of the *Arthashastra* and under his successors this became the bible of Mauryan statecraft. Supposedly written by his Brahmin chief minister Kautilya, the *Arthashastra* (Science of Material Gain) was an eminently practical, dispassionate and deeply sceptical guide to the art of government. Its primary concern was to ensure the power and authority of the ruler, and the efficiency of his government. In this cause the *Arthashastra* laid down careful guidelines as to how the state should be organized, how the economy should be run, and the way in which war and diplomacy should be conducted.

> The primary duty of a king consists of the protection of his subjects and the constant keeping under control of evil elements. These two cannot be accomplished without the science of policy.

The policy of statecraft was taken very seriously by all the Mauryans, who took great pains to follow Kautilya's advice. Many of Asoka's pronouncements, for example, often seem only to echo the carefully considered tones of the *Arthashastra*.

The chief arm of Mauryan government was its methodically organized and efficient bureaucracy which carefully supervised almost every aspect of daily life. The empire was divided into four great regions, each administered by a viceroy who was either a member of the imperial family or a trusted associate of the emperor. Under the viceroy were the governors of the provinces, who were also appointed by the state. This, however, was not enough for the emperor and inspectors were sent round every five years to check on the provincial administration. The provinces in turn were subdivided into districts of several groups of villages, each staffed with an official who maintained the boundaries and kept a record of the population and the ownership of land and livestock within the area. Thus the roots of Mauryan power extended right down to the individual village itself which was the final unit of its administration.

The administration of the towns and the cities was just as highly organized. They too were governed by centrally appointed officials, foremost among whom was the superintendent who was responsible for law and order and the general cleanliness of the city. He was assisted by two other officials, an accountant and a tax collector. As for the capital, Pataliputra was governed by a board of thirty officials. This board was divided into six committees which between them regulated almost every aspect of city life. The first committee concerned itself with the register of all births and deaths; the second dealt with industry and manufacturing, while the third regulated the sale of all manufactured goods; the fourth supervised trade and commercial matters, the fifth oversaw the collection of taxes on all gold articles, and the sixth had special responsibility for the welfare of all the foreigners in the capital.

The Mauryan civil service was organized with great precision and there were different departments for the various areas – trade, revenue, agriculture, taxation, navigation, mines and arsenals. Very careful records were kept by each department of its spending and its income, all of which had to be accounted for to the Treasury. All officials were paid regular salaries, the higher ones in particular being very well paid. Indeed, their salaries accounted for almost a quarter of the entire budget. Yet at the same time the imperial government kept a careful watch over its bureaucrats and their activities were tightly controlled. 'Government servants', warned the *Arthashastra*, 'should be constantly kept under vigilance in their duties, for men are by nature fickle and temperamental.' According to the creed, the Mauryan bureaucrats worked only as directed, and nothing was done without the knowledge and approval of their superiors.

As with Mohenjo-Daro and Harappa, the power of the state seemed to extend into every walk of life. The currency, the system of weights and measures, even the drinking of alcohol, all were carefully controlled by the state. The government also owned all the important industries – mining, shipbuilding, the making of weapons, spinning and weaving. There was a rigorous code of conduct for all artisans and workers which was very strictly enforced. For example, workers who failed to fulfil their contracts were fined a quarter of their wages and could be imprisoned. Similarly, doctors whose patients died of neglect or negligence could expect to be very harshly dealt with. The sight of washermen beating their cloths clean over a bed of stones is still a familiar sight in India. In Mauryan times, however, these washermen (dhobis) knew they would be severely punished if they beat their laundry over any but the smoothest stones. Today thankfully the dhobi can breathe rather more easily about the quality of his work.

The whole system was held together by the prodigious energy of the emperor, supported by a ruthlessly efficient secret police and an enormous standing army. In the *Arthashastra* there were two qualities which a successful ruler had to have: he had to be 'energetic' and 'ever watchful'. Certainly the first three Mauryas had an almost religious dedication to the business of government, especially Asoka who was constantly travelling throughout his dominions in order to keep in touch with his subjects. But a king also had to be watchful, for in order to control his subjects he had to know what they were doing. To this end the *Arthashastra* advocated the use of spies and informers from every walk of life: thus householders, merchants, prostitutes, students and even holy men were employed to keep the emperor informed of what was happening in every part of his realm.

The other arm of the Mauryan state was the armed forces. Megasthenes tells us that in Chandragupta's time the army consisted of 600,000 infantry, 30,000 cavalry, 8,000 chariots and 9,000 elephants. Even if these figures were exaggerated, and it is more than likely that they were, it still suggests a huge number of men under arms, and it is not surprising to learn that soldiers were the most numerous class in society. Like everything else, the Mauryan army was very highly organized. Its affairs were handled by six different departments, one for each corps, plus a commissariat to deal with transport and supplies, and a sixth department whose business it was to co-ordinate movements with the fleet. Unlike many armies in the ancient world, the Mauryan army seems to have been a professional standing army; it was paid on a regular basis and its only function seems to have been to fight.

All this – the spies, the army and the huge civil service – was maintained by harsh laws and heavy taxation. All land was regarded as belonging to the state – farmers, for example, could be moved if the imperial officials were not satisfied with their methods. Whole communities on occasion were dispersed to clear forest land and establish new settlements. For all Asoka's humanity, one cannot ignore the fact that there are at least eighteen kinds of torture listed in the *Arthashastra*, punishments which he did little, if anything, to have repealed. However, the most pressing concern of the Mauryan administration was finance. The greatest danger to the security of the state, warned the *Arthashastra*, lay in an empty treasury. To combat this, the Mauryans taxed every possible commodity and source of wealth, whether gold, trade, livestock or, of course, land. One quarter of all crops and produce raised was taken by the government; out of this the peasant can have been left with little more than the barest subsistence.

ASOKA'S LEGACY

Yet for all this, Mauryan India seems to have enjoyed a very high level of prosperity and contentment. Harsh though they may have been, the laws of the Mauryans maintained the security of life and property which was so essential for a stable society. According to Megasthenes, theft was so rare that houses and property were often left quite unguarded. What the government took out in the form of taxes and levies it also put back in. Along with the payment of salaries, the largest element in the imperial expenditure was devoted to public works. This covered a wide range of activities, such as the construction of public buildings, the maintenance of roads and the development of wells and irrigation projects. The greatest public work of all was the Royal Road, one of the great wonders of the ancient world, and along which Megasthenes travelled on his way to the Mauryan court. It ran for 1,150 miles right across northern India, from the north-west frontier to Pataliputra. Every mile was marked by a stone indicating by-roads and distances. Trees planted on either side provided shade, while resthouses and wells at regular intervals supplied the traveller with shelter, food and water.

Megasthenes describes the Mauryan capital as the largest and greatest city in the world. It stretched for nine miles along the banks of the Ganges and was more than a mile and a half wide in many places. Even to the modern mind, its dimensions remain quite breathtaking. The outermost boundary was a moat connected to the river, 30 feet deep and 900 feet wide, which enclosed a mighty wall built entirely of wood, with 570 towers and 64 gates. By all accounts, Pataliputra was a sophisticated and vital place. The well-planned streets contained bazaars, theatres, racetracks, inns and public meeting places, all teeming with every kind of human life. At the centre of the city was the Imperial Palace. This stood by itself in a walled park, with trees and shrubs of every description, ornamental lakes for boating and all kinds of exotic

All that remains of Pataliputra

birds. The palace itself, although also made of wood, glittered with gold and silver and was adorned with elegant carving and inlaid sculpture. Asoka's palace was still standing six centuries later when the Chinese pilgrim Fa-hsien visited India. Fa-hsien was convinced that this magnificent building must be the work of spirits; only spirits, he believed, could have piled up the stones, raised the walls and executed the decoration in such a marvellous fashion. Today there is little to be seen, although there are some remains of gigantic wooden walls or palisades which can now been seen at the Patna museum.

Of the art of the Mauryan empire very little survives today, for nearly all the major works were created out of wood. Nevertheless it was in the Asokan period that stone first began to be substituted for wood and brick, to become the medium par excellence of Indian artists. The earliest surviving examples of Indian architecture, the rock-cut chambers in the Barabar Hills in Bihar, are thought to have been executed

A typical Asokan stone column made out of a single shaft of stone

on the orders of Asoka himself. These chambers were carved out of the living rock in the style of a wooden building in order to provide a retreat for the holy men of the area.

Asoka is also said to have constructed many Buddhist temples or stupas all over northern India. The stupa was originally a brick burial mound faced with stone which was raised over a relic belonging to the Buddha. Shaped like a huge dome, it has since become one of the most enduring images of ancient India. The most famous of Asoka's stupas is the Great Stupa of Sanchi near Bhopal; however, along with nearly all the other temples of the era, this has been completely transformed by subsequent alterations. What remains now really belongs to a much later period.

The most vivid monuments of the Asokan era were the polished stone columns which he had erected all over his empire. Made out of a single shaft of stone, at least 40 feet high and weighing almost 50 tons,

The magnificent lion capital on the pillar erected at Sarnath by Asoka

these pillars are a triumph of craftsmanship and engineering. In 1370, for example, the Muslim ruler of Delhi had a pillar moved there from where it stood. This one pillar required the labour of 8,400 men pulling a cart with 42 wheels. The polish left on these pillars by the Mauryan stonecutters was so highly finished that even in the sixteenth and seventeenth centuries they continued to dazzle travellers, who were convinced that they were made out of metal. The finest carving of all was reserved for the capitals of the pillars, which were crowned with lions and bulls which are in turn masterpieces of style and technique. The most famous and eloquent of these is the capital of the pillar erected at Sarnath which has at its summit a quartet of snarling imperial lions standing back to back, their eyes staring outwards, an image of imperial unity prevailing over diversity. The Sarnath capital, the quintessence of the Indian identity, is still the national symbol of the republic of India and today it appears in the centre of the Indian flag.

Asoka died in 232 BC. Following his death the Mauryan empire began to disintegrate. The coinage was debased and the frontiers of the empire contracted as governors of great provinces like Taxila in the north-west became virtually independent. Nevertheless, Asoka's successors continued to rule over central India and the Gangetic Plain for another fifty years. In 184 BC, however, Brihadratha, the last of the Mauryans, was deposed by his Brahmin commander-in-chief, Pushyamitra Shunga, who murdered him and seized the throne. India's first great unification had lasted almost 140 years, but in the end the strain of maintaining such a huge and all-encompassing administration proved too much. Faced with what must have been a huge drain of their resources and lacking the driving will of their great predecessors, the successors of Asoka found themselves unequal to the task of sustaining their inheritance.

Pillar capital from Pataliputra

CHAPTER FIVE

The Golden Age of Indian Civilization, 184 BC – AD 647

The collapse of Mauryan power saw the break-up of India into several different kingdoms, as new dynasties grew up to take control of various parts of the subcontinent. This state of affairs was to last for almost 500 years, until the rise of India's next great imperial dynasty, the Guptas. Despite this lack of political unity, this period was not one of stagnation but of increasing trade and prosperity, combined with great cultural enrichment.

The Heirs of the Mauryas

Pushyamitra Shunga, the usurper of the Mauryan throne, founded a new kingdom in central India which lasted for 112 years. Unlike Asoka, he was a devoted adherent of Hinduism and is said to have destroyed several monasteries and killed many monks. However, later evidence suggests that the monarchs who followed him did not share his attitudes, for nearly all the finest monuments of the Shunga period are Buddhist creations. One of the most spectacular of these was the great Buddhist stupa which was erected at Bharhut in Madhya Pradesh. This once huge and elaborate temple has been so completely despoiled that all that remains are beautifully carved fragments which now exist only in museums. The giant sculpture of the Buddhist temple at Bhaja (Maharashtra) also dates from the same era. Here the entire rock face has been carved away to create a monumental hall of worship (Chaitya) extending deep into the hillside. Originally built of wood, the Chaitya was a long chamber with a carved, vaulted roof, supported on either side by a row of columns. At Bhaja all the features of the earlier wooden

A stone carving showing a warrior at the temple at Bharhut

buildings have been painstakingly reproduced out of the living stone. The end result is quite remarkable.

In 72 BC the Shungas were overthrown by a new dynasty, the Kanvas. The last Shunga, Devabhimi, was killed, poetically enough, by his own chief minister, Vasudeva Kanva. However, the kingdom which he founded proved to be far shorter-lived than its predecessor and by 30 BC it too had disappeared.

In the east Kalinga, Asoka's last great conquest, had been one of the first states to throw off the Mauryan yoke. Under its king Kharavela, who ascended the throne in 183, at about the same time as Pushyamitra, Kalinga reached the peak of its power. Kharavela launched three invasions of northern India, bringing the kingdom of Magadha to its knees and sacking the once proud imperial city of Pataliputra.

Meanwhile, in the south a new power had assumed the mantle of the Mauryas. Shortly after the death of Asoka a hitherto obscure people, the Satavahanas, had carved out an independent state in the Deccan. Between the second centuries BC and AD, the Satavahanas (or Andhras as they became known) spread across much of western and central India. By the second century AD the Andhra kingdom had reached the zenith of its power and dominated the Deccan plateau from coast to coast. (The state of Andhra Pradesh, which was established in 1956, was founded in memory of their rule.)

The wealth which was garnered by the Andhras' control over the rich trade routes and seaports of the south was lavished on building and they have left behind them some of the most famous monuments in India. Towards the end of the first century BC they completely rebuilt Asoka's stupa at Sanchi, making it one of the most magnificent Buddhist temples in the subcontinent. Fortunately, Sanchi has been almost completely preserved and it remains an imposing sight to this day. Adorning the gateways and the railings are gloriously fashioned sculptures of flowers, animals and human figures: many of these still seem as fresh and as vital as when they were carved. The Andhras also built a number of temples in the area south of the Deccan, between the Krishna and Godavari rivers. The largest and most splendid was the Great Stupa at Amaravati, which was said to have been 162 feet in diameter and embellished with the most elaborate carving and decoration. Sadly these stupas were all but destroyed during the nineteenth century and all that is left is a series of crumbled remains. Nevertheless, many of the reliefs and sculptures have survived and together they rank as one of the finest flowerings of Indian sculpture. A number of these works can today be seen at the British Museum and at the Government Museum in Madras.

From here we move, once again, to the north-west, which was subject to yet another series of foreign invasions. By the end of Asoka's reign the Greek colony of Bactria (modern Afghanistan) had shaken off Seleucid control and made itself a powerful independent kingdom. In 190 BC Demetrius, the Greek king of Bactria, crossed the Hindu Kush and invaded north-western India. This invasion saw the creation of a new Indo-Greek kingdom, occupying the Gandharan region and the entire Punjab. This new state acted as a bridge between east and west, bringing about a fusion of Greek and Indian ideas which was to have a profound influence on Indian culture. Its most enduring legacy was the art of Gandhara. Here the adoption of Greek values led to the evolution of a classical form of Buddhist art, renowned for its naturalism and vitality.

The Kushan Period

The Greeks maintained their hold over north-western India until the middle of the first century BC. Then following the unification of China under the imperial Han dynasty, the Chinese began to advance their western frontiers. This forced the nomadic tribesmen who inhabited these areas to migrate even further westwards and triggered off a wave of invasions of India and western Europe. The first of these central Asian invaders were the Scythians or Shakas. They poured into Bactria and from there into India, where they completely destroyed Greek power in the north-west. The Shakas in turn were driven out of this area by another, more powerful, tribe, the Yueh-chi, and were forced further south into the area around Gujarat while the Yueh-chi established themselves in the Gandhara region. Here they founded the powerful new Kushan kingdom.

As the hub of the trade routes linking India, China and the West, the Kushan kingdom steadily grew in wealth and influence during the first century AD. It reached the height of its power during the reign of its third king, Kanishka (r.78–114) the greatest and most celebrated of the Kushan rulers. In his reign, the frontiers of the Kushan state extended from Gandhara and Kashmir to touch Benares in the east and Sanchi in the south. Tradition has it that Kanishka, like Asoka, converted to Buddhism and became a great devotee and patron of the faith. He is said to have convened the Fourth Buddhist Council and he built a number of magnificent Buddhist monasteries.

Kanishka took a great interest in art and literature and his court attracted artists, poets and musicians from all over Asia. The most famous of these was the Sanskrit poet Ashvaghosha, whose *Buddhacharita* (Life of the Buddha) is one of the earliest classical Sanskrit poems. Under Kanishka's patronage the Gandharan school of art reached its peak, producing Buddhist sculptures which are masterpieces of the fusion

Bodhisattva from Gandhara

between east and west. Inspired by the Greek and Roman models of the west, the stone carvers of Gandhara created a uniquely beautiful style, embodying vivid realism with great calm and serenity. Mathura, 35 miles south of Delhi on the Yamuna river, was the other great artistic centre of the Kushans. Here another school of Buddhist art flourished which was completely free of Greek influences and almost entirely Indian in character. Recent excavations have uncovered a number of these sculptures, most of them exuberantly carved out of the local red sandstone.

Despite his conversion to Buddhism and for all his patronage of the arts, Kanishka remained obsessed with war. He was not a popular ruler. In the words of a contemporary, 'The king is greedy, cruel and unreasonable: his campaigns and continued conquests have wearied the mass of his servants. He knows not how to be content.' His overweening ambition and insatiable lust for war finally proved too much for his own men, who smothered him to death in his camp. The Kushan kingdom, however, outlived him and survived for almost another hundred years.

The Rise of the Guptas

At the beginning of the fourth century AD, India was fragmented into a number of small states. Out of this seeming chaos there arose a new Chandragupta, whose aim it was to restore the lost glory of the Mauryans. Chandragupta founded the Gupta empire, one of the mightiest dynasties in Indian history.

Unlike Chandragupta Maurya, who was little more than an adventurer, the founder of the Gupta dynasty came from a background of inherited wealth and position. He belonged to a well-established and prosperous family of landowners who had lived in the area around Magadha for several generations. He made an important dynastic marriage with a princess of the Licchavi clan, one of the oldest and most powerful families in the region, and this, more than anything else, set the seal on his rise to power and enabled him to establish himself as the ruler of Magadha. In 320 he had himself enthroned at Pataliputra, the old imperial capital of the Mauryas, proclaiming himself 'Maharajadhiraja', 'king of kings', and his coins announced the beginning of the Gupta era.

The rule of the Guptas saw the creation of a new empire which was to dominate the whole of northern India. It lasted for almost 150 years and saw such a brilliant outpouring of science, art, music and literature that it has been hailed as the 'Golden Age' of ancient India.

On his death in 335, Chandragupta was succeeded by his son, Samudragupta (r.335–75). It is reputed that Chandragupta's last words to his son were: 'Thou are worthy, rule this whole world.' Inspired by this ambition, Samudragupta's dream was to make himself master of the entire subcontinent, in pursuit of which aim he waged numerous military campaigns all over India and the records speak of his victorious march across the country. He extended Gupta authority throughout northern India and his power reached from the Punjab to Assam in the east. He also marched into the Deccan and established his overlordship over the various kingdoms of the south, although he did not bring them

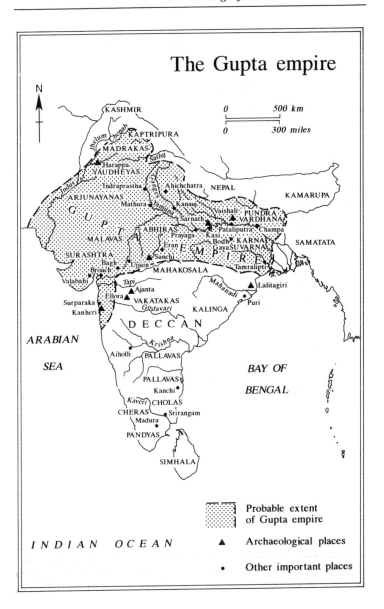

The Gupta empire

N

KASHMIR

0   500 km
0   300 miles

Jhelum Chenab
KAPTRIPURA
MADRAKAS
Satluj
Harappa
YAUDHEYAS
Indus
Indraprastha   Ahichchatra   NEPAL   KAMARUPA
ARJUNAYANAS   Mathura   Kanauj
Ganges Yamuna   Vaishali   PUNDRA
G U P T A   Sarnath   Pataliputra   VARDHANA
ABHIRAS   Prayaga   Kasi   Champa
MALAVAS   Bodh   KARNA   SAMATATA
E M P I R E   Gaya SUVARNA
SURASHTRA   Eran   Sanchi
Bagh   Ujjain   Tamralipti
Broach   MAHAKOSALA
Valabahi   Mahanadi   Lalitagiri
Tapi   Ajanta   Puri
Surparaka   Ellora   VAKATAKAS
Kanheri   Godavari   KALINGA
D E C C A N

ARABIAN   Krishna

SEA   Aiholli   PALLAVAS   BAY OF

PALLAVAS   BENGAL
Kanchi
Kaveri   CHOLAS
CHERAS   Srirangam
Madura
PANDYAS

SIMHALA

```
        Probable extent
        of Gupta empire

▲       Archaeological places

•       Other important places
```

INDIAN OCEAN

under his direct control. In western India he marched against the Shakas; here, however, he did not prove so successful and the Shakas were to remain unconquered until the reign of Chandragupta II. Nevertheless, under Samudragupta Pataliputra was once again the centre of a great empire, comprising almost the whole of northern India.

For all his military prowess, Samudragupta was also a man of great culture and learning. He was a musician and a poet and his inscriptions refer to him as 'Kaviraja', the poet king. His reign saw the beginnings of a brilliant artistic revival and Pataliputra became once more the cultural capital of India.

He was succeeded by Ramagupta who, unlike his father and grandfather, was supposed to have been a weak ruler. He is said to have been defeated in battle by the Shakas, and was forced to conclude a humiliating treaty with them. According to the popular Sanskrit drama *The Queen and Chandra Gupta*, which was written in the sixth century, Ramagupta was compelled to surrender his wife Dhruvadevi as part of the peace terms. Outraged by this, his younger brother Chandragupta disguised himself as the queen and entered the Shaka king's palace in her stead. He killed the Shaka king and became an instant hero with his people. In doing so, however, he had made a bitter enemy of his brother and he found himself left with no alternative but to kill him too. Having assassinated Ramagupta, he married Dhruvadevi and assumed the throne. The story itself is probably very much exaggerated but many of the details are true. What we do know is that Ramagupta did exist and that he was succeeded very rapidly by his younger brother, whose wife's name was indeed Dhruvadevi.

CHANDRAGUPTA II

Despite the rather murky circumstances surrounding Chandragupta's accession, there is no doubting his abilities. Chandragupta II was the greatest of the Guptas and his reign (375–415) marks the high point of the dynasty's power and glory. The Gupta empire reached its greatest extent and Chandragupta assumed the title of 'Vikramaditiya' ('He whose splendour equalled the Sun'). Taking up the work of his father, he launched a series of campaigns against the Shakas, and in 409 the Shaka kingdom was finally defeated and the whole of western India annexed to the Gupta empire. Chandragupta's realm now extended to the Arabian Sea, commanding the rich routes of trade and commerce with the western world. By marrying his daughter, Prabhavati, to the ruler of the Deccan, he also ensured friendly relations with the south. Gupta influence now stretched from Kashmir in the north to the Deccan, and from Bengal in the east to the Arabian Sea.

The prosperity and order of Chandragupta's great empire made a deep impression on travellers. The Chinese monk Fa-hsien, who was in India from 405 to 411, was struck by the peacefulness of the country and wondered at the mildness of the administration and the rarity of serious crime. According to Fa-hsien, respect for the law was so great that it was possible to journey from one end of country to the other without the slightest danger; even passports, he said, were not needed. Chandragupta II's reign also marked the culmination of the intellectual and cultural revival which had begun under his father. Under the patronage of 'Vikramaditiya' there was a glorious flowering of the arts and sciences. We are told that the court glittered with the glow of nine jewels, nine gifted men of arts and letters who graced the imperial capital. Of these the most brilliant was Khalidasa, who is regarded as the greatest poet and playwright ever to have lived in India.

CHANDRAGUPTA'S SUCCESSORS

After the death of Chandragupta II, the empire was governed by his son, Kumaragupta I. His reign, which lasted for almost forty years (415–54), saw a long period of peace and prosperity. Towards its end, however, the very existence of the empire was threatened by the appearance of terrifying new invaders from the north, the Hunas or Huns. Pouring down from the steppes of central Asia, the Huns crossed the mountains and swarmed across the plains of India. They were kept at bay only with the greatest difficulty and the imperial army suffered some very serious reverses. However, the tide was turned by the emperor's warrior son Skandagupta, who ascended the throne upon his father's death. He inflicted a crushing defeat on the Huns and drove them out of India. His victory was so complete that the subcontinent remained free from their depredations for almost half a century. Skandagupta had succeeded in turning back the same ferocious hordes who had overrun most of

Europe and Asia, reducing all its towns and cities to a desolate waste. It was a remarkable achievement, perhaps the greatest military achievement in Indian history.

Skandagupta (r.454–67) was the last of the great Guptas. He restored the empire and by the end of 455 it was once more at peace. However, the arduous military campaigns had been an enormous drain on the resources of the empire and left it gravely weakened. One of the most telling signs of this lies in the great scarcity of gold coins, which had once been minted in such profusion and variety by his predecessors. Nevertheless, on his death Skandagupta had the unique satisfaction of leaving behind him the same mighty empire which had been built up by his forebears.

His death, however, saw the rapid decline of the empire. Towards the end of the fifth century the Huns returned, invading India in even greater numbers. But this time there was no Skandagupta to lead a united India, only a decaying empire weakened by internal conflict and continual war. This new invasion shattered the last remnants of Gupta power, and by the middle of the sixth century the once imperial dynasty had all but disappeared. The Huns seized the Punjab and western India, which they held for about thirty years from AD 500. Under the leadership of their king Mihirakula they conquered much of the Gangetic Plain and had advanced as far as Gwalior in Madhya Pradesh. In 530 Mihirikula was defeated by Yashodharman, a former vassal of the Guptas who had built a large empire for himself in northern India. Although this victory ended the Hun kingdom in India, Yashodharman's own empire did not last very much longer and disappeared with his death in 540.

The Gupta Empire

The Gupta empire was organized in a similar fashion to the empire of the Mauryas, which it consciously sought to emulate. As in the Mauryan system, the king stood at the centre of government while princes or close relations acted as viceroys of the great provinces. In a similar vein, the empire was divided into provinces (*desha*), which were then subdivided into a number of districts (*pradesha*). Each particular section had its own set of officials who acted as the link between imperial authority and the local government. The power of the Guptas, however, was nowhere near as great as that of the Mauryan emperors and they were never able to exercise as much direct control over their administration. Whereas the Mauryans had insisted on knowing and controlling the doings of the lowest official, under the Guptas local government was more or less independent of the centre and decisions were generally taken locally. In the cities too the pattern was very similar. On the surface the city was run by a council, in a manner very reminiscent of the Mauryans; but in practice this council consisted not of officials appointed by the government but of representatives of the local community, such as local merchants and artisans. The revenue still continued to be collected by the emperor's officials but they were no longer paid in cash but with grants of land. This meant a considerable reduction in the authority of the king, who was no longer able to exercise so much control over the owners of the land.

The economic structure of the state, however, had not changed all that much since Mauryan times. Land was still the mainstay of the economy and continued to be heavily taxed. The state still took a large share of every harvest, there was a tax on cattle and gold, and the peasants also had to make over one sixth of their possessions in trees, meat, honey, fruit and herbs. Forced labour too was usually demanded for one day of every month, in order to maintain the roads, wells and irrigation systems. The state also continued to own industries of special importance, such as the mines, the mint, weaving and spinning mills, and gold and silver workshops. The amount of this ownership, however, was far less all-encompassing than it had been before. The evidence also suggests that, despite the number of taxes, the level of taxation was nowhere near as high as it had been under the Mauryas.

> People are prosperous and happy, without registration or official restrictions. Only those who till the king's land have to pay so much on the profit they make.   (Fa-hsien)

Commerce was widely carried on and India enjoyed a thriving trade with China and south-east Asia as well as with the West. Fa-hsien was particularly impressed by the prosperity of the towns and the volume of the trade which passed through them. Silk, muslin, calico, linen and wool were all produced in great quantities, for there was a vast domestic market to satisfy as well as a very considerable foreign demand. Ivory work was very highly valued and there was a great call for stone-cutting and carving. Metal-working was another major industry and used up large quantities of copper, iron and lead, as well as gold and silver. India's exports did not differ very greatly from earlier times and she continued to export spices, pepper, sandalwood, pearls, precious stones, perfume and herbs. However, imported commodities were now quite different and included Chinese silk, which was brought in in great quantities as was ivory from Ethiopia. Horses too were in great demand and came from Arabia, Iran and Bactria. As often as not these goods were carried in Indian ships, which now regularly sailed the Arabian Sea, the Indian Ocean and the China Seas. The authority of the Guptas ensured that these goods were moved swiftly and easily to all parts of the subcontinent. On the roads pack animals and ox-drawn carts were used and in eastern areas elephants too, while the lower reaches of the large rivers – the Ganges, Yamuna, Narmada, Godavari and Krishna – all served as major waterways.

The standard of living also was quite high, especially for the prosperous town dwellers who lived a cultured and refined existence. We are given a glimpse of this in Vatsyayana's famous fourth-century treatise on the art of love, the *Kama Sutra*. According to the *Kama Sutra*, the well-off citizen enjoyed a comfortable and relaxed life-style, though not necessarily a very luxurious one. His life was enhanced by well-seasoned foods, delicate perfumes and flowers; much of his time was devoted to poetry, painting and music, all arts at which he was expected to excel. Music in particular was considered a very necessary accomplishment, especially the playing of the lute, the most popular instrument. The sophisticated man of the world also had to be well versed in the art of love and it was with this purpose in mind that the *Kama Sutra* was written. As a manual on the art of love it is remarkable for its sophistication, analysing and discussing the whole question of love and lovemaking clearly and in great detail. In doing so, it gives us a very distinct picture of the society of its day. The comfortable life-style depicted was not confined only to the wealthy classes. Many finds of copper and iron objects suggest that the prevailing level of prosperity also included a large part of the middle classes – but not the outcasts who lived on the outskirts of the town, in slums which were not very different from today's shanty towns.

India had, however, changed a great deal since Mauryan times some 500 years earlier. Although the Guptas lavished patronage on Buddhism and Jainism, they themselves were Hindu and the society which travellers now found was predominantly Hindu. Caste had become much more important than before and great emphasis was laid on the concept of Brahmin purity. Fa-hsien speaks of the great fear of pollution from low castes and untouchables, to whom he refers as causing pollution 'on approach'. The foundations of society were clearly based on Hindu codes – the concept of the joint family, for example, was now firmly established and all the male members enjoyed an equal right to each other's property.

The most important legal treatises were also now derived directly from the Hindu canons, and the Gupta period saw the genesis of many of the main elements of later Hinduism. The temple started to become the focus of social and religious life and it was during this period that images began to be worshipped. There was also an upsurge in the popular worship of Shiva and Vishnu, who now overshadowed the other gods in the Hindu pantheon. As a result Hinduism itself assumed a new form and began to divide into two main sects – the Vaishnavites, the worshippers of Vishnu, and the Shaivites, the worshippers of Shiva.

The influence of Buddhism and Jainism had gradually modified Indian society and it was now far more gentle and humane than in Mauryan days. Gone were the harsh laws and the overbearing administration. According to Fa-hsien, the citizen no longer had to register his household or his property, nor observe so many rules. The peasant was much freer because he was no longer tied to the land: if he wanted to go, he could. Gone too were the harsh laws and the savage punishments: criminals were no longer executed, but fined, lightly or heavily, depending on the circumstances. 'Even in cases of repeated attempts at wicked rebellion, they only have their right hands cut off,' said Fa-hsien. In the West, European civilization had degenerated into chaos as the Roman Empire neared its end, while further to the east China was racked by troubles in the period between the two great dynasties of the Hans and the T'angs. To many of the travellers who visited it, India under the rule of the Guptas must have seemed the happiest and most peaceful country on earth.

The Classical Style

The Gupta period is one of the most important epochs in the development of Indian culture. Their lavish patronage of art and literature saw the evolution of a classical style which was to become the standard for subsequent developments. Sanskrit had already become the language of the ruling classes and the reign of the Guptas saw a flourishing of Sanskrit literature. The classical Sanskrit style reached its peak in the poetry and drama of Khalidasa, the 'Shakespeare' of India.

Very little is known about Khalidasa other than his work, which shows a gentle and happy man, a great lover of nature and of pomp, but possessed at the same time of a deep understanding of sorrow and the moods of women and children. He was the author of three plays and four poems, all of which have since become an integral part of the Indian literary tradition.

His most famous and beautiful work is the play *Shakuntala*, one of the classics of world literature. It is named after its heroine, the orphaned forest nymph Shakuntala, who captures the heart of King Dushyanta while he is out hunting in the forest. Her beauty so bewitches the king that he completely forgets his wife and kingdom and takes her for his bride. He lives with her for a time, leaving her with child, but then returns to his kingdom where he soon forgets everything that has happened. Thus when Shakuntala appears at his court with the heir that she has borne him, the king refuses to acknowledge her or his son. Only much later, after much grief and great suffering, does his memory return to him; only then does he recognize and acknowledge the youth who is his true son and heir.

One of the most popular of Khalidasa's other works is the poem 'Meghaduta', or 'Cloud Messenger', universally recognized as one of the gems of Sanskrit poetry. An imaginary Yakha or devil is separated from his lover by the curse of his master. Maddened by sorrow and longing he implores a cloud to act as his messenger to his beloved, and assure her of his undying love:

> I see your body in the sinuous creeper, your gaze in the startled eyes of deer, your cheek in the moon, your hair in the plumage of peacocks, and in the tiny ripples of the river, I see your sidelong glances, but alas, my dearest, nowhere do I find your whole likeness.   (Meghaduta. 19,21)

Giant though he was, Khalidasa was only the symbol of the literary achievement of this period. Both poetry and drama enjoyed great popularity and this encouraging climate produced a number of notable literary figures. One of the more unusual was the playwright Shudraka, author of a tragic and very realistic play about a poor Brahmin hopelessly in love with a courtesan. Most of the plays of this era tended to be romantic comedies for it was thought that the main purpose of the theatre was to entertain. Painful or distressing themes were largely avoided and Shudraka's work ranks as India's first real tragedy. There was also a major reworking of the traditional legends and stories. During this period the *Mahabharata* was compiled and rewritten in the form which has come down to us today. All the myths concerning Vishnu and Shiva were also collected together into a series of eighteen Sanskrit poems, known as the Puranas, and today they are regarded as the bible of popular Hinduism.

The Gupta age heralded a new epoch in Indian architecture. Until then Hindu temples had been built mostly out of wood, now for the first time they were built of dressed stone. The temple became the home of the god, where his devotees went to pray and offer gifts; it was in this form that it continued to be built in future. Gupta art reached its highest form of development in the field of sculpture. Technical skill was perfected and combined with a quest for spiritualism to create an entirely new vision. The human body, which had previously been described in an earthy and fleshy form, was now depicted in an abstract manner, characterized by its serenity, calm and inner tranquillity. The two great centres of Gupta sculpture were Mathura and Sarnath, near Benares. Together these two schools perfected a style which was personified by its refined simplicity and its calm serene air, and is

An early Hindu temple from the Gupta period

reflected in the beautiful Buddha images from both places which today are among the outstanding masterpieces of Indian art.

ART AND LEARNING

The Gupta style is also to be found in the magnificent sculptures which decorated the cave temples of Ajanta and Ellora in Maharashtra. The caves at Ajanta also provide us with our first glimpses of Indian painting and they are perhaps the finest example of Hindu art. Hidden in the carved cliffs of a remote valley north-west of Bombay, the caves remained forgotten for almost 1,200 years. They were rediscovered only in 1817 when a party of British officers out tiger hunting stumbled into them. Many of the caves themselves are masterpieces of Gupta architecture: a breathtaking variety of pillars, halls and temples all wrought from solid stone. Adorning them are numbers of softly and delicately carved figures, a clear echo of the art of Sarnath and Mathura. The wall-paintings, however, overshadow everything else: never again does Indian art achieve such freedom and such virtuosity. These frescos embody the spirit of the Gupta age and they are full of the life of the times – court scenes, love scenes, feasts, elephant processions, dancers and even a lady putting on her lipstick. They evoke a timeless world of

A painting of a princess from the cave at the Ajanta temple

refined elegance, peopled by graceful, aristocratic men and women living in harmony with exuberant nature. In this world, even the gold coins minted by the Gupta treasury were of such magnificence that they too seemed to be works of art.

Learning was at its peak and this period witnessed a great interest in the sciences, especially astronomy, astrology and in particular mathematics, which made great progress. Under the Guptas, Indian mathematics was more advanced than in any other part of the world; India's scholars had already invented the zero symbol and the decimal system, which were both to have a profound impact on the development of science. From India this knowledge was carried by the Arabs to Europe. In astronomy the leading figures were Aryhabhata and Varahamihare, whose works displayed a wide knowledge of Greek astronomy. Aryhabhata was by far the most brilliant and original thinker; he was the first Indian to hold that the earth was a sphere which rotated round its axis and that it revolved around the sun. Aryabhata was the most scientific of all Indian astronomers and it was largely through his efforts that the subject came to be recognized as a separate discipline from mathematics. His fertile and enquiring mind inspired several other discoveries, many of which have since become a part of our everyday terms of reference; he developed a remarkably accurate method, for instance, of forecasting the length of a year, coming as close as 365 days in his estimate. It is also to Aryabhata that we owe our first true explanation of the lunar eclipse, which he attributed to the shadow of the earth falling on the moon.

Universities and institutions of learning flourished in this fertile climate. The most famous was the Buddhist monastery of Nalanda, near Patna in Bihar. The largest monastery in the subcontinent, Nalanda was one of the most celebrated universities in Asia and its reputation extended as far as China. Modern excavations have revealed the foundations of a huge complex of monasteries and temples which once accommodated 10,000 monks and students. Although the ruins themselves are rather disappointing, there are still traces of temples built high on raised platforms and approached by long flights of steps. These are all that are left to conjure up the image remembered by one pilgrim – of a temple city, its lofty towers lost in the morning mists.

Harsha Vardhana 606–47

The fall of the Gupta empire saw northern India break up once more into a cluster of small kingdoms, very similar to that which had preceded Chandragupta's rise to power. In 606 a remarkable young monarch, Harsha Vardhana, ascended the throne of Thanesar, a small kingdom north of Delhi. Harsha had come to power at a very critical moment. Thanesar was right in the middle of a war with a neighbouring power and its whole future seemed in doubt. Although he was only sixteen, Harsha, who had been destined for a Buddhist monastery, proved himself equal to the challenge, rallying his forces and saving his kingdom.

Harsha's great ambition was to revive the empire of the Guptas. The task of empire builder, however, was now much more difficult that it had been in Chandragupta's day. Harsha's military expeditions were not always successful and the best he was able to do was to establish a state which was loosely bound together by feudal ties. Nevertheless, after six years of almost continuous campaigning, he had made himself the most powerful ruler in northern India. The empire which he built up stretched from Gujarat in the west to Bengal in the east, and as far as Kashmir in the north. Its capital was Kanauj, in western Uttar Pradesh, which became one of the largest and most important cultural centres in North India. It replaced Pataliputra as the new imperial capital and it remained a key city well into the medieval period. However, hardly anything has survived and the only trace of its former glory is a series of mounds and the outlines of a few fortifications. Although Harsha tried to extend his power across the Narbada river into southern India, he was thoroughly defeated by Pulakesin II (r.610–43), the ruler of the Deccan, and he did not make the attempt again.

Thanks to the existence of a record of his reign, we know a great deal about Harsha. The *Harshacarita* (Life of Harsha), compiled by his court poet Bana, was the first important historical biography written in the subcontinent and it is regarded as the finest example of Sanskrit prose. The Harsha who emerges was clearly a man of great gifts and prodigious energy. He was constantly on the move, controlling his kingdom by ceaselessly travelling from province to province, conducting military campaigns and dispensing justice. He is described as hearing the complaints of his humbler subjects with unwearying patience, not in a grand audience hall but in a small travelling pavilion by the road. Yet at the same time Harsha loved pomp and ceremony, travelling across the country in great state accompanied by an enormous train of officials, courtiers, attendants, Buddhist monks and brahmins.

Harsha was a great champion of Buddhism and under him Nalanda reached the height of its splendour. However, like the Guptas before him, Harsha was an enlightened supporter of all religions. A lover of philosophy and literature, he himself was an excellent scholar and his court attracted many literary men. Despite his huge burden of work, Harsha also found time to write three plays, two comedies in the classical Gupta style about life in the harem, and a serious play about religion.

Harsha ruled for forty-one years. For the latter part of this long period his empire was more or less at peace. Despite this the power of the king was no longer as great as it had been under the Guptas: in reality his empire was a loose confederation of states bound together by a series of feudal ties and personal loyalties. Thus the control of the central government was much looser and law and order were not quite so well maintained. Hsuang Tsang, another Chinese pilgrim, was twice robbed on his journey through Harsha's domains and on one occasion he was nearly sacrificed by river pirates. Harsha died in 647 without leaving an heir. The empire which he built had been carved out by his own achievements and had been held together by the force of his personality; it is not surprising that it fell to pieces after his death.

CHAPTER SIX

The Rise of Islam, 647–1565

The later years of Harsha's reign saw the origin of new developments in the Middle East which were to have a momentous impact on the course of Indian history. At about the time that Hsuan Tsang was wandering through Harsha's dominions, a new religion, Islam, was beginning to make its appearance in Arabia. Its followers were Muslims.

Islam, meaning 'Submission to the will of God', originates with the figure of the founder Muhammad (570–632), a merchant of Mecca. Muhammad is regarded as the Prophet or Messenger of God and he was said to have received revelations from God in the form of visions. He translated these visions into a set of precise rules which he embodied in the Quran, the holy book of Islam. Unlike Hinduism, these doctrines were clear-cut and definite and advocated a specific way of life. All Muslims formed part of a brotherhood overriding all distinctions of class, race and colour, in which each man was equal before God. Everything that could not be understood or controlled was the will of God, Allah, whose dictates must be completely obeyed. As with Christianity, from whose traditions it derived many of its influences, Islam recognized only one God. According to Muhammad there could be no other way. God was absolute and indivisible. He could not be represented in any other form or by any sort of image. 'There is no God but God and Muhammad is the Prophet of God.'

Inspired by this stern, uncompromising message, Muhammad's followers swept through the Middle East waging holy war (Jihad) against those who failed to acknowledge the will of Allah. By the time of Harsha's death, Islam was already well on its way to becoming a world religion. From Arabia and Syria it burst across Asia Minor, north Africa and Spain, only to be halted in the heart of France at the battle of Tours in 732. Eastwards it knew no bounds and from Persia it spread rapidly across Asia towards India. The first invasions of the subcontinent came towards the end of the seventh century when Arab raids were launched on Sind, now the southernmost province of Pakistan. By the early years of the eighth century Sind had been conquered by the Arabs; it has remained Muslim ever since. This, however, was not destined to be the route by which Islam would come to India, for the Arabs halted at Sind and did not attempt to penetrate any further. The real threat was not to come for another 300 years and it was to arrive from a very different direction.

These early invasions were soon forgotten and north India settled down to enjoy a long and unaccustomed respite from foreign aggression. This is not to say that the subcontinent was free of the perennial power struggles and internecine conflicts which characterized so much of its history. Indeed, for the next several centuries northern and central India was divided between different warring powers. Although several powerful kingdoms were established, many were short-lived and did not survive the rulers who had founded them. The flourishing commercial and cultural intercourse which India had once enjoyed with the outside world declined sharply as she became more and more preoccupied with her own affairs.

This process was accompanied by a growing stagnation in the state of knowledge and learning. So much so that when the famous Muslim physician, astronomer, philosopher and historian Al-Biruni arrived in India in 1030, he could find barely a trace of the brilliant intellectual culture of the Gupta age. Indian learning, he observed, seemed to be little more than a confused jumble of ideas completely lacking in any clarity or order. 'I can only compare their mathematical and astronomical knowledge to a mixture of pearls and sour dates, or of pearls and dung.' In his great study of India, the *Tarikh al Hind* (A History of India), Al-Biruni gives a penetrating description of the subcontinent and its people on the eve of the Muslim invasions. He was particularly struck by the insularity of Hindu culture which, as he observed, seemed to have completely closed in on itself. The Hindu outlook, he noted, combined an enormous pride in its own civilization with a complete contempt for all things alien; this was accompanied by a singular reluctance to communicate anything at all about its own culture and learning.

The Rajputs

The history of northern and central India during this period is dominated by the Rajputs, whose name means 'Sons of Kings'. They were thought to be descended from the Huns who had settled in India during the fifth and sixth centuries and were quickly assimilated within the Hindu structure, forming themselves into a number of warrior clans claiming descent from the sun, the moon and fire. These clans gradually rose to power during the ninth and tenth centuries until they formed most of the ruling dynasties of the north. Foremost amongst them were the Chauhans, the Chaulukyas, the Pratiharas and the Paramaras, all of whom described themselves as the 'Agnikula', the fire family. For most of the eleventh and twelfth centuries, these clans fought each other incessantly for mastery. As in medieval Europe, war became part of a way of life and the Rajputs acquired an undying reputation for valour, heroism and lofty chivalric ideals. They were to all intents and purposes the knights of medieval India. Indian legends and songs are full of their deeds.

The most celebrated and romantic figure of all was Prithviraj III, the last of the Chauhan kings, the most powerful of the Rajput dynasties which had established itself in the area around Delhi. His deeds are commemorated in a long epic poem, the *Prithvirajaso*, which tells the romantic story of how Prithviraj fell in love with the daughter of his bitter enemy, the king of Kanauj, and how he won her in the face of her father's unrelenting opposition. When the time came for the princess to marry, all the suitors were assembled at the court of Kanauj so that she could make her choice. Prithviraj, however, had not been invited; instead, a statue of him as the doorkeeper had been placed outside as an insult. But the princess had already made her choice, and she walked straight up to the statue and placed her garland around its neck, whereupon Prithviraj, who had been lying concealed nearby, galloped up and carried her off to his capital.

Despite the decay of learning, both art and literature flourished under Rajput patronage. Indeed, the medieval period was India's great age of temple building – magnificent examples can be found all over northern and southern India. Most remarkable of all are the temples of Khajuraho in central India which were built between 950 and 1050. Today some twenty temples survive out of a total of more than eighty; many of these are richly decorated with lush, erotic sculpture and they rank among the greatest works of medieval Hindu art. The largest and finest is the Kandariya Mahadeo Temple dedicated to Shiva. Almost every yard is covered with carving, a profusion of riotous figures coupled in every conceivable kind of embrace. In the west, on top of Mount Abu in south-west Rajasthan, stand the shimmering marble temples of the Jains. Seen from the outside they often appear quite ordinary; on the inside, however, they are quite breathtaking – a wonder of shining marble carved into delicate and infinitely complex patterns, the interior of each temple is as intricately and elaborately worked as an ivory trinket; only the floor itself remains smooth.

In the east, almost on the other side of India, are the temples of Orissa – at Bhubaneshwar, Puri and Konarak. Although they share many common characteristics, such as their monumental beehive-shaped towers, the most striking image of all is provided by the sun temple at Konarak (1238–64). Here the whole temple is conceived in the form of a gigantic stone chariot, the vehicle of the sun god, Surya, in his path across the skies.

The Turkish Invasions

The conquest of Sind had been just a passing episode. The major Muslim invasions were launched not by the Arabs but by the Seljuk Turks, who were to be the real standard-bearers of Islam in India. Yet another people of central Asian origin, the Turks had already come to dominate the Muslim world and in 1071 they burst upon the west. They overthrew the Byzantine empire and overran Asia Minor, founding what was to become the modern state of Turkey. By the tenth century they had established themselves in Afghanistan, and it was from here that they launched themselves on India.

In 962 an independent Turkish kingdom was founded at Ghazni, between Kabul and Kandahar in modern Afghanistan. Under its third ruler, Mahmud (971–1030), Ghazni became a formidable power and it was from here that the first shattering blows were delivered. Beginning in 977 Mahmud, who became known as the sword of Islam, led seventeen brutal bloody raids into India. Fuelled by Islamic zeal and lured by the prospect of loot, he launched himself against the temple cities of north India. Enriched by the donations of the pious, these temples were renowned for their vast quantities of gold, silver, jewels and precious stones which had been accumulated over the centuries; they were also the home of countless Hindu idols and images, an abomination in the eyes of Islam. Between 1010 and 1026 Mahmud sacked and destroyed Mathura, Thanesar, Kanauj, Nagarkot and, richest and most fabulous of all, Somnath, on the seashore at Kathiawar in Gujarat. It contained a huge temple with a pyramidal roof of 13 storeys surmounted by 14 golden domes. The whole structure was supported by 56 huge wooden pillars carved and set with precious stones. Most wonderful of all was the image of a 'Siva' lingam, a phallus which seemed to float in mid-air without any visible support from above or below – it was in fact held in place by a magnetic force-field. A thirteenth century Arab source tells how the inhabitants of Somnath watched Mahmud's preparations with indifference and amusement, confident in the protection of their deity. The 'Siva' lingam however proved of no avail. 'The Indians made a desperate resistance. They would go weeping and crying for help in the temple and then issue forth to battle and fight till all were killed.' More than 50,000 were killed: those who remained were put to the sword. The temple itself was razed to the ground and the Siva lingam broken into pieces.

By the end of Mahmud's reign, the Punjab had become part of his empire and north-western India had been brought firmly within the Muslim sphere. The vast wealth he brought back was used to beautify and enrich his own capital, transforming Ghazni into one of the greatest Islamic cultural centres of its day. However, despite the savagery of these raids they failed to make any real impact on the rest of India: to most Indian rulers the Muslims were just another wave of barbarians (*mlecchas*) like the Sakas and the Huns. It was thought that in time they too would be absorbed and assimilated within the fold of Hindu civilization. But the Turks were not on the same primitive level as previous invaders, for they had been deeply influenced by the sophisticated Islamic culture of the Persian world. They represented a religion and a culture which would remain entirely separate from the Hindu structure. For the first time a completely foreign culture was inserted into the Indian fabric, one which could not and would not be absorbed. To this day Muslim communities exist side by side with Hindu communities, each with its own distinctive customs. It was a development which had profound implications for the future of the subcontinent.

With the death of Mahmud of Ghazni, the threat from the north-west was soon forgotten and the Indian rulers returned to their internal rivalries. Thus when the second wave of attacks came, India was as completely unprepared as she had been before. Ghazni was succeeded by another Turkish dynasty, the Sultanate of Ghur. Almost 150 years after Mahmud's death, the onslaught on India was resumed by Sultan Muhammed of Ghur. Together with his slave lieutenant Qutb-ud-Din, Muhammed made his first attack on India in 1175. His purpose, however, was not just to loot and plunder but to establish a kingdom. Having established his authority over Sind, he proceeded to conquer the Punjab, taking Peshawar in 1179 and Lahore, the capital of the Punjab, in 1186.

From there he attacked the Rajput kingdoms controlling the Gangetic Plain. Momentarily forgetting their bitter internal rivalries, the Rajput clans rallied together under the leadership of their great hero Prithviraj III. In 1191 the two sides met at Tarain, about 80 miles from Delhi. Under the onslaught of the massed ranks of Rajput cavalry, both the left and right wings of the sultan's army broke down and fled, followed soon after by the centre. The sultan himself was wounded and had to flee the field. However, this great victory was not followed up and in the following year, Muhammed of Ghur returned with a fresh army.

Once again the two sides faced each other at Tarain. This time fortune was not with Prithviraj. The simmering jealousies between him and the other Rajput kings burst into the open and he was deserted by his allies. Rajput chivalry and courage proved of no avail and Prithviraj and his army were defeated and destroyed.

> For miles the stricken field was bestrewn with castaway flags and spears and shields, and heaped bows, jewelled swords and plumed casques, exquisitely chiselled and damascened gauntlets, breastplates and gaily dyed scarves, intermingled with the countless dead.

In true Rajput tradition, Prithviraj's princess, dressed in all her bridal jewels, mounted her husband's funeral pyre and threw herself into the flames. Prithviraj's kingdom of Delhi fell to Muhammed of Ghur, who returned to Afghanistan leaving Qutb-ud-Din in charge. The following year saw the overthrow of the Jai Chand, the Rajput ruler of Kanauj who had deserted Prithviraj on the field of Tarain. His kingdom, whose territories covered roughly the same area as the modern state of Uttar Pradesh, was annexed to the new Islamic state. In 1202 Bengal was conquered, and with it Bihar, Orissa and Assam were all overrun. The conquest of Bihar saw the systematic destruction of all the remaining Buddhist monasteries and the wanton slaughter of all the monks. Nalanda, the greatest centre of Buddhism in India with over 10,000 monks living and studying there, was completely sacked. The ruthless fanaticism of the new conquerors led to the complete disappearance of Buddhism from the land of its birth.

The Delhi Sultanate, 1206–1526

Following the assassination of Muhammed of Ghur in 1206, Qutb-ud-Din made himself ruler of Delhi, founding the Delhi Sultanate which was to last 320 years under five successive Turkish and Afghan dynasties. Despite its longevity this was to be a very turbulent period, marked by court intrigue, palace revolutions and full-scale rebellions.

THE EARLY DYNASTIES, 1206–1320

The first Turkish dynasty is often called the Slave dynasty, after its early rulers who had been military slaves of the sultan. By this system, young children were taken from their homes and brought up in the service of

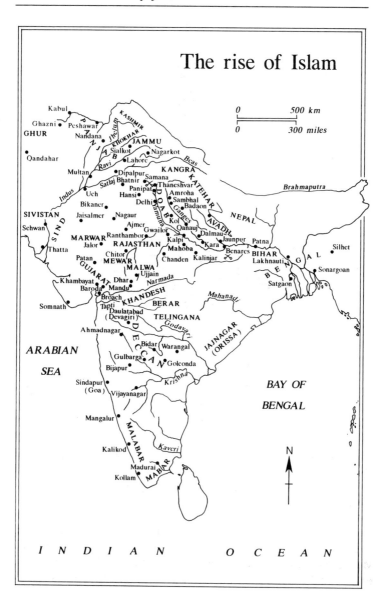

The rise of Islam

The colossal Qutb Minar in Delhi erected as a symbol of victory by
Qutb-ud-Din the Turkish Conqueror

the sultan. They were drafted into either the army or the civil service
and many rose through the ranks to exercise positions of the highest
authority. Qutb-ud-Din was such a man, a soldier and administrator of
considerable ability. In the heart of his new capital (now on the outskirts
of modern Delhi) he erected a stupendous monument, the Qutb Minar.
Fifty-two feet at its base and a colossal 260 feet high, the Qutb Minar
was every inch a tower of victory. Carved with sentences from the
Quran, each letter a yard high, it cast the long shadow of God over the
conquered city of the Hindus.

The tower was completed in 1236 by Qutb-ud-Din's son-in-law and
successor, Iltutmish. Iltutmish (1211–36) ruled at Delhi for twenty-five
years, during which time he did his best to weld the loosely conquered
Muslim territories into some form of political unity. By 1220 he had
established the northern frontier of the sultanate along the Indus river

and had managed to impose his authority on the turbulent Turkish nobles. In his efforts to consolidate his hold over the Gangetic Plain, he launched several campaigns against the Rajputs but they continued to resist stubbornly. Nevertheless, by the time of his death Iltutmish had succeeded in establishing the most powerful state in north India.

Iltutmish was followed by his daughter Raziya (r.1237–40). The only Muslim woman ever to rule in India, Raziya seems to have been a remarkable figure. Abandoning female dress and manners, she threw herself into the workings of the administration, held open court and rode out at the head of her troops. According to contemporaries she was endowed with all the virtues of a king, but as one of them remarked, 'not born of the right sex, and so, in the estimation of men, all these virtues were worthless'. After barely three years she was murdered by her own palace guard.

During the period which followed her killers jostled with each other for power. The foremost of these conspirators, Balban, ruled as Grand Chamberlain for almost twenty years, until 1266 when he assumed the title of Sultan. Thereafter he reigned for another twenty years, dying in 1287. In order to protect the sanctity of the office which he himself had violated, Balban surrounded himself with pomp and ceremony. The king's presence became almost unapproachable; he was surrounded at all times by his bodyguard; and he never spoke in public except to his officials. Balban's ruthless and effective methods held the sultanate together and his reign established the foundations of the Delhi state.

In the early stages the court at Delhi remained very aloof from indigenous life, and Indians, whether Muslim or not, were excluded from positions of authority. The court relied almost entirely on immigrants from central and western Asia – Mongols, Turks, Afghans, Persians and Arabs. Thus India attracted a steady stream of immigrants, adventurers and soldiers of fortune from all over Asia. Under the Khalji dynasty, however, this policy was reversed and Indian Muslims were gradually admitted to high office. This action served to strengthen the foundations of the sultanate and marked another step in its growing Indianization.

The Khaljis were another group of Turks, who came to power in 1290 when Balban's general Firuz Khalji seized the throne. Under them

(1290–1320) the Delhi state began to approach the peak of its power. The authority of the sultan was firmly enforced over the nobility and tight economic controls were introduced. The Rajputs were pressed back into central India and into the deserts of Rajasthan. In 1299 Gujarat was conquered and the first incursions were made into the Deccan, even as far as Tamil Nadu in the deep south.

MUHAMMED TUGHLUQ

Five miles from the Qutb Minar, on top of a range of sandstone hills are the massive ruins of Tughluqabad, the huge fortress-citadel of fourteenth-century Delhi. For most of that century Delhi was ruled by the Tughluqs, a dynasty of mixed Mongol and Turkish origin. It was founded by Ghiyas-ud-Din Tughluq, a military commander who seized the throne in 1320. Upon his accidental death, he was succeeded by his second son Muhammed-ibn-Tughluq (r.1325–51). Of all the monarchs who ever sat upon the throne of Delhi, Muhammed Tughluq is perhaps the greatest enigma. No ruler in medieval India has aroused so much discussion and provoked so many conflicting opinions. Brilliant, eccentric and capricious, he has been described as 'of all men the fondest of making gifts and shedding blood'. An energetic, hardworking ruler and a capable general, he was one of the most learned and accomplished men of his age. At the same time he was also capable of the most horrifying acts of cruelty and violence. He extended the Delhi sultanate to its furthest limits and by the early part of his reign his control stretched deep into southern India. However, his policies gave rise to widespread economic and social discontent, culminating in rebellion and breakdown.

The Delhi empire reached its highest point only to collapse, and before his death Muhammed Tughluq had lost everything south of the Vindhyas. In 1338 Bengal threw off its allegiance to Delhi and established itself as a separate Muslim kingdom. In the south, too, there was rebellion. In 1345 the Muslim nobles of the Deccan revolted and set up a new sultanate. This was the Bahmani kingdom, which survived from 1346 to 1482, leaving a profound mark on the Muslim culture of the south – many of its monuments can still be found all over the Deccan. This period also saw the re-emergence of Hindu power. In

1336 the Hindu kingdom of Vijayanagar was founded (see p.106); it was to become famous as the greatest centre of Hindu culture in India. Over the next two centuries its power spread from sea to sea across the whole peninsula.

Muhammed Tughluq was succeeded by his first cousin Firuz Shah. Although he was more than forty when he came to the throne, Firuz Shah reigned for thirty-seven years (1351–88). Learning from the revolts of the preceding reign he relaxed many of the policies which had been imposed by his predecessor. Much of his time was devoted to building and during his reign Delhi became a city of gardens, mosques and splendid public buildings. What is left of his capital, Firuzabad, is now a pleasant public park much favoured by strollers, readers and picnickers to relax in.

The death of Firuz Shah was followed by a period of rapid deterioration. This was accelerated by the invasion of the terrible central Asian conqueror Timur the Lame (Tamerlane). Taking advantage of the dissensions in Delhi, Timur swooped down through the passes to ravage the Punjab. In 1398 he captured Delhi itself. The city was savagely plundered and so completely destroyed that it was abandoned for almost 100 years. The inhabitants were slaughtered and those who survived were dragged away as living booty to a life of slavery. As Timur himself remarked grimly, 'The pen of fate had written down this destiny for the people of this city.' In his wake he left behind a desolate wilderness, marked only by macabre towers of human flesh, piled high with the heads and bodies of slaughtered Hindus. 'The city was utterly ruined; the inhabitants who were left, died, and for two months not a bird moved a wing in Delhi.'

THE FIFTEENTH CENTURY

Independent sultanates appeared in western and central India, in Jaunpur (1400), Malwa (1406) and Gujarat (1407). Gujarat, with its thriving trade with the west, flourished and its capital at Ahmedabad became one of the most splendid cities in India. Rajput power re-emerged, and in Rajasthan two new Hindu kingdoms, Marwar (Jodhpur) and Mewar (Udaipur) appeared on the scene. The Delhi sultanate had become only one of a number of Muslim states in northern India.

The mausoleum of Firuz Shah in Delhi

The fifteenth century was dominated by two dynasties who inherited what was left of the Delhi kingdom. First were the Sayyids, who were displaced in 1450 by an Afghan dynasty, the Lodhis, who largely restored the power of the sultanate. The first of them, Bahlul Lodhi (r.1451–89), brought the whole area from the Punjab to Benares once more under the rule of Delhi. He was followed by his son Sikander Lodhi (r.1489–1517), who is commonly regarded as the most remark-able of all the sultans of Delhi. A ruler of great energy and ability, Sikander Lodhi moved the capital to Agra, from where he ruled with a strong hand. He also found the time to stimulate the growth of learning and the creative arts and his reign saw the beginnings of a fusion between several aspects of Muslim and Hindu culture in literature, art and religion. Some of the blue-domed tombs of the Lodhi rulers can still be found in a pretty park called the Lodhi Gardens, but unfortunately their tombs are all they have left us.

The first two Lodhi kings had relied a great deal on Afghan tribal loyalty and they had tried to rule with the support of the Afghan nobles. However, Sikander's successor, Ibrahim Lodhi (r.1517–26), tried to reassert the absolute power of the sultan. Not surprisingly this met with fierce opposition and his reign saw a continuous struggle between him and the nobles which finally culminated in the governors of the Punjab calling for foreign assistance to overthrow him. Babur, the ruler of Kabul, was invited to invade; in 1526 the two armies met at Panipat where Babur defeated and killed Ibrahim (see p. 110). His victory ushered in a new era in India's history, the Mughal era.

The Interaction of Islam and Hinduism

The Turks and the Afghans brought with them new influences which were to modify and alter Indian culture. First of these was a new language, Persian, which supplanted Sanskrit as the official language throughout northern India and was to prove an important new literary influence. Throughout the succeeding centuries Persian became the lingua franca of much of south Asia, and the cultivation of Persian literature became one of the cornerstones of Indo-Muslim culture. The period of the Delhi sultanate marked one of the early peaks of Indo-Persian literature. History in particular was held in great esteem; one of its leading lights was the Muslim cleric Barani (d.1358) whose *Tarikh-i-Firozshahi* chronicled the rise of Muslim power up to the reign of Firuz Shah. The dominant figure of this period was the poet Amir Khusrau (1253–1325). Nicknamed the 'Tuti-i-Hindi' (The Parrot of India) on account of the quantity and quality of his poetry, Amir Khusrau was the finest of all Indian-born Persian poets and is today regarded as the father-figure of Indo-Muslim culture. Persian literature also introduced a new art form, for many of the books were illustrated with exquisite miniature paintings by Persian artists. This style of art was taken over by the Indians and during the later sixteenth and seventeenth centuries it was to reach brilliant new heights.

The most visible change in the Indian landscape came with the introduction of a new architectural style. The Turkish invaders brought with them the traditions of Arab and Persian architecture. Wherever they went they built vast forts, palaces, tombs and places of worship, decorated with floral and geometric patterns and texts from the Quran. Thanks to them the mosque, the mausoleum, the arch, the dome and the minaret have all become an integral part of India's scenery. The most important structure was the mosque, the ritual centre where Muslims gathered to pray. Either square or rectangular, it was surrounded on three sides with cloisters or pillared arcades. Those at prayer faced the wall to the west, towards Mecca, the spiritual capital of Islam. At each corner was a minaret, a slender pointed tower from which the muezzin, or crier, called the faithful to prayer. The other main structure was the mausoleum. This was a tomb enclosed in an octagonal or square-shaped room which was then surmounted by a dome. In contrast to the rich and varied decoration of Hindu architecture, these buildings were austere and monumental with very little in the way of ornamentation. In accordance with the doctrines of Islam, no living thing or image of any kind was represented. The earliest mosque of all was the Quwwat ul Islam or 'Might of Islam', which was erected by Qutb-ud-Din. As befitting its name, the mosque was built on the site of Delhi's largest Hindu temple to commemorate the triumph of Islam over the Hindus.

In the field of religion the doctrines of Islam were to have a powerful impact. The Islamic concept of one God and its attack on caste and image worship had a profound effect on Hindu thought. It encouraged the emergence of several spiritual sects which preached against asceticism, ritual and caste and advocated a single, universal religion. The Hindu doctrine of *bhakti*, which preached the spiritual love of God, inspired a Muslim weaver called Kabir (1440–1518) to attempt a synthesis of Hindu and Muslim ideas. Kabir preached that

> God is one, whether we worship him as Allah or Rama . . . The Hindu God lives at Benares, the Muslim God at Mecca; but He who made the world lives not in a city made by hands. There is one Father of Hindu and Muslim.

His teachings inspired millions of Muslims and Hindus, who abandoned their respective faith to embrace the simple love of God. The democratic doctrines of Islam also encouraged the growth of Sikhism in the Punjab which became the best known of these movements. It was founded by Guru Nanak (1469–1538), a Hindu who had rejected the strictures of caste. He too preached a religion which centred on one God who was the creator of all things.

Vijayanagar and the South

Vijayanagar, which means 'City of Victory', was an immense fortified city and the capital of a Hindu empire which flourished from 1336 to 1565. Situated on the banks of the Tungabhadra river, in the state of Andhra Pradesh, it was the wonder of its time. A garden city, almost twenty-four miles round, Vijayanagar was ringed by seven concentric walls whose lines stretched for nearly sixty miles. Said in its heyday to have housed half a million inhabitants, the city contained palaces of marble, colossal stone elephant stables, delicate ladies' pavilions, baths, bazaars and, of course, hundreds of temples. Foreigners who visited Vijayanagar – Italians, Persians, Portuguese, Russians – were all quite overwhelmed by what they found. In 1522 Paes, a Portuguese traveller who had come to India after visiting the Italian cities of the Renaissance, spoke with awe of a city as large and as splendid as Rome, full of charm and wonder with innumerable lakes, waterways and fruit gardens. As well as being an important religious centre, Vijayanagar was also a magnet for trade in pearls and coral, elephants and horses, camphor, pepper, sandalwood and musk. Through its seaports on the Coromandel and Malabar coasts it traded with countries as far away as China, Burma, Malaya, Persia, Africa and Portugal.

Vijayanagar was founded by two brothers, Harihara and Bukka, who had been defeated by the armies of Muhammed Tughluq and taken as his prisoners to Delhi. Here they converted to Islam and gained the confidence of the sultan. When a rebellion broke out amongst the Hindus of the south, they were given the task of restoring order to the region. However, Muhammed Tughluq's troubles with his own Muslim nobles encouraged the brothers to declare themselves independent and they reverted to Hinduism.

For much of its history Vijayanagar was at war with the neighbouring Muslim kingdoms of the Deccan. The disintegration of the Bahmani sultanate towards the end of the fifteenth century saw the growth of several independent Muslim states – Bidar, Ahmednagar, Bijapur, Golconda and Berar. However, they were all successfully kept at bay and during the reign of Krishna Deva Raya (1509–29) Vijayanagar reached the height of its prestige and prosperity. Krishna Deva Raya was the ablest of Vijayanagar's kings and its greatest military leader. A fascinating personality, he was even more noted for his personal qualities, his moral conduct, his tolerance and his love of literature. In the words of an admiring Portuguese visitor:

> He is the most learned and perfect king that one could possibly be. He is a great ruler and a man of such justice . . . He is by rank a greater lord than any but it seems nothing compared to what a man like him ought to have, so gallant and perfect is he in all things.

His court, it seems, only mirrored his splendour. Renowned for its magnificent sculpture and decoration, it was rich with silk hangings, silver furnishings and beautiful gems, fragrant with the smoke of incense and filled with gifted Sanskrit and Telugu poets and philosophers. There are still traces of Krishna Deva's Hall of Audience and the platform on which his throne stood, both of them built to grand proportions. On the outer walls of the platform one can see carvings of elephants, dancing girls, camels and scenes from the *Ramayana*.

Krishna Deva Raya proved to be the last great Hindu king of southern India. The ambition of his successors drove the Muslim sultans of the Deccan finally to sink their differences and unite together. At the battle of Talikota in 1565 the Hindus suffered a catastrophic defeat. Vijayanagar was completely obliterated. According to some accounts the destruction of this vast citadel took five months; others say it took the best part of a year. What remains today are a few grandiose buildings and a huge tumble-down mass of ruins scattered over a vast area. Of the clumps of stone that litter the ten-mile-square site, scarcely one can be lifted without a crowbar and tackle.

CHAPTER SEVEN

The Mughal Empire,
1526–1707

The Mughal period is one of the most glorious and fascinating episodes in Indian history. It describes the reign of India's most splendid Muslim dynasty, whose rule held the subcontinent together for nearly two centuries. Like so many previous conquerors the Mughals had their roots in Central Asia, and the word Mughal itself is an Indian spelling of Mongol.

The English version of the word, Mogul, is still very much in use and as 'mogul' is often employed to describe the great power and influence exercised by press and industrial tycoons. When applied to Indian history where it has its origins, its significance is even more breathtaking: it conjures up images of fabulous wealth, dazzling splendour, awesome power and savage ruthlessness. For Western travellers to the subcontinent in the sixteenth and seventeenth centuries, India was the land of the 'Great Mogul'. Although so much has changed and the Mughal empire itself has long since vanished, it is a perception which still remains with us. Today's visitor will still see a landscape which is dominated by the beauty and the grandeur of the Mughal legacy. The sublime memory of the Taj Mahal, the imposing grandeur of the Red Fort, the silent splendour of Fatehpur-Sikri – for many these will be the most abiding images of India. Like his earlier counterpart, the most vivid and enduring memory for today's traveller will still be that of Mughal India.

The memory of the Mughal period is not only to be found in its monuments. There are traces of its influence almost everywhere in Indian society – in its languages, its customs, its dress and its food. In history its importance is profound. For the first time since the death of

Harsha Vardhana, almost 1,000 years earlier, we see the return of a stable, unifying force to the Indian scene. Instead of the divisive, fragmentary pattern of the preceding centuries, we see a growing political, administrative and cultural unity spreading through the subcontinent. By the latter half of the sixteenth century, almost all of northern India was once more under the control of a single empire. By the end of the seventeenth century, it had spread still further and now dominated almost the entire subcontinent.

Unlike so many other areas of Indian history, we have a wealth of information for the Mughal period from a variety of sources, both Indian and European. It reveals to us a rich gallery of striking personalities, both men and women. As much as anything else, it is this which accounts for the fascination of the period.

Babur: The Founding of an Empire

Babur (1483–1530), the founder of the Mughal empire, is also one of its most fascinating and attractive personalities. A poet and a man of letters, he was also an adventurer of iron nerves and powerful determination. A keen diarist, he recorded his experiences in his memoirs, the *Tuzuk-i-Baburi*, which are an important source for the history of the period. These memoirs speak of a tremendous zest for life, a man of boundless energy and optimism, a dedicated drunkard and a wholehearted sportsman and polo player. They also reveal an artistic nature of great sensitivity and refinement. Wherever he went Babur laid out Persian gardens, and his memoirs are full of references to the beauties of nature. Cold-blooded and ruthless at times, he was also capable of great generosity and chivalry, and his memories are laced with that rare quality – an endearing sense of humour.

Heir to a small principality in central Asia, Babur was the direct descendant of two great central Asian conquerors: on his father's side Tamerlane, the destroyer of Delhi, and on his mother's side the Mongol warlord, Genghis Khan. Most of his early years were spent trying to recover his ancestral seat of Samarkand, the glittering capital of central Asia. Catapulted into authority as an eleven-year-old boy, he lived a freebooting existence, wandering from place to place with a small band of followers in search of food, wealth and a kingdom. On one sorry occasion, Babur tells us, his army numbered scarcely 200 men, most of them 'on foot with sandals on their feet, clubs in their hands and long frocks over their shoulders'. These were years of constant danger, immense hardship and great distress. Babur once again sums it up rather well: 'It passed through my mind that to wander from mountain to mountain, homeless and houseless had nothing to recommend it.'

In 1504, by a stroke of luck, Babur gained control of Kabul in Afghanistan. From here on his fortunes prospered and he was able to carve out a new kingdom for himself in Afghanistan. Having established himself he began to turn his attentions elsewhere and in 1517 he made his first raid into India.

At the time, India was divided into four spheres of influence, two Muslim and two Hindu. The first Muslim zone stretched from the Indus river to the Bay of Bengal, covering Sind, Delhi, Punjab, Bengal and Bihar, while the second encompassed Gujarat and Malwa in the west and the Bahmani kingdoms of the Deccan in the south. As for the Hindu areas, the first consisted of Rajasthan and the Rajput states, the second, far to the south, the Hindu kingdom of Vijayanagar. Urged on by his discontented Afghan nobles Babur invaded India in 1525.

In the spring of 1526 Babur met Ibrahim Lodhi at Panipat, 50 miles from Delhi, which was to become the decisive battleground of India. Babur was heavily outnumbered, with little more than 25,000 troops while Ibrahim Lodhi's army is said to have been as many as 100,000. Typically undaunted, Babur dug himself in behind a barricade of 700 carts, behind which he entrenched his artillery under the command of Turkish gunners from Constantinople. On the wings he positioned his other great weapon, his cavalry which had been trained in the Turkish tactic of wheeling and flanking. Ibrahim Lodhi's huge army ground to a halt before the earthworks and the artillery. Then at the critical moment Babur launched his cavalry which wheeled and attacked from both flanks. The result was a resounding victory. Babur occupied Delhi and pushed on to Agra where his first act was to lay out a garden.

Important though it was, Babur's victory at Panipat did not mark the end of his problems. His own chiefs had regarded the invasion only as a great raid and they had no intention of settling down in their new conquests. Complaining bitterly about the heat and the dust, they demanded to be led back to the cool Afghan hills. However, Babur's great powers of leadership prevailed and he was able to win over his supporters. It was as well that he did, for they now had to face an even more formidable enemy. Realizing that he intended to stay, the Rajput princes combined together once more. Led by another veteran hero, the one-eyed, one-armed Rana Sangha of Mewar, a Rajput army of 80,000 marched on Agra. Completely demoralized by the size of this new threat, the Mughal army would have melted away had not Babur rallied them once more. In a dramatic speech Babur, the lover of wine, renounced alcohol for ever – not for the first time! He broke up his cherished golden wine goblets, declaring, 'With fame, even if I die, I am contented; let fame be mine, since my body is Death's.'

The battle of Khanua was fought on 16 March 1527 about 40 miles west of Agra. The same tactics were employed as at Panipat and the Mughal position was defended by a series of entrenchments, behind which were the artillery and the matchlock men. The Rajputs, however refused to be daunted or to modify their traditional ideas of warfare; riding stirrup to stirrup, as was their custom, they launched a series of magnificent mass charges against the Mughal positions. In Babur's own words:

> Still the gallant Rajputs were not appalled. They made repeated and desperate attacks on the Emperor's [Babur's] position, in the hopes of recovering the day, but were bravely and steadily received, and swept away in great numbers. Towards evening, the confusion was complete, and the slaughter was consequently dreadful.

Finally as evening fell after ten hours of fighting, the Rajputs were completely routed. Panipat had only unseated an unstable dynasty; Khanua shattered the dream of a Rajput revival. Although they retained control of Rajasthan, their offensive power was destroyed for ever and they were never again to aspire to the mastery of India. Victory left Babur fairly secure and gave him undisputed control of a large area of northern India. However, he still had to deal with the Afghan chiefs of Bengal and Bihar who refused to accept his authority. In 1529 Babur fought his third and last great battle, near Patna where he defeated a coalition of Afghan chiefs under Mahmud Lodhi, Ibrahim's brother.

With relatively meagre resources Babur had managed to make himself master of most of northern India; still only forty-five he now found himself in control of an empire stretching from Afghanistan to the borders of Bengal. However, like many of his countrymen he too longed for the lush greenery of his homeland. Indeed, his first impressions of his new kingdom were not favourable. Hindustan, he wrote in his diary, had little to recommend it. 'No good horses, no good fish, no grapes, muskmelons, no good fruits, no ice or cold water.' Even candlesticks and torches he complained bitterly, could scarcely be found.

> If you want to read or write by night, you must have a filthy, half-naked fellow standing over you holding a wood tripod with a wick on which they let trickle a thin thread of oil when necessary.

However, he noted realistically that 'Hindustan was a large country and had an abundance of gold and silver'.

HUMAYUN

Whatever he may have thought about it, Babur did not live long enough to consolidate his newly-won kingdom. His health had been ruined by a lifetime of exertion and hard drinking and within a year of his last victory he was dead. His much-loved eldest son Humayun (r.1508–56) inherited a vast, newly-conquered, unsettled and unconsolidated empire. His army, too, was not wholly reliable, a mixed body of Turks, Persians, Afghans and Indians who had been held together only by his father's magnetic personality.

Humayun is almost as interesting and attractive a character as his father, although he commands much less respect. A mercurial figure, he was brilliant, charming, good humoured and affectionate, a brave soldier and good general who could inspire his followers and endure great hardship. Yet he was also wayward, unstable and profoundly self-indulgent, dominated by an overweening love of pleasure which periodically got the better of his natural energy and good sense. After a string of brilliant achievements he would settle down to gorge himself

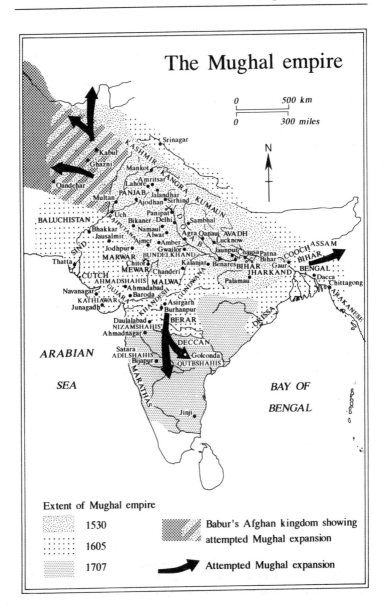

The Mughal empire

Extent of Mughal empire

(dotted)	1530
(dotted)	1605
(shaded)	1707

Babur's Afghan kingdom showing attempted Mughal expansion

Attempted Mughal expansion

on wine, opium and poetry. In the prolonged fit of indolence and carelessness which followed, everything he had worked so hard to gain would be needlessly frittered away.

Upon ascending the throne, Humayun gave a rousing display of what he was capable of. In 1531 he easily defeated the renewed challenge of Mahmud Lodhi. Then in 1534–5 he took Malwa and Gujarat in a brilliant campaign. Following this he lapsed into one of his characteristic stupors and indulged himself at Agra for almost a year. Not surprisingly he lost both his newly-conquered provinces and watched idly as a new threat built up in the east. This took shape in the form of a new Afghan leader, Sher Khan, who was to prove far more dangerous than any of his previous opponents. However, instead of destroying him Humayun allowed him to build up his power in Bihar. Only when Sher Khan moved against Bengal with all its wealth and treasure was he finally galvanized into activity. By then of course it was too late.

INTERREGNUM, 1540–1555

By 1540, after two resounding defeats, Humayun found himself a fugitive. He wandered from kingdom to kingdom with an ever-dwindling band of followers seeking help. On his wanderings he met Hamida, the daughter of a local ruler in Sind. Although only fourteen at the time, she was not much impressed with this debauched and hunted fugitive and it took Humayun nearly a month to persuade her to marry him. These were difficult times for Humayun and he stumbled from disappointment to disappointment. His fortunes reached their lowest ebb during the crossing of the Sind desert. Hamida, who was now pregnant, found herself without a horse, but in spite of her condition none of Humayun's followers would give up their mounts for her. Finally Humayun gave up his own horse and clambered on top of one of the baggage camels. He travelled in this fashion for several miles, perched ingloriously on top of the camel, before the humiliating spectacle finally proved too much for his followers and one of his officers eventually offered him his own horse. It was here in the Sind desert, on 15 October 1542, that Humayun's heir, Akbar, the greatest of all the Mughals was born. His birth proved to be the turning-point in his father's fortunes and Humayun finally found refuge at the court of the

Shah of Persia.

Meanwhile Sher Khan had himself enthroned as Sher Shah. He established himself at Delhi from where he proceeded to assert his authority over most of northern India. Within five years he had reorganized the whole government and had built up the beginnings of an administrative structure. His great ambition was to build a monument grander than anything found in Delhi, 'that my name might remain honoured upon earth until the day of resurrection'. In this cause he greatly enlarged the new citadel which Humayun had begun to lay out at Delhi – the Purana Quila ('Old Fort'). As befitting its name, this is a giant ruined shell of a fort dominated by two great gateways and massive, rugged walls. Although not much else remains of Sher Shah's capital, the sheer size and scale of the ruins themselves are a fitting tribute to his ambition. His masterpiece, however, was the tomb which he had constructed for himself at Sasaram in Bihar. A grand five-storey mausoleum, picturesquely set in the middle of a lake, it is a scene of great romantic beauty which for sheer charm far surpasses many of the other monuments of this era. Had he lived, it is unlikely that the Mughals would ever have re-established themselves in India. Fortunately for Humayun, Sher Shah was killed in 1545 at the siege of Kalinjar, one of the great Rajput strongholds of central India. Upon his death the empire which he had built collapsed into several parts.

THE RETURN OF HUMAYUN

In the meantime Humayun had gained the support of the Shah of Persia who agreed to help him regain his heritage. In 1545, the year of Sher Shah's death, Humayun regained Kabul and Kandahar with the aid of Persian forces. Then, after several years preparation, he was finally ready and in 1554 set out for India. Under the leadership of his general Bairam Khan, his army achieved two resounding victories and Humayun was able to reoccupy Agra and Delhi. The Mughal episode which had seemed destined to come to an inglorious end had been revived. Humayun, however, did not live to enjoy his triumph and within six months he was dead – killed by the effects of a fall down the stairs of his library, an eight-sided pavilion called the Sher Mandal which still stands inside the Purana Quila. After a discussion with his astrologers on the roof of the Sher Mandal, Humayun had began to descend the steps when he heard the muezzin calling the hour of prayer. Turning to bow his knee in respect he slipped and fell headlong down the stairs. As one unsympathetic chronicler rather unkindly put it, 'He stumbled out of life as he had stumbled through it.'

In his memory his widow Hamida raised a magnificent tomb of white marble and red sandstone. Barely a mile away from the spot where he died, Humayun's tomb is set in the most glorious surroundings amidst gardens, fountains and pools of water. The tomb, which stands on a red sandstone platform, consists of a central octagon surmounted by a dome and flanked by lesser domes and towers. Quite apart from its beauty, the tomb is also important for architectural reasons: here for the first time the Mughals combined their inherited love of gardens and water to enhance the symmetry of the buildings and the harmony of the colour scheme. It was a process which reached its perfection in their most famous monument of all – the Taj Mahal.

The comparisons with his father are many. When Humayun died he was nearly forty-eight, almost the same age as Babur when he died. The lives of both men had been characterized by huge fluctuations and had seen an extraordinary combination of triumph and disaster, good luck and misfortune. For all his romanticism Babur remained eminently practical and clear-headed, whereas Humayun allowed his romantic side to cloud his better judgement. Babur, for example, had once taken a practical decision for astrological reasons but had regretted it almost immediately. Humayun, on the other hand, would spend hours shooting arrows into the air marked with his name and that of the Shah of Persia. He would then spend almost as much time trying to determine how the arrows had fallen, so that he could work out which nation would become the greater.

The Age of Akbar

Humayun had died before he could begin to establish his authority and at his death the Mughal position seemed as insecure as when Babur had first taken Agra, almost thirty years before. All the work of both Babur and Humayun would probably have come to nothing had it not been for the genius of Akbar (1542–1605).

Only thirteen years old when he came to the throne, Akbar owed his survival to the faithful guardianship of his father's general, Bairam Khan. An able general, a seasoned politician and deeply loyal, Bairam Khan steered Akbar through the early challenges of his reign. The new regime was established with a victory on the now historic field of Panipat in 1556. Here Bairam Khan and Akbar defeated the forces of another challenger, Hemu, a Hindu general who had usurped control of Delhi and Agra. At the time of Humayun's death Bairam Khan and Akbar were far away in the Punjab, and when Delhi fell to Hemu the nobles advised Bairam Khan to retreat to Kabul with his young protégé. Refusing to be intimidated by Hemu's strength, they advanced to meet him. It was a bold and decisive move and it set the tone for the rest of the reign. For the next four years Akbar allowed himself to be guided by Bairam Khan, who gradually consolidated the Mughal position in northern India. In 1560, however, now in his eighteenth year and already increasingly masterful, Akbar dismissed him and shortly afterwards assumed the reins of power himself.

The reign of Akbar is one of the most significant and decisive epochs in the history of India. It was during this period that the Mughal empire became a political fact over almost half of India and a factor which has influenced her ever since. The whole period is indelibly stamped with the personality of Akbar, who next to Asoka is perhaps the greatest figure in Indian history. One of the most famous of all Indian characters, Akbar is also one of the most complex. Although he never learned to read or write, he had a prodigious memory and a keen intellect. He made up for his illiteracy by having every manner of book on philosophy, history, poetry and theology read out to him. By nature humane and gentle, he was essentially a man of action, renowned for his great physical strength and personal courage. A consummate politician and soldier, he was a man of boundless energy and ambition and often only slept for three hours a night. The number of descriptions which exist of Akbar suggest an energetic, powerful and often very sensitive man. Perhaps the most revealing of these is from the memoirs of his son Jahangir, who embittered his declining years:

although he was illiterate, so much became clear to him through constant intercourse with the learned and the wise in his conversations with them that no one knew him to be illiterate, and he was so well acquainted with the niceties of verse and prose composition that his deficiency was not well thought of. He passed his nights in wakefulness and slept little in the day . . . He counted his wakefulness at night as so much added to his life. His courage and boldness were such that he could mount raging, rutting elephants, and subdue to obedience murderous elephants.

AKBAR'S CONQUESTS

Akbar's achievements transformed the Mughal empire from an alien, foreign dynasty into part of the accepted order of things. The first great turning point in his reign was the Rajput war (1568–9). Then as now Rajasthan, with its semi-arid wastes and its rocky desert strongholds, seemed to represent the very heart of Hindu India. Indeed, apart from the southernmost tip of the subcontinent it was now the only part of India which remained entirely Hindu. Although their ambitions had been severely checked by Babur, the Rajputs still represented a permanent threat to Mughal progress.

The leading Rajput power was the state of Mewar, led by Udai Singh (r.1537–72) who proudly scorned any dealings with the new rulers of Delhi. In 1568 Akbar laid siege to Udai Singh's capital of Chitor, a vast rocky crag in the middle of the desert. After a fierce struggle the fortress was captured but there was to be no surrender. As was their custom, the Rajputs preferred death for all before dishonour. In a terrible ritual known as the 'Jauhar', the women and children threw themselves into the flames of the funeral pyre while the men sallied out to fight to the death. All the Rajput warriors duly died in the ensuing battle. Those who survived the holocaust, some 30,000 or so, were massacred on Akbar's orders as a warning to others. The lesson had the desired effect. The great Rajput fortresses of Ranthambor and Kalinjar surrendered the following year and the rest of Rajasthan accepted Mughal supremacy. Chitor, the scene of Rajput valour and heroism for almost a thousand years, was left desolate. Its ruins are still an awesome sight today: one of the finest surviving examples of medieval Hindu fortifications, its walls tower some 500 feet above the plain. A still silence hangs over the walls, the deserted pavilions and the ruined temples – the brooding memory of a savage past.

Akbar's next conquest, the rich province of Gujarat, extended the Mughal empire to the Arabian Sea. This was done in a campaign of almost dazzling speed. Hearing that a revolt had broken out in the capital of Ahmedabad, Akbar set out with a small force of 3,000 horsemen. He covered 600 miles in nine days, arriving on the eleventh day to defeat an astonished army of rebels before marching back to his capital in another 32 days. His next target was Bengal, then the wealthiest province in north India, which he had annexed in 1576, and over the next few years he gradually conquered Kashmir (1586), Orissa (1592), Sind and Baluchistan (1590–5). By 1590 Akbar had established himself as the undisputed master of north India and he began to turn his attention to the Muslim states of the Deccan. Progress here was slower but he still managed to make substantial inroads.

One enemy, however, continued to defy him. This was Udai Singh of Mewar, who with luminous spirit vowed never to go to Delhi while India was ruled by foreigners. It was only after Independence in 1947 that a descendant of his house was finally to visit Delhi. To replace Chitor, Udai Singh built himself a new capital at Udaipur. Nestling within a ring of stark, brown mountains surrounded by rippling lakes and dotted with fairy-tale palaces, it is one of the most beautiful cities in India. At its heart is the Jag Niwas or Lake Palace (1754), a dreamlike creation of marble amidst a sea of luminous blue. Still owned by the descendants of Udai Singh, it is now one of the most romantic hotels anywhere in the world.

The Consolidation of Mughal Power

Akbar recognized that a real settlement could not be achieved by conquest alone. Looking back on successive Muslim dynasties, not one had lasted more than forty years, and he had the wisdom to realize that no empire in India could hope to be secure unless it commanded the support of the Hindu population, nor could it seriously hope to influence the country without a proper administrative structure. Up till then Mughal authority had rested on the support of several near-independent feudal chiefs who were occasionally disciplined from the centre. Beyond this, neither Babur or Humayun had any means of enforcing their decisions or policies. Sher Shah, however, had begun to lay the foundations of a more concrete system and it was his work that Akbar built on.

His first step was to come to a series of understandings with the Rajputs. Through a number of marriage alliances and by the grant of personal privileges, Akbar managed to bring them into the service of the empire. In return for allegiance and loyal service, the Rajput chiefs were made partners in the Mughal empire. Left in control of their own territories, they were given imperial honours and positions of authority in the Mughal administration: Rajput rajas became governors of Mughal provinces and commanders of Mughal armies. To many the Rajputs were the leaders of Hindu India and through them the rest of the Hindu community gradually began to accept Mughal authority.

Akbar's partnership with the Rajputs was accompanied by a new policy of religious toleration and freedom of worship. Whereas previous Muslim rulers had always maintained the supremacy of Islam, Akbar worked hard to ensure that both Islam and Hinduism were treated on the same footing. He recognized that there could be no integration of the two communities unless Hindus felt that their religion and their customs were respected. In this cause he went to great lengths to safeguard Hindu temples from destruction and he encouraged the building of new ones. Indeed, in the latter half of his reign it was said that Hindu temples were even safer from interference than mosques.

Akbar also abolished two taxes which the mass of the Hindu community found particularly oppressive. The first was the lucrative pilgrimage tax which was exacted from the streams of pilgrims who travelled to worship at the innumerable Hindu shrines and holy places. Even more hated was the 'jizya' tax, a poll tax which was levied on all non-Muslims. Even though it was not always oppressive, the Jizya was bitterly resented by nearly all Hindus, who regarded it as a symbol of servitude. These measures and many others like them had the effect of transforming Akbar in the eyes of his Hindu subjects. To them he was no longer just the leader of a foreign minority, and they regarded him more and more as the accepted ruler of all India. Rather like Asoka had been, the Mughal emperor became the protector of his people and the guardian of all religions.

To a great extent Akbar also succeeded in restoring the concept of imperial sanctity which had surrounded the earlier Buddhist and Hindu emperors. A freethinker, fascinated by all religions, Akbar was motivated by a searching curiosity about the nature of religion. He would spend hours in conversation with Brahmins, Jains, Muslims, Sikhs and Christians, trying to discover the truth about religion. Inspired by these different strands he inaugurated a new religion – 'Din-i-Ilahi', the Divine Faith. This was an attempt to found a national religion which would enable Muslims and Hindus to worship together. It revolved around the figure of the emperor, who was presented as a semi-divine figure whose authority was almost sacred. Obedience was a near-religious duty while it was almost sacrilege to disobey or to oppose. Although Akbar's new religion died with him, it had the effect of surrounding the Mughal throne with an air of almost divine authority which set it above the general run of Indian kings and princes, and enabled the Mughal empire to command the allegiance of both Hindus and Muslims.

Akbar gave his empire a firm basis by providing it with a well-developed, clearly organized system of government. This was perhaps his greatest achievement. As in Mauryan times, the whole system was cemented together by a centralized bureaucracy controlled by the king. Akbar created a fixed, impartial civil service, arranged into thirty-three grades with regular ranks and fixed salaries. The officers were called 'mansabdars' or 'holders of commands' and they performed both military and civil duties. Each rank was classified by the number of cavalry an official could be expected to lead and they ranked from commands of 10 to commands of 5,000. In Akbar's day all these officers were paid in cash, something which must have imposed a huge strain on the imperial revenues. Under his successors, however, officers were given assignments on tracts of lands from which they collected the revenue in lieu of salary. The system was designed to provide a structure in which talent and ambition could find its outlet in the service of the state. The dangers of rebellion were averted by constant rotation, every officer moving every three to four years. At the death of an official all his property was resumed by the state. Thus the next generation had to start from the bottom of the ladder.

Akbar's empire was organized into eighteen provinces or soubahs, which were divided into districts called 'sarkars' and into subdistricts or 'parganas'. Each province was governed by its imperial governor, the 'Subadar', who commanded the troops and was responsible for law and order. He was matched by a 'Diwan', who was responsible for collecting the revenue and paying the troops. This division of authority was carefully calculated to reduce the chances of rebellion. It meant that an over-ambitious subadar had no money to pay his troops while the diwan had no troops to command. As under the Mauryans, the towns and cities were governed by a separate set of officials who in turn supervised the various municipal boards.

The land-revenue system, which continued to be the main source of income, was completely reorganized in an effort to make it fairer and more efficient. Under Akbar's brilliant Hindu finance minister, Raja Todar Mal, virtually all the cultivated land in north India was recorded and graded. Land was assessed according to the soil and crop-bearing potential. An average yield was estimated which then formed the basis for the revenue assessment. All this had the effect of making taxation much fairer, more systematic and more efficient than it had been for centuries. This, together with the other parts of Akbar's administrative machine, was maintained by his successors and survived until well into the eighteenth century. Akbar had inherited a state founded on little more than feudal loyalties and personal power, but within the space of a lifetime he had created an efficient administrative structure which would tie the whole country together.

FATEHPUR SIKRI

The most evocative expression of Akbar's genius is his royal capital at Fatehpur Sikri, one of the most spectacular sites in the whole of India. Situated in a remote desert town some twenty-six miles west of Agra, it was built between 1571 and 1586. It owes its creation to the prophecy of a Muslim saint who had predicted the birth of Akbar's son and heir, the future emperor Jahangir. Inspired by the fulfilment of the prophecy, Akbar built a completely new city on the site of the holy man's retreat. A characteristic product of Akbar's demonic energy, the city was constructed at a phenomenal rate. Jahangir recalled how in the space of barely fifteen years a whole network of buildings appeared as if by magic out of the desert air.

Akbar's capital was only inhabited for fourteen years before it was abandoned once more to the desert. Almost untouched by the passage of time, Fatehpur Sikri is a perfectly preserved ghost town – a silent complex of splendid palaces, pavilions, tombs, reflecting pools and a great mosque, all elaborately carved from red sandstone. The nature of the decoration is so complex and so ornate that it often seems that it could only have been fashioned from wood. But everything in this city – the doors, the lintels, the screens and even the floorboards – is hewn entirely from stone. Everywhere there is a conscious fusion of Islamic and Hindu elements, the reflection of Akbar's desire to integrate the different cultures of his empire. The whole picture is dominated by the towering bulk of the Buland-i-Darwaza, a huge triumphal gateway. Architecturally this is the most perfect gateway in India and it is the largest of its kind anywhere in the world. Standing 176 feet high at the head of a massive flight of steps, it is a potent reminder of the power and the majesty of Akbar's empire.

Probably the most fascinating building of all is the Diwan-i-Khas, the Hall of Private Audience, for it is this which best reflects Akbar's idea of himself. Housed in a freestanding pavilion with deep eaves and elegant arches, it is a high chamber in the midst of which stands a sturdy, swelling pillar. At the top of this pillar was a circular platform on which the imperial throne was situated. The pillar was connected to the rest of the room, and by implication the rest of the world, by four delicate bridges which joined it with balconies suspended halfway up the wall. The symbol of divine majesty, Akbar would sit enthroned on the platform high above the heads of his courtiers, while those seeking an audience could only watch and wonder below.

The Flowering of Indo-Muslim Culture

Akbar's rich and fertile mind found its outlet in a wide range of interests which in addition to architecture included literature, music and painting. Under his inspiration the influence of Persian culture spread throughout India. Persian became the polite language of the country and it was adopted by the Hindu courts of the north and the south. It brought with it the influence of Persian dress and Persian manners, the imprint of which is still visible in many parts of north India. It also led to the development of a new language, Urdu, an offshoot of Persian, which mixed with Hindi to become one of the great languages of the subcontinent.

LITERATURE AND MUSIC

Under Akbar's inspiration Persian literature flourished. There were the poems of Faizi (d.1595), Akbar's poet laureate, and the work of his brother, Abul Fazl, who was the greatest historian of the period. A close friend and confidant of the emperor, Abul Fazl's greatest achievement was the *Akbar Nama*, the Life of Akbar. A perceptive and detailed work, it provides us with our most intimate picture of the mind and personality of Akbar.

> From early childhood, he had passed through the most diverse phases of religious practices and beliefs and had collected with a peculiar talent in selection all books can teach, and thus there gradually grew in his mind the conviction that there were sensible men in all religions and austere thinkers and men with miraculous gifts in all nations. If some truth were thus found everywhere, why should Truth be restricted to one religion.

Despite his lavish support for Persian and Urdu, Akbar also took a keen interest in Hindu culture. He encouraged the study of Hindu texts and made great efforts to have them translated from Sanskrit into Persian. As with Persian, Akbar appointed a court poet – Raja Birbal – for Hindi, now India's national language for Sanskrit had long since fallen into disuse. As a result of his interest, Hindi literature made great strides during his reign. Indeed this period produced perhaps the greatest figure in Hindi literature in the form of the poet Tulsi Das (1532–1623). Described as the glory of his age, Tulsi Das's reputation rests on his great work, the *Ramcharitmanas*, the Hindi *Ramayana*. Writing in the language most commonly spoken by the majority of Hindus, Tulsi Das retold the ancient story of Rama or Ram, now no longer a dead hero but a living saviour:

> I have told you the story as best as I am able
> though at first I had chosen to keep it well hid;
> when I saw the extent of your heartfelt devotion
> I recited the story of Ram.

The *Ramcharitmanas* is still recited by village storytellers all over northern India, and even today it is through the verse of Tulsi Das that millions of illiterate Indians hear the story of Ram for the first time.

Hindu and Muslim culture merged more in music than in anything else and during Akbar's time Hindi music reached its zenith. Akbar loved music and kept as many as thirty-six singers at his court. The most gifted of these was the vocalist and instrumentalist Tansen. Most modern Hindi musicians trace their descent from Tansen and today he is widely regarded as the father figure of Hindi music.

PAINTING

Next to architecture, Akbar's most visible contribution lies in the creation of a Mughal school of painting. It was in this field that his fusion of Islamic and Hindu culture was to reach its highest point of development. Although the portrayal of any form of creation was strictly forbidden by Islam, Akbar regarded painting as a way of coming closer to the spirit of God.

> It appears to me as if a painter had acquired a peculiar means of recognizing God; for a painter in sketching anything that has life . . . is thus forced to think of God, the Giver of Life and will thus increase in knowledge.

When he returned from Persia, Humayun had brought with him two Persian master painters, Mir Sayyid Ali and Abdul Samad. Building on this start, Akbar established a state workshop of ten artists from all parts of his empire, most of them Hindus. He placed them under the direction of the Persian masters and often supervised their productions himself. His influence ushered in a new era in the history of Indian art. From this period book painting or individual miniature painting replaced murals and wall paintings as the most vital form of art. Persian refinement and technique were combined with Indian vigour and colour to create the famous Mughal school of painting, one of the most magnificent treasures of Indian civilization.

Akbar's mausoleum in Sikandra

The first production of the studio was a series of illustrations to accompany the Persian romance, the *Hamza-Nama*, a rambling adventure story. This consisted of almost 1,400 individual paintings on cloth, two feet high and with the text written on the back so that they could be displayed while the story was read aloud. The later years of Akbar's reign produced a steady stream of these illustrated manuscripts which were characterized by their blend of intricate decoration with glowing colour and vivid realism. The *Akbar Nama*, now in the Victoria and Albert Museum in London, is one of the finest works of this period. Full of dramatic, densely-peopled scenes of life at court, in camp, out hunting and on the battlefield, it is a vivid illustration of the age of Akbar.

In 1605 Akbar died. He lies at Sikandra, a few miles from Agra, in a beautifully proportioned mausoleum. In the true Mughal style the dimensions of the building were matched by those of the terraces, the fountains, the flower-beds and the aqueducts, which were all carefully arranged to harmonize with each other. Here at Sikandra his son Jahangir built the first minarets to be erected in India since the Qutb Minar at Delhi four centuries earlier.

The Seventeenth Century: The Era of Magnificence

The seventeenth century was the great age of the Mughal empire. During this period Indian society was more stable, more prosperous and more splendid than it had been for almost 1,000 years. Akbar's work was continued by his successors, Jahangir (r.1605–27) and Shah Jahan (r.1628–57), and their reigns saw the achievement of brilliant new heights in painting and architecture.

JAHANGIR

Akbar's eldest son and heir, Prince Salim, on becoming emperor took the title of Jahangir, 'World Grasper'. Although not the giant his father had been, Jahangir was a striking personality in his own right. Cruel and quick-tempered, he was at the same time genial and good-humoured. A deeply cultured man with an acute sensibility for art and nature, in many ways he resembled his grandfather more than his father. Although a very capable ruler, like Humayun he had an overwhelming love of pleasure which progressively got the better of him as the years went on. He became addicted to wine and opium and he himself tells us how he graduated from wine to arrack (a potent, double-distilled spirit) and finally to opium. By his late twenties, Jahangir admits he was drinking as many as twenty cups a day of arrack laced with opium. All this is recorded with characteristic frankness in his diary, the *Tuzuk-i-Jahangiri*. As fresh and immediate as Babur's memoirs, they leave behind a day-by-day account of Jahangir's perceptions of nature, science and art.

During Jahangir's reign Udaipur, which had defied Mughal authority for so long, was finally forced to come to terms. This was achieved in a brilliant campaign by Jahangir's son, Prince Khurram, later to become the emperor Shah Jahan. By ruthlessly devastating the entire countryside surrounding Udaipur, Khurram finally brought the Rana to open negotiations. He then showed even greater political wisdom by making the conditions comparatively easy. Thus a settlement was achieved whereby the Rana was able to acknowledge Mughal authority without renouncing his independence. Mughal power also continued to expand in the south and during Jahangir's reign several campaigns were launched into the Deccan. Although many of them were to prove inconclusive, the effect of so much Mughal pressure finally achieved a result and in 1616 the kingdom of Ahmednagar fell to the Mughals. However, the most important development of Jahangir's reign was the rise to power of his queen, Nur Jahan.

NUR JAHAN

Mehrunissa, or Nur Jahan (Light of the World) as she was later known, was the daughter of a high-ranking Persian official. One of the great beauties of her day, she had first met Jahangir at a court entertainment where she so captivated him that he married her barely two months later. A lady of great energy and many talents, Nur Jahan had a refined taste for poetry and art; she was also a renowned hunter and on one occasion it is said that she killed four tigers with only six bullets. Jahangir always remained deeply devoted to her and as his powers became less and less effective Nur Jahan came to exercise increasing control over the government of the empire. Special gold coins (*mohurs*) were issued showing her ruling alongside her husband, and imperial decrees (*firmans*) often carried her name as well as his. However, Nur Jahan's ambitions led to numerous intrigues and provoked several power struggles which led on more than one occasion to open rebellion. The latter part of Jahangir's reign was characterized by a bitter struggle between Nur Jahan and her stepson, the emperor's heir, Prince Khurram. From 1624–7 Prince Khurram was in open revolt against his father.

Upon the death of Jahangir in 1627, one of the first acts of the new emperor was to force Nur Jahan into retirement, where she consoled herself by building one of the most beautiful of all Mughal monuments. In memory of her father Itimad-ud-Daula, Nur Jahan erected an exquisite mausoleum at Agra, on the north bank of the Yamuna River. About three miles down from the Taj, the tomb of Itimad-ud-Daula marks the beginning of the most lavish phase of

Mughal building. Akbar's sandstone was now replaced by a profusion of white marble, gold and precious stones, all worked into the most subtle and delicate patterns. Seen from a distance the whole thing has the appearance of a sumptuously jewelled casket, marvellously and intricately decorated.

THE ARTS

Like his father, Jahangir was a great connoisseur of art and under him Mughal painting reached its peak. To help him record his daily impressions for his diary, Jahangir had his studio of painters travel everywhere with him and he used them to record everything he saw. This released Mughal art from its dependence on the text of the manuscript and opened out a whole new world. Instead of just illustrating manuscripts, the artist was now free to record his impressions of everyday life, to paint individuals, animals, birds and flowers. In Jahangir's time the imperial studio became an élite group of masters, producing individual paintings of the highest quality which were mounted in lavishly decorated albums. The exquisite portraits of individuals and the delicate, finely observed pictures of animals, birds and flowers which we can still see today are all the result of this change of direction.

The evolution of Mughal painting was matched by a brilliant artistic flowering in the Muslim courts of the Deccan. By temperament pleasure-seekers and lovers of beauty, the sultans of Ahmednagar, Bijapur and Golconda developed a court culture of their own which was quite distinct from the Mughal influences of the north. This produced an opulent style of painting, elaborately detailed and rich with gold and brilliant colour. The greatest patron was the Sultan of Bijapur, Ibrahim Adil Shah (r.1580–1627), an outstanding artist, musician and poet, for whom some of the finest works were painted. He died in the same year as Jahangir, to be succeeded by Muhammed Adil Shah (r.1627–56) who constructed Bijapur's most striking monument, the Gol Gumbaz or 'Round Dome', a vast domed mausoleum flanked by four seven-storeyed towers, one at each corner. Enclosed within is the largest domed space in the world; the dome itself is 178 feet high, second only to that of St Peter's in Rome.

Shah Jahan

The accession of Shah Jahan marked the high point of Mughal power and glory. A much greater man than his father, he combined great military, political and administrative ability with a refined artistic sense. He was particularly renowned for his love of the magnificent, which was responsible for some of the most majestic buildings in India. Shah Jahan governed India firmly for almost thirty years, during which the Mughal empire enjoyed an almost unbroken period of peace. Despite the loss of the great Afghan fortress of Kandahar to Persia in 1649, there were no foreign invasions and to the south there were some signal military successes. Shah Jahan followed a more aggressive Deccan policy than either his father or his grandfather and his rule saw the final absorption of Ahmednagar into the Mughal empire. This left the two neighbouring Muslim kingdoms of Bijapur and Golconda as the only remaining obstacles to the Mughal domination of the whole subcontinent. Both were forced to pay tribute, and when in 1653 the advance was renewed by the emperor's third son, Aurangzeb, their final demise seemed only a matter of time.

THE TAJ MAHAL

Although a ruthless politician, Shah Jahan had a great capacity for love and affection. His greatest work, the Taj Mahal, India's most famous monument, is a tribute to his undying love for his queen Mumtaz Mahal. Like her aunt, Nur Jahan, Mumtaz Mahal (1594–1630) was said to have been a woman of dazzling beauty and great intellect. Married at the age of eighteen to Shah Jahan, she wielded great influence over her husband who always remained deeply devoted to her. Shah Jahan discussed all state affairs with her and she accompanied him everywhere, on every one of his campaigns. Her death in 1630 left a profound gap in his life: 'Empire has no sweetness, life itself has no relish left for me now.' He was almost inconsolable and is reported to have lived in a state of complete mourning for nearly two years.

In 1632, determined to give a concrete shape to his grief, the emperor began the construction of a mausoleum for his queen at Agra. The work was to take almost twenty-two years and it consumed the energies of

The Taj Mahal

more than 20,000 labourers and craftsmen. Described as a dream in marble, the Taj Mahal is Mughal India's greatest masterpiece. It marks the peak of that blend of careful harmony and intricate decoration which had come to characterize the Mughal style. Set in a formal Persian garden backed by the Yamuna river, the whole conception is carefully arranged to present a picture of the most perfect harmony, so that for all its mammoth size the overall effect is one of lightness and delicacy. As with the tomb of Itimad-ud-Daula, the marble itself is sumptuously decorated and worked in subtle contrasting patterns. The Taj Mahal is considered by many to be the most beautiful building in the world. One awestruck traveller exclaimed: 'Henceforth, let the inhabitants of the world be divided into two classes – them as has seen the Taj Mahal, and them as hasn't'. (Edward Lear, 1874).

The best place to see the Taj is from the central archway of the entrance portal. From here the building looms to a height of about 100 feet, presenting a magnificent picture of a snowy white monument framed against a luxuriant garden broken up by rippling watercourses. Another famous visitor, Eleanor Roosevelt, wrote,

> This is a beauty that enters the soul. With its minarets rising at each corner, its dome and tapering spire, it creates a sense of air, almost floating lightness, looking at it, I decided I had never known what perfect properties were before.   (*India and the Awakening East*, 1954)

Luminous though it is, the Taj is not Shah Jahan's only achievement. At Agra he built the Moti Masjid or Pearl Mosque (1648–55), an exquisite marble gem crowned by three beautifully shaped domes. He also added a series of palaces to the Red Fort which had been built by his grandfather. Characterized by their striking elegance, these later additions seem a world away from the robust sandstone buildings of his predecessors.

MUGHAL DELHI

In the end, however, Shah Jahan tired of Agra, and in 1638 he moved his capital to Delhi. Here he began laying out a new city, Shahjahanabad – 'the City of the Ruler of the World' – which is now the walled city of Old Delhi. Here he built himself an imposing new palace fortress, the Red Fort – so called, as at Agra, because of its massive red walls. Rising to 100 feet in places, these thick battlemented walls with their massive round bastions enclose the finest and most magnificent of all Mughal palaces. The Red Fort housed a complex of halls, palaces, pavilions and gardens of almost overwhelming beauty and splendour. It was adorned with marble, decorated with gold and precious stones, and inlaid with delicate multi-coloured mosaics, all polished to a glittering smoothness. At the heart of it all was the emperor's throne room, where letters of gold written on the ceiling proclaimed: 'If there is a paradise on earth, it is this, it is this, it is this.'

Not far from his palace Shah Jahan built the largest mosque in India, the Jami Masjid (Friday Mosque). Standing on a lofty pavement, it is clearly silhouetted against the Delhi sky – a shadowy outline of three bulbous domes and two slender minarets. The Jami Masjid is approached by three broad stairways leading to three grand gates at the north, the west and the east; the east gate was opened only for the emperor in person. Designed to accommodate 10,000 worshippers, it is one of the largest mosques in the world. A grand and imposing place of worship, it was the spiritual counterpart of the Red Fort; together with the imperial palace it provided a majestic focus for the capital of an empire.

> I stood on the high platform of the Great Mosque, one of the noblest buildings in India and the world. Profound thankfulness filled me. The sky was now intensely blue, the kites circled round the pearl grey domes and the red frontispiece of sandstone. E.M. Forster (*Hill of Devi*, 1953)

The seat of Mughal government for almost 200 years, the Red Fort was the centre of Shah Jahan's world. Here he lived a luxurious but extremely busy life in a setting of great pomp and ceremony. Shortly after sunrise he would appear on a public balcony of the palace, called the *jharokha*, where he would show himself to the public. This ceremony was called the *darshan*, meaning the sight of something high or holy, and it would last for about 45 minutes. The area below the balcony would then be cleared and elephant fights, of which the emperor was particularly fond, would be staged. Shah Jahan and his entourage would then proceed to the Diwan-i-Am (Hall of Public Audience), where for two hours he would give audiences, pass on orders, make appointments and receive petitions. This must have been a gorgeous scene; 50 feet long and 24 feet wide and open on three sides, the hall was a place of overwhelming majesty; the roof was covered with silver inlaid with gold and there were 32 columns, all plastered with powdered marble. At one end was a raised platform which housed the emperor's seat, the fabulous Peacock Throne. Made of gem-encrusted gold and standing on massive golden feet, the throne took its name from the figures of two peacocks which stood behind it, their tails outstretched and inlaid with sapphires, rubies, emeralds and other precious stones, all representing the different colours of life. Between the two peacocks stood the figure of a parrot, said to have been carved out of a single emerald; overhead hung a canopy of gold and rubies. To the left and right of the throne were Shah Jahan's sons, while in the hall itself stood the courtiers, nobles and officers of state, their backs to the open sides. They stood facing the emperor in ranks according to their authority, in strict silence and decorum. Lining the wall to one side were the imperial standard-bearers, all holding golden banners. All those whose rank did not entitle them to be in the Diwan-i-Am, the lesser officials, nobles and guards, stood in an outside courtyard covered with velvet canopies embroidered in gold.

From the Diwan-i-Am Shah Jahan would proceed to the Diwan-i-Khas (Hall of Private Audience). Here, under a ceiling lined with silver and amidst walls inlaid with jewels, he would discuss important state matters with his principal ministers and attend to his correspondence. After another two hours, the emperor would leave for the Shah Burj or Royal Tower. Only the princes of the blood and the most trusted officers were allowed to be present, for it was here that the most secret affairs were discussed. At midday the emperor retired to the harem, where he would eat and sleep for about an hour. Afterwards he heard petitions from widows, orphans and other women, which would be brought to him by the ladies of the harem. At about 3 p.m. a second and shorter audience or 'durbar' was held and the emperor would return to Diwan-i-Am if business called for it.

In the evening the Diwan-i-Khas was lit with candles and a less formal gathering was held where business was combined with pleasure. There were musical performances and displays of singing and dancing, all mixed in with discussion and conversation. As the English ambassador to the Mughal court, Sir Thomas Roe, described, it was a good time to put your point to the emperor while he was still in the mood to take it all in. Later, after his evening prayer, Shah Jahan would return to the Shah Burj. At about 8.30 p.m. he would retire for the night to the harem. Here he would hear songs sung by the women and listen to readings from his favourite books, most often travel or lives of the saints and histories of former kings.

THE SUCCESSION

In 1657 Shah Jahan fell seriously ill and it was rumoured that he was dead. During this time a bitter war of succession was fought between his four sons. The eldest, Dara Shikoh (1615–58) was his father's favourite and chosen heir apparent. A brilliant and artistic intellectual,

An exquisitely decorated ewer from the Mughal period

he was renowned for his liberalism and his religious tolerance. In the eyes of many of his contemporaries he seemed the true successor to the liberal policies of Akbar. Dara Shikoh, however, proved no match for his younger brother, Aurangzeb, an experienced campaigner who commanded the Mughal armies in the Deccan. Cool, calculating and extremely capable, Aurangzeb had already proved himself in the Deccan wars. In a series of bold and subtle moves he outmanoeuvred and outfought the vain and over-confident Dara Shikoh. He then turned his attention to his other rivals, his brothers Shah Shuja, the governor of Bengal, and the youngest, Murad. In a display of chilling ruthlessness, Aurangzeb executed Dara Shikoh and Murad, and drove Shah Shuja out of India. Even his aged father did not escape his suspicions. Shah Jahan finally recovered from his illness, only to be imprisoned in his own palace at Agra. For the remaining eight years of his life he remained a prisoner in the Red Fort which he himself had embellished so beautifully, brooding on his fate; every sunset he would sit on the battlements, staring mournfully down the Yamuna river towards the Taj Mahal.

Conquest, Rebellion, and Decline: The Reign of Aurangzeb

Aurangzeb's rise to power earned him a reputation for suspicion and ruthlessness and his name today is still a byword for cunning and duplicity. Given the standards of the time, however, his actions were no more ruthless than those of his predecessors – Shah Jahan, for example, had secured his accession by executing all his closest male relatives. An efficient soldier and a skilled politician, Aurangzeb governed India for over forty-eight years (1658–1707), nearly as long as his great ancestor Akbar. Like Akbar he left the empire much larger than he found it, and at his death Mughal power extended down into the very tip of the subcontinent.

A stern, austere figure, Aurangzeb dominated India for the rest of the seventeenth century, retaining his grip on power right up to his death at the age of eighty-eight. Although he lacked the charisma of Shah Jahan and Akbar, he was a firm and capable ruler. He inspired an awe and even terror of his own, and it is said that his eldest son never received a letter from him without trembling. Where he differs from his predecessors is in his attitude to religion and it is this which accounts for his widespread unpopularity in modern-day India.

A strict orthodox Muslim, Aurangzeb saw himself as a model Muslim ruler whose duty it was to reassert the supremacy of Islam. From the very beginning he seems to have pursued an anti-Hindu policy. In 1664 he prohibited the repair of all Hindu temples and in 1669 he stopped the building of new ones. This policy seems to have intensified after 1679 when, despite bitter protests, he reintroduced the hated Jizya or poll tax. New custom duties were also introduced, with a separate rate for Hindus which was twice what it was for Muslims. All this was accompanied by the increasing destruction of Hindu temples, and on occasion their replacement by mosques. At Benares, for example, Aurangzeb demolished a Hindu temple to make way for a mosque, which is still standing today and dominates the sacred city of Hinduism in much the same way as the Qutb Minar commands the skyline of Delhi. Not surprisingly these measures were bitterly resented by the majority of the empire's Hindu subjects and succeeded only in undermining the foundations of Mughal authority. Akbar had built his empire on a spirit of impartiality and integration and had worked hard to instil these principles into his administration. Aurangzeb's policy antagonized and alienated the many different communities who made up the empire. Increasingly they began to feel that the emperor no longer represented their interests. The result was a series of revolts against Mughal authority.

In 1669 and 1689 Aurangzeb had to face a series of uprisings by the Jats, an agricultural Hindu caste who inhabited the region to the west of Delhi. Both these rebellions were bloodily put down but the Jats continued their raids even after their leaders had all been killed. In the Punjab, too, there was trouble with the Sikhs. Originally a peaceful religious sect, persistent Muslim hostility transformed them into the beginnings of an independent nation. Aurangzeb's summary execution of their leaders for refusing to embrace Islam only inflamed the situation. Fearing annihilation the Sikhs organized themselves along military lines, and by the end of the seventeenth century they had become bitter enemies of the Mughals. Even the Rajputs who for so long had been a pillar of the Mughal empire began to be estranged: in 1679 a new Rajput war broke out caused by the emperor's attempt to annex the state of Marwar. Although the Mughal giant eventually broke the back of Rajput resistance, hostilities in Rajasthan did not cease but continued to the end of Aurangzeb's reign.

THE CONQUEST OF SOUTHERN INDIA

From 1681 onwards, for almost all of the last twenty-six years of his life, Aurangzeb virtually transferred his capital to the Deccan. His head-quarters was a moving city of tents some thirty miles in circumference, housing more than half a million soldiers and camp followers. Here he finally achieved what no other Mughal emperor had been able to do – the conquest of southern India. In 1664, 1676 and 1682 a series of attacks had been launched on the kingdom of Bijapur. All had failed and finally Aurangzeb had to come himself. In 1685 his army settled down to besiege the vast fortress city.

Situated on an open plain, Bijapur did not have the natural defences common to many Indian strongholds. Instead it relied on its gigantic city walls, almost six miles round and studded with 100 bastions, all of them adapted for artillery and some of them with their cannon still in place. However, these defences proved to no avail, and after a desperate 18-month siege the city finally surrendered. Its garrison had been so depleted by starvation that there were only 2,000 defenders left. The capital of one of the most liberal and enlightened cultures of the Deccan, Bijapur is a city littered with mosques, tombs and splendid public buildings. Although most of those which remain are well preserved, today Bijapur is a backwater full of nondescript buildings which cluster around the mosques and tombs of the sultans.

Barely six weeks after the fall of Bijapur, Aurangzeb moved against Golconda, now the last independent kingdom in the Deccan. Mughal troops occupied the city of Hyderabad which was renowned throughout India for its wealth and luxury. It was even more famous for its decadence and was reported to have had as many as 20,000 registered prostitutes. The sultan Abul-Hassan (r.1672–87) retreated to his citadel, the vast, high fortress of Golconda. Seen from across the Deccan plains, Golconda is a dramatic sight. A glinting mass of minarets, terraces, pavilions, domes and arches, it seems to rise in tier upon tier until it reaches the summit of the rock on which it is built. Hitherto the triple-walled defences of the fort had proved virtually impregnable and it was one of the strongest places in southern India. For nearly nine months it resisted fiercely against a combination of bombardment, mining and infantry assault. Finally bribery succeeded where all else failed and in 1687 Golconda too capitulated. Its conquest brought almost the whole of southern India under Aurangzeb's authority. The Mughals now controlled almost the whole of the subcontinent. Not since the reign of Asoka had one single dynasty dominated so much of India.

The Marathas

Aurangzeb's triumph in 1687 seemed to mark the peak of Mughal power. This impression, however, is misleading. Far from subduing the Deccan, Aurangzeb was to spend the remaining years of his life fighting a new enemy, the Marathas. They were a hardy, tenacious people who inhabited the parched, barren mountain ranges of the western Ghats. During the early part of Aurangzeb's reign they emerged as fierce opponents of Mughal rule, led by their great leader Shivaji (1627–80). Seizing a number of key mountain-top plateaus as his strongholds, Shivaji carved out a large principality for himself in the western Ghats, in what is today known as Maharashtra. From these strongholds, Shivaji and his followers would swoop down and plunder the caravans that travelled through Maharashtra. Many of these hill-forts are still in existence today: perched on the top of massive, rugged peaks, many of them are so extraordinarily situated that one wonders how they could ever have been taken by force.

A daring and brilliant guerilla leader, Shivaji humiliated the armies which were sent against him by both Bijapur (1659) and the Mughals (1660–4). In 1664 he sacked the great Mughal port of Surat on the western coast of Gujarat. He had become too much of a threat to ignore and a powerful Mughal army was sent against him. Shivaji was forced to come to terms and he agreed to come to the Mughal court at Agra to pay his respects. There suspicion between Shivaji and Aurangzeb flared up into open hostility. In a thrilling episode Shivaji escaped from Agra hidden in a basket of sweets. Disguised as a Hindu priest, his face covered in ashes, he made his way back to the Deccan where he renewed the struggle against the Mughals, and by the time of his death in 1680 he had moulded the Maratha peoples into the beginnings of a nation. Today Shivaji is regarded as a national hero, a Hindu leader who had risen from comparatively humble beginnings to shake the mighty Mughal empire. He was succeeded by his son Sambhaji, a weak ruler with little of his father's ability. He proved no match for the remorseless Aurangzeb and in 1689 he was captured. After two weeks of torture, during which he maintained a constant stream of abuse against Aurangzeb, Sambhaji was hacked to death. As each piece of his body was cut off it was fed to the dogs.

Nevertheless, the Marathas continued to resist and they waged an unending guerilla war against the Mughals. Like an old bear plagued by a swarm of bees, the aged Aurangzeb spent his last years hounding the Marathas. The huge Mughal army dragged itself across the bleached Deccan landscape to besiege one precipitous fort after another, only for the Marathas to return and reoccupy the last one. It was a futile exercise – a huge drain on the empire's resources which served only to exhaust its energy and demoralize its army. Aurangzeb's long absence in the Deccan also led to the growing erosion of Mughal power in the north: while his armies captured the forts of the Marathas, his officials in the north found themselves unable to collect the revenues from their territories. The Rajputs still remained in revolt and in other parts of the subcontinent local rulers began to assert themselves. All these developments were carefully watched by the great nobles of the empire and they too began to consolidate their own positions.

For all his determination and his ability, Aurangzeb did not have the flexibility to realize that the welfare and stability of his vast empire depended on accommodating the different castes, races and religions which comprised it. His failure to understand this rendered all his successes and conquests meaningless; for in imposing Islam over everything else and putting down every sign of dissent, he was only serving to encourage it. Although he managed to retain control until the very end, Aurangzeb had succeeded only in undermining the foundation of his own power. Towards the end there were signs that Aurangzeb himself was beginning to realize that, in spite of everything, somehow he had failed. Before his death he wrote: 'The days that have been spent except in austerities have left only regret behind them. Life so valuable, has gone away for nothing.'

CHAPTER EIGHT

A Receding Tide Uncovering Rocks: The Eighteenth Century, 1707–85

The eighteenth century in India was a period of great change and fluctuation. It was dominated by the declining power of the Mughal empire. Like the tide, Mughal power gradually rolled back to reveal the rocks which now remained: rocks which were to prove the foundations of future states and nations.

In the absence of their all-embracing grip, the century witnessed the emergence of new forces on the Indian scene. Nations like the Marathas and the Sikhs, which had been so savagely repressed during the previous century, built themselves into powerful new states, competing for influence with the new independent Muslim states which succeeded Mughal rule. The last factor in this equation was the growing involvement of the European commercial companies.

During the course of the seventeenth century the Portuguese, the Dutch, the British and the French had all established themselves in India. They had come to trade and at first this was their only concern. However, the collapse of the Mughal authority left behind a power vacuum which inevitably drew them in.

In order to safeguard their all-important trade, the European companies gradually became involved in Indian politics. By the middle of the eighteenth century they too had become a force to be reckoned with. Rather like the Muslims when they first arrived on the scene, at first the Europeans were not taken very seriously. In the final analysis, however, they proved to be the most powerful influence of all.

The Disintegration of the Mughal Empire

Aurangzeb's son, Bahadur Shah (r.1707–12) was effectively the last of the 'Great Moguls'. After his death the empire began to disintegrate as Delhi gradually lost control over events in the provinces. However, he temporarily succeeded in covering up the cracks which had begun to appear towards the end of his father's reign. He brought an end to the long-running war in Rajasthan by making peace with the Rajputs, and he fiercely put down a revolt by the Sikhs. He also managed to neutralize the Marathas. By skilful and cunning diplomacy he set off a civil war amongst them, so that they spent most of his reign fighting each other. Already sixty-three when he came to the throne, Bahadur Shah did not live long enough to provide the leadership and the energy the empire needed to survive. His death was followed by a series of struggles for the succession, leading inevitably to the erosion of Mughal prestige and authority. The 'Great Mogul' became little more than a pawn in the hands of different court factions, a mere shadow of the awesome figure he had once been. This culminated in 1719 when the emperor Farrukhsiyar was dragged from the harem, blinded and poisoned by his own courtiers. Firm leadership and personality had always been one of the cornerstones of the Mughal empire; it was a principle which was embodied in monumental works of architecture all over India. The eighteenth century saw as many as fourteen different rulers at Delhi. Not one of them was powerful enough or governed for long enough to erect a single building of any note.

This vacuum at the centre was accompanied by an increasing loss of control in the provinces. The great nobles who had formerly governed on behalf of the emperor now began to build up their own power bases. The great officers of Subhadar and Diwan, which the Mughals had worked so hard to keep separate, gradually became merged into one. In their place new hereditary kingdoms took shape. In Bihar there was the kingdom of Oudh or Awadh, with its capital at Lucknow, a luxury city famous for its silks, perfumes and jewellery. Hyderabad too became the capital of a new state, one which was to outlast the Mughal empire; its founder was Nizam-ul-Mulk (r.1724–48), who had previously been the chief minister of the Mughal emperor. Frustrated in his attempts to

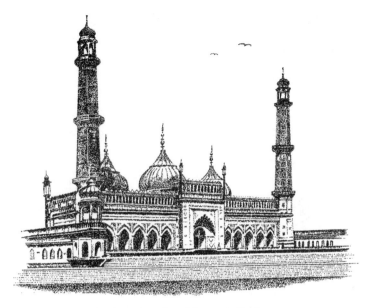

The Great Imambara Mosque in Lucknow

reform the empire, Nizam-ul-Mulk retired to the Deccan, established his capital at Hyderabad and set himself up as the virtually independent ruler of the southern half of the empire. Another Mughal noble, Murshid Quli Khan (r.1703–27) established himself in Bengal, creating a new regime and a new capital which he named after himself, Murshidabad. There was a growing exodus of soldiers, civil servants, intellectuals, artists and craftsmen from Delhi to these provincial cities. Whereas Delhi declined, Hyderabad, Lucknow and Murshidabad all developed into important new centres of Mughal culture.

The revival of Maratha power in the 1720s and 1730s accelerated the process of disintegration. Now no longer on the defensive, the Marathas had begun to launch great raids deep into central India. The Mughal armies were helpless in the face of these repeated incursions, and by 1738 the Marathas were even raiding the suburbs of Delhi. All attempts to drive them back failed and in the same year the Mughals were forced to cede the province of Malwa in central India. This had the effect of separating the empire's northern territories from its possessions in the Deccan, virtually dividing it into two halves.

The empire's weakness was revealed even more dramatically in 1739 by the sack of Delhi. In 1738, while the empire was busy fending off the Marathas, Nadir Shah, the ruler of Persia, had invaded India. Easily defeating the Mughal armies sent against him, Nadir Shah marched on the imperial capital. Delhi was brutally sacked and its inhabitants slaughtered in a massacre which lasted for almost six hours. Almost 30,000 people are supposed to have died in this orgy of killing. 'The streets were strewn with corpses like a garden with dead leaves. The city reduced to ashes looked like a burnt plain.'

Nadir Shah returned to Persia with a fabulous plunder in gold, jewels and precious stones. With him went the fabled Peacock Throne of Shah Jahan which provided a brilliant new setting for its future owners, the Shahs of Persia. As one historian remarked, 'The accumulated wealth of 348 years changed hands in a moment.' Gone for ever was the dazzling wealth and splendour which had once been the hallmark of the Mughal empire. Although the empire continued to linger on, it was barely a shadow of its former self. What had been an empire became little more than the kingdom of Delhi, its emperor a puppet in the hands of other, more powerful rulers.

In 1761 a new invasion sealed the fate of the empire. After the death of Nadir Shah, his lieutenant, an Afghan general named Ahmed Shah Abdali, set up an independent kingdom for himself in Afghanistan. Following the example of his master, he looked towards India in search of easy pickings. From 1756 onwards he began a series of raids into the Punjab, gradually establishing his control over the region. In desperation the Mughals turned to their old enemy the Marathas for help. Even they, however, failed to stop Ahmed Shah and an exhausted Delhi was sacked once more. Only Ahmed Shah's decision to return to Afghanistan saved the empire from complete extinction; nevertheless his invasion had signalled the end of Delhi's independence. The emperor he left behind, Shah Alam (r.1788–1806), ceded what was left of his power to the Marathas. In 1788 he himself was blinded when a half-mad Afghan robber chief attacked Delhi and captured the Red Fort. In the heyday of Mughal power Jahangir, Shah Jahan and Aurangzeb had all removed their rivals from contention by blinding them; as in Constantinople, another great imperial capital, blinding effectively disqualified a candidate from power, for a blind man could not rule an empire. The blinding of the emperor Shah Alam was in many ways a deeply symbolic act; it signified that by 1788 the Mughal empire had ceased to play an effective role in Indian politics.

The Maratha Confederacy

Although Aurangzeb's long campaigns against them did not destroy Maratha resistance, they broke up the compact kingdom which Shivaji had built up. This transformed the Marathas into a loosely-knit confederacy of peoples, headed by a hereditary chief minister called the Peshwa. Lightly armed and mounted on hardy little ponies, noted for their speed and endurance, the Marathas had developed a taste for plunder and guerilla warfare. As their homeland of Maharashtra was poor and barren, they turned their attentions to the rest of India which now seemed wide open. Within a few years they had acquired a similar reputation to the Vikings and were feared all over India for their sudden, devastating raids.

By 1750 Maratha power had spread right across central India and was already starting to reach deep into the north. Overall authority was exercised by the Peshwa from his base at Poona, in the heart of Maharashtra. From here he supervised and tried to control (not always successfully) the activities of the Maratha chiefs who had established themselves in different parts of India. In the west was Gujarat, which was ruled by the Gaekwar from his capital at Baroda. Situated amidst one of India's richest agricultural regions, under the British it became one of the wealthiest and most powerful of all princely states. Although the princely order has been officially abolished, much of its former splendour still remains. Modern Baroda is a neat, well-maintained city with broad tree-lined avenues, extensive parks and many distinguished public buildings. It is decorated with a series of enormous palaces, the most famous of which is probably the fabulous Laxmi Vilas Palace (1880–1900), the most expensive building erected by any private individual in the nineteenth century.

Central India was controlled by another general, Bhonsla, who had established himself at Nagpur, now a rather grimy industrial city. Further to the north, at Indore and Gwalior, were the two other great Maratha states. Indore was ruled by the Holkar, while Gwalior was ruled by the Scindia. Taken by the Marathas in 1754, the medieval fortress capital of Gwalior is one of the great sights of India. Perched on a high sandstone precipice 300 feet above the plain, it is defended by huge towering walls set with massive round towers surmounted by open-domed cupolas. A vast complex comprising several different palaces, it is entered by a steep ascent which twists and climbs its way through five great gateways passing under five different palaces. Located in the heart of Madhya Pradesh, Gwalior was for centuries the key to central India.

On the invasion of Ahmed Shah in 1756, the Mughals called upon the Marathas to drive the invader out of India. Dreams of a new empire began to open out before Maratha eyes and the Peshwa accepted the challenge. He dispatched an army of crack Maratha horsemen under the command of his cousin, the Bhao Sahib, and they met up with the Afghans at Panipat on 13 January 1761. This, the third battle of Panipat, was to be the fiercest struggle of all, but it was arguably to prove the least decisive. Both armies had entrenched themselves behind strong fortifications but the Marathas found themselves outmanoeuvred by the Afghan cavalry patrols. The Afghans succeeded in cutting the Maratha communications and the Marathas found themselves unable to obtain either food or supplies. Their horses and soldiers were soon starving and their ammunition almost exhausted. They had no option but to abandon their defences and attack the Afghan positions, although they were much stronger and much better positioned. In the ensuing battle the Maratha army was almost completely annihilated, 75,000 slaughtered and another 30,000 taken prisoner. For the Marathas this disaster completely exploded any ambitions which they might have had. The Peshwa himself died a few months later, shattered by the news of the defeat.

Ahmed Shah, however, could not take advantage of his stunning victory, for his troops mutinied and forced him to return to Afghanistan. His departure left a political void in northern India which the Marathas were too exhausted to fill. It took them almost a decade to recover; not until the 1770s were they once more a major force on the Indian scene. Ahmed Shah's departure was also good news for the Sikhs who had been steadily rebuilding their power in the Punjab. Taking advantage of the chaos and anarchy following the collapse of Mughal rule, they gradually consolidated their position. By the end of the eighteenth century they had established a powerful kingdom which sprawled across the Punjab, Kashmir and Afganistan.

European Inroads

The other major story of this period concerns the expansion of European power. At first it was slow and steady, but as the century progressed it became more and more spectacular. The European merchants had originally come to India in search of exotic and expensive commodities like spices and silks, for which there was an increasing demand in Europe. At first this trade had been dominated by the Portuguese from their great base at Goa on the west coast of India. This was the hub of Portugal's empire in Asia, a commercial empire which stretched from the shores of western India as far as the Philippines. Founded in 1510, Goa was the first Christian colony in the subcontinent and it remained in Portuguese hands until 1961 when Indian troops were sent in to seize the territory. Not surprisingly, the Portuguese connection is very much in evidence today – in the names of its inhabitants, in the white-painted, crumbling villas, and in the gracious baroque churches which are still an important part of everyday life. Today, however, Goa is more famous for its fabulous golden beaches, an attraction which for better or worse has made it the tourist capital of India.

The strong position which the Portuguese had built up gradually passed to the Dutch, but by 1740 they had been overtaken by a new rival, the English East India Company. During the seventeenth century the English had established three major commercial centres on the coast. The first was on the Coromandel Coast, where in 1639 permission was obtained to set up a fortified trading post on the site of a small village. This village was to become the settlement of Madras, one of India's great capital cities. The heart of the settlement centred around its fort, Fort St George, which still dominates the sea front. The first headquarters of British India, Fort St George has been greatly altered and enlarged over the years; nevertheless it still remains full of history. Nestling within its confines is the oldest Anglican place of worship in India, the completely English-looking St Mary's Church (1678). Near by are the houses occupied by some of the great heroes of British India – Robert Clive and Sir Arthur Wellesley (later the Duke of Wellington). Clive was married in St Mary's, as was Elihu Yale, governor of Madras from 1687 to 1692, who later gave his name to Yale University. Today Madras is the capital of the southern state of Tamil Nadu, a clean, pleasant city with broad streets which sprawls in a leisurely way over 50 square miles.

In 1688 the East India Company gained another foothold when they received the Portuguese settlement of Bombay on the west coast. Originally a string of malarial islands, these were gradually joined up as Bombay developed from a fort into a port and then into a city. The financial and business centre of India, Bombay has its own special character: one formed by its teeming skyscrapers, its offices, its banks and its business houses. The personification of India's extremes of sophisticated wealth and abject poverty, for the British Bombay became the 'gateway to India'. This is the name given to the gigantic triumphal archway which still dominates the quayside; erected by the British, it commemorates the visit of King George V and Queen Mary in 1911. In 1948 it was the point of departure from which the last British troops left India.

The last and most important settlement of all was set up in 1609 in Bengal. This small settlement on the banks of the river Hughli was to become the city of Calcutta, the first capital of the British Empire in India. Although it is no longer the capital, Calcutta is still one of the largest cities in the world, a densely packed mass of crowded, bustling humanity.

As the East India Company's trade grew these settlements expanded at a spectacular rate, spreading rapidly into the hinterland. By 1750, for example, Calcutta already had a population of well over 100,000. Each town became a local centre for Company operations, run by its own governor and council. Madras, Calcutta and Bombay all became the capitals of separate administrative regions, or presidencies as they were called. The focus of each settlement was the 'white town', where the Company servants lived, together with a small garrison of European soldiers and private merchants. Separate from this was the 'black town', which housed the rapidly growing Indian population. This consisted of Indian merchants and traders who did business with the Company as well as the artisans, servants and labourers employed by the Company's officials.

THE ANGLO-FRENCH WARS

By the early eighteenth century, the English East India Company was shipping more Indian goods to Europe than any of its rivals. However, the English were beginning to feel themselves increasingly threatened by the French. The French East India Company, the Compagnie des Indes, had established itself in India in 1674. Its headquarters was Pondicherry, a coastal town 85 miles south of Madras. Although it had started rather slowly, between 1720 and 1740 the French Company's trade increased to such an extent that it amounted to nearly half that of the East India Company. As their stake in India grew the two Companies began to display increasing commercial and political rivalry.

The collapse of the Mughal empire had left a power vacuum in southern India. As a result both the English at Madras and the French at Pondicherry became involved in local politics and began supporting local candidates. In 1748 Nizam-ul-Mulk, the ruler of the Deccan, died. The governor of Pondicherry at the time was Joseph François Dupleix (1697–1764), a man of remarkable energy and diplomatic skill, not to mention huge ambition. Under his leadership the French took this opportunity to place their own candidate on the throne. The result was a long-drawn out struggle between the French and the British, who feared that French ambition would endanger their trade. From 1748 onward, small armies of English and French soldiers, regiments of trained Indian troops (sepoys) and the forces of their Indian allies fought each other for control of various strategic points in south India. The most important of these was the fort of Trichinopoly, situated on top of a great rock which rose some 250 feet above the level plain of Tamil Nadu. Although the French enjoyed some significant successes, the

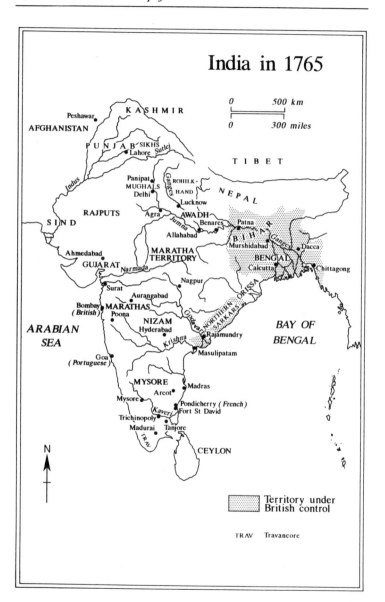

India in 1765

| 0 | 500 km |
| 0 | 300 miles |

AFGHANISTAN

Peshawar

KASHMIR

PUNJAB SIKHS
Lahore Sutlej

Indus

TIBET

Panipat
MUGHALS
Delhi

Ganges

ROHILK-
HAND

NEPAL

Lucknow

RAJPUTS

Agra

AWADH

Jumna

Benares

Patna

Allahabad

Ganges

BIHAR

SIND

Ahmedabad

MARATHA
TERRITORY

Murshidabad

Dacca

GUJARAT

Narmada

BENGAL

Calcutta

Chittagong

Surat

Nagpur

Aurangabad

Bombay
(British)

MARATHAS

Poona

NIZAM

Hyderabad

Godavari

NORTHERN   ORISSA
SARKARS

BAY OF
BENGAL

ARABIAN
SEA

Krishna

Rajamundry

Masulipatam

Goa
(Portuguese)

MYSORE

Madras

Arcot

Mysore

Pondicherry (French)
Fort St David

Trichinopoly

Kaveri

Madurai

Tanjore

TRAV

CEYLON

N

Territory under
British control

TRAV   Travancore

weight of superior sea power combined with greater resources and steadier support from home finally turned the balance in favour of the British. In 1760 the French were decisively defeated at the battle of Wandiwash. A year later Pondicherry, the capital of French India, fell to the British. Like Goa, Pondicherry too has an interesting history. It was later returned to the French, and was treated as a district of France until 1954 when it was ceded to India. Today it is the home of the largest concentration of French speakers in India. All the road signs are in English and French which, together with the elegant, white-washed façades, give Pondicherry the air of a French seaside town.

The defeat of the French cleared the field for the British, who had begun to establish themselves as an important force in Indian politics. They were aided by a significant change in the military balance of power. The Anglo–French wars had shown that small numbers of disciplined European troops, with the superior fire-power of their muskets and cannon, could repel much larger numbers of undisciplined Indian troops. This superior fire power neutralized the threat of the main Indian arm, the cavalry, as it meant that a cavalry charge could be broken up well before it reached the infantry line. These developments provided the English with a great advantage over their Indian rivals and they played a significant role in their subsequent successes.

The Conquest of Bengal

The event which really confirmed the British as an important political power was the conquest of Bengal in 1757. In 1756 the British settlement at Calcutta had been overrun by the forces of the Muslim ruler, the Nawab of Bengal, Siraj-ud-Daula (r.1756–70). Angered by the independent attitude of the English community, Siraj-ud-Daula ransacked and destroyed the settlement. In an infamous episode known as the Black Hole of Calcutta, all the European captives were imprisoned in a tiny airless cell measuring only 14 by 18 feet. It was reported that as many as 146 Europeans were imprisoned in this cell, out of whom only 23 survived until the next day. This event, however, is surrounded by a great deal of hysteria and recent studies suggest that only 64 people were imprisoned, 21 of whom survived. Siraj-ud-Daula himself is not even supposed to have known about the atrocity, let alone ordered it. Nevertheless, the Black Hole has become almost legendary as an example of Indian cruelty. Today the unfortunate Siraj-ud-Daula is more famous for being a cruel and vicious monster than being the last independent ruler of Bengal.

Siraj-ud-Daula's outrage was quickly punished. An expedition was sent up the coast from Madras and by the beginning of 1757 Calcutta had been recaptured. Determined that there would be no repetition of the Black Hole episode, the British developed a new fortress which was one of the most advanced forts of its time. The centre of the European community, Fort William is the most famous of all Anglo–Indian military forts. An eight-sided stronghold, defended by heavily fortified walls and redoubts, it was surrounded by a deep, wide moat that could be filled from the river. Beyond this lay an expanse of bare grassland which had been cleared to provide a field of fire. Called the Maidan, this stretch of parkland still plays an important part in the life of Calcutta. Fort William is still there, a warren of barracks, stables and storehouses, but it is the Maidan which is now the centre of activity. One of the few open spaces left in Calcutta, it comes alive in the mornings and evenings when it is crowded and buzzing with life.

ROBERT CLIVE

The British army which had recaptured Calcutta was commanded by Colonel Robert Clive (1725–74). Formerly a civilian in the service of the East India Company, he had already distinguished himself in the Anglo–French wars. An ambitious, energetic and extremely resourceful character, Clive's exploits were to lead to a dramatic expansion of the Company's role in India. His orders had been only to retake Calcutta, for the Company was only concerned about regaining its commercial position in Bengal. Bengal, however, was still the richest province in India and Clive realized that there were huge gains to be made in overthrowing Siraj-ud-Daula, not just for the Company but also for himself. Ignoring orders from Madras to return, he continued his campaign in Bengal. On 23 June 1757 he and his tiny army of 800 Europeans and 2,000 sepoys met Siraj-ud-Daula's army of more than 50,000 at the famous battle of Plassey, which founded British power in

India. Despite its significance, the battle does not rank as a great military victory; it was really more of a successful conspiracy, for Clive's cunning diplomacy had already made sure that the bulk of the Nawab's army would desert him on the battlefield.

Clive's triumph enabled the British to instal their own nominee on the throne of Bengal, which became a British client state governed by a puppet ruler whose only duty was to satisfy the Company's financial expectations. Between 1757 and 1765 a series of ruthless financial and commercial demands gradually drained Bengal of its seemingly inexhaustible wealth. As Clive had anticipated, the rewards proved enormous and huge fortunes were made by the Company's servants; he himself became one of the richest men in England almost overnight, with a fortune of £234,000 plus an annual income worth £30,000. The new Nawab, however, proved unequal to the task of satisfying British expectations, and in 1765 the Company began to take over the administration of the province for itself. Within a few years the East India Company had become the real ruler of Bengal and Calcutta became the seat of government for the whole province.

Warren Hastings and the Establishment of British Power

In 1774 Warren Hastings (1732–1818) was appointed as governor-general of all the Company's territories in India. A man of outstanding ability, under his determined leadership the Company's influence continued to expand. By a policy of treaty alliances and outright annexations, Hastings gradually built up the British position in India. His greatest achievement, however, was to preserve the Company's settlements in the south from a coalition of the strongest Indian powers. First of all there were the Marathas, who were once again re-emerging as a force to be reckoned with. Then there was the ruler of the Deccan, the Nizam of Hyderabad as he later became known; the only surviving portion of the Mughal empire, Hyderabad was dominated by a Muslim aristocracy which ruled over a Hindu majority. The newest addition to the scene was the state of Mysore, a prosperous and militarily powerful kingdom in the southern Deccan.

Warren Hastings, Governor-General of India from 1774–1785

Mysore's rise to prominence had been founded largely on the efforts of its dynamic ruler Haidar Ali (r.1761–82). He was a Muslim soldier who had risen through the ranks to displace the Hindu Raja of Mysore. He remodelled the army on western lines, and during his reign and that of his gifted son Tipu Sultan (r.1782–99), Mysore posed a powerful military threat to the British. Haidar Ali in particular was very adept at outthinking and outmanoeuvring the British forces sent against him:

> I will march your troops until their legs swell to the size of their bodies. You shall not have a blade of grass, nor a drop of water. I will hear of you every time your drum beats, but you shall not know where I am once in a month.

It was only in 1799, after a series of bitterly contested wars over a period of almost twenty years that Mysore finally capitulated. Even then the struggle ended only with the death of Tipu Sultan himself, who was killed fighting on the walls of his capital Seringapatam. Tipu was buried with full military honours by the British to the peals of an extraordinary thunderstorm; the storm was so severe that two British officers who had survived the assault unscathed were suddenly struck dead by lightning. Tipu's remains, along with those of his father, were entombed in an austere monument some way outside their citadel. Approached by an avenue of tall cypress trees the mausoleum of Haidar Ali and Tipu Sultan (1799) is a rather severe, domed building surrounded by a corridor of polished wooden pillars. In the crypt below lie the remains of Haidar Ali and his brilliant but erratic son. Both tombs are usually covered with shawls, black or purple for Haidar and red for Tipu, as befitting a martyr of the faith.

At various times during his governorship (1774–85), Hastings had to fend off attacks from either the Marathas, Haidar Ali or the Nizam; on one occasion he found himself having to face all three at the same time. His energy and his unwavering determination saw the Company through this troubled period at a time when it was still very vulnerable. His success gave the East India Company the time it so desperately needed to build up its strength. A scholar and a student of Indian languages, Hastings did a great deal to encourage the study of Indian culture by British scholars. It has been said that his personality was more attuned to studying Latin, Greek, Persian and Urdu than making forced marches or defending breached walls. Yet by the time he left India in 1785 he had done more than any other Englishman to secure British power. He returned home to England but not to the hero's welcome which had greeted Clive; he was attacked and persecuted on all sides, accused of corruption and misuse of power. The rest of his life was spent fighting off these charges, a process which was to cost him his entire fortune, his property and ultimately his health.

CHAPTER NINE

'The Jewel in the Crown': The British Raj, 1785–1914

Throughout the nineteenth century and for most of the first half of the twentieth India was dominated by the British. It became the most glittering prize of the British empire, the brightest jewel in the imperial crown. The British governed the subcontinent for almost 150 years, completely transforming its appearance, its institutions and its culture. Everywhere they went they built palatial mansions, universities, city halls, museums, public libraries and schools, all connected from city to city by a network of roads, railways and bridges. They even built a completely new capital, New Delhi: a city whose gigantic architecture and huge proportions completely eclipsed anything ever built in India. A city of 33 square miles, almost five times the size of Shah Jahan's capital, New Delhi consisted of 60 miles of main streets, all as straight as an arrow and many of them still beautifully lined with trees.

At the heart of New Delhi is the gigantic Viceroy's Palace. Even larger than the Palace of Versailles, it is probably the last great royal palace in history. Standing on top of Raisina Hill, its silhouette is dominated by a great copper dome, 180 feet high, rising above the rest of the city. On either side, on a suitably lower level but just as huge and awe-inspiring, are the massive secretariat and legislature buildings. Together with the palace, they formed the powerhouse of the 'Raj', as British rule in India came to be known. Described by the writer, Robert Byron, as being 'like the shout of the imperial suggestion – a slap in the face of the average man with his second-hand ideals', New Delhi was the centrepiece of the British empire in India.

Although today New Delhi houses the government of independent India and the Viceroy's Palace (Rashtrapati Bhawan) is now the residence of the President of India, for many it remains the very symbol of the Raj. It is a period which is still regarded with great fascination in the West and its glamour has inspired countless books, films and dramas. The best-known of these is probably David Lean's film of E.M. Forster's classic novel, *A Passage to India.* In this, his most famous work, Forster (1879–1970) describes the relationship so potently expressed in the buildings of New Delhi. He focused on the way the British saw India and the way in which the two societies – one European and one Indian – reacted to each other. Published in 1924, *A Passage to India* is a sensitive and sympathetic portrait of India under the British: in many ways it provides an ideal introduction to the world of the Raj.

The Permanent Settlement

The arrival of Lord Cornwallis (r.1786–93) to replace Warren Hastings as governor-general signalled the beginning of a new phase in the history of British India. An aristocrat and soldier who had fought in the American War of Independence, his task was to reorganize the Company's administration. The East India Company had previously been a mainly commercial body, whose servants had regarded administration purely as a sideline to the main business of making money. Cornwallis, however, changed all this. Whereas the Company had previously shared the business of government with the local rulers, he set up a new system of administration and taxation which was to be run by the British themselves; in Bengal it was known as the Permanent Settlement. Under this system agreements were made with the local landlords, who agreed to keep the peace and pay regular sums of money to the British; in return they were guaranteed possession of their lands.

To run this new system Cornwallis established what was the beginnings of a civil service, staffed by salaried officials who were forbidden to trade. Indians were deliberately excluded and all the high posts were reserved for Europeans. Cornwallis himself entertained a very low opinion of Indian honesty and efficiency: 'Every native of India, I verily believe is corrupt.' Thus he introduced the idea that it would be far more efficient and much better for the Indians themselves if the British kept the administration in their own hands, and ran it on

European rather than Indian lines. This policy was a very significant break with the past. Not only did it reflect the deep mistrust and estrangement which had begun to develop between Europeans and Indians, it also gave a foreign complexion and a completely alien character to the nature of British rule. Unlike the Mauryas, the Guptas, and most recently the Mughals, the British did not seek to merge or adapt themselves to Indian conditions. Almost from the beginning theirs was a completely foreign empire.

Conquest and Expansion: 'No greater blessing'

The governorship of Lord Wellesley (1798–1805) saw a dramatic expansion in British power. By now the East India Company had become convinced that the cheapest and most practical way of securing trade was to advance. Better to conquer and police one large tract of land than fritter away resources waging campaign after campaign against the same persistent enemies. Wellesley himself, ambitious and energetic, was an ardent champion of this policy: 'No greater blessing can be conferred on the native inhabitants than the extension of British authority.' He arrived in India with a clear blueprint for conquest. The new governor-general was assisted by the military skills of his brother Arthur Wellesley, later the Duke of Wellington and the future victor of Waterloo. Cleverly combining war and diplomacy, he succeeded in taming the leading Indian powers of the day – Mysore, Hyderabad and the Marathas.

In addition to his victories, Lord Wellesley also succeeded in building up the prestige and dignity of the governor-general's office. Determined that Britain's premier representative should have a residence worthy of his status, he constructed the first great palace of British India, Government House at Calcutta, which is now the home of the governor of Bengal. An enormous classical mansion, it was built in the style of an English country house; all its rooms were of huge proportions and they were embellished with vast marble floors and high ceilings of polished oak. It was in perfect tune with Wellesley's sentiments; as one admirer of his declared, 'India should be ruled from a palace not a counting house.'

The Company's best organized and most determined enemy was Tipu Sultan and it was against Mysore that Wellesley first turned his attention. After a short, fierce campaign Tipu was overthrown and half his state annexed; the other half was restored to the child heir of the dispossessed Hindu raja. In order to further British influence, Wellesley evolved a new policy for dealing with the rulers of the Indian states. The British would guarantee the security of a threatened state in return for control over its foreign policy. A contingent of Company troops would then be stationed in the capital under the charge of a British official, who became known as the Resident. All this was maintained and paid for by the local ruler himself who had more or less surrendered his independence in return for British protection. At the slightest difficulty the Company's troops were already at his throat. By this method, known as 'subsidiary alliances', Wellesley was able to annex large tracts of southern India – right down the eastern coast and across the southern peninsula. In the north the same tactic was used to put pressure on the client state of Oudh, whose ruler was forced to cede half his kingdom.

In 1798 Wellesley concluded a treaty with Hyderabad whose ruler, the Nizam, was terrified of both Mysore and the Marathas. Hyderabad happily accepted British protection and it remained a separate client state until independence in 1948. An enclave of Muslim culture in the Deccan, Hyderabad was to become better known for the almost legendary wealth of its last and tenth ruler, Nizam Usman Ali (r.1911–48), reputedly the richest man in the world. The Nizam's wealth was not tucked away in bills or bonds but lay scattered about his palace in an *Arabian Nights* dream, piled into stacks of gold bricks, chests of diamonds and mountains of silver rupees.

THE MARATHA WARS

The British advance was made easier by the disunited condition of their other great enemy, the Marathas, whose chiefs were involved in a bitter power struggle amongst themselves. In 1802 the Maratha Peshwa, harassed and threatened by his own chiefs, asked for British protection and signed a treaty agreeing to a British Resident in his capital and accepting a subsidiary position. This, however, proved too much for the Maratha chiefs and it led to the outbreak of the Second Maratha War (1802–5). The Scindia of Gwalior and the Bhonsla of Nagpur both took the field against the British, but the Holkar of Indore, the most powerful of the chiefs, remained aloof. In the Deccan the Marathas were checked by Arthur Wellesley who defeated them in a hard-fought campaign. Bhonsla capitulated and, following further defeats in the north by another British army, Scindia too sued for peace. The defeat of Scindia who had previously dominated northern India, gave the British possession of both Agra and Delhi, extending their authority right up to the banks of the Yamuna river. The British entered the old Mughal capital in triumph, to be confronted with the pathetic, broken-down figure of the Mughal emperor, Shah Alam: 'Oppressed by the calamities of old age, degraded authority, extreme poverty, and loss of sight, seated upon a small tattered canopy, the remnant of his royal state.' The emperor was taken under the protection of the new conquerors and became a pensioner of the British.

In the south, too, the British were able to make considerable gains, which enabled them to link up their territories in Bengal and Madras. Jashwant Rao Holkar (r.1798–1811), however, remained defiant and undefeated:

> My country and property are upon the saddle of my horse, and please God, to whatever side the reins of the horses of my warriors may be turned, the whole of the country shall come into my possession.

In 1804 he entered the struggle, inflicting a series of reverses on the British forces. The news of these setbacks together with the enormous cost of these wars proved too much for the Company. An uneasy peace with Holkar was patched up and Wellesley was recalled to England. The simple commercial minds of the directors of the East India Company had found his empire-building too costly and too troublesome. Like Warren Hastings before him, Wellesley was pilloried rather than celebrated for his achievements, accused of having 'goaded the whole country into a state of revolt'.

The Third Maratha War (1817–19) finally broke the power of the great Maratha chiefs who were once again defeated one by one. Like Scindia before him, Holkar was forced to accept client status while most of Nagpur was occupied and a new ruler placed on the throne. The Peshwa himself was deposed and his territories annexed to the Bombay presidency. Rajasthan, which for so long had been under Maratha control, also submitted to the British. Led by Jaipur, Udaipur and Jodhpur, the Rajput states concluded a series of treaties with the British, accepting subsidiary status. The end of the Maratha Wars had clearly established the British as the largest and strongest power in India. Only in the north-west, in the Punjab, did the British have a serious rival left. This was the Sikh kingdom of Ranjit Singh.

THE SIKH WARS, 1839–1848

Short, ill-favoured and with only one eye, Ranjit Singh (1780–1839) does not present a very attractive figure. Nevertheless, by sheer dynamism and ability he had managed to weld the Sikhs into a powerful military state which dominated Kashmir and the whole Punjab. His army, trained by French and Italian generals, was a formidable force, and while Ranjit Singh lived even the British dared not provoke a conflict. Until 1839 the two powers maintained a very cautious attitude towards each other and preserved a carefully guarded peace. His death, however, set in train a series of bitter disputes over the succession. Sikh unity, which he had so carefully nurtured, was torn apart in a nightmare of blood and intrigue. In the chaos which followed the leaderless Sikh army was pushed into a trial of strength with the British.

The First Sikh War (1845–6) resulted in a series of bloody, brutal battles – Mudki, Firozshah and Sobraon. The Sikhs fought so fiercely that casualties on both sides were very high. Surveying the slaughter after the battle of Firozshah one British commander exclaimed, 'Another such victory and we are undone.' Nevertheless, after three months' bitter fighting the Sikhs began to give way and the British conquered Lahore, the capital of the Sikh empire. The Sikhs were forced to cede some of the most fertile tracts of the Punjab as well as the beautiful mountain region of Kashmir. Although a predominantly Muslim area, Kashmir was then sold by the British to the highest bidder, who turned out to be a Hindu chieftain, Gulab Singh.

The first war, however, proved inconclusive and within two years hostilities had broken out again. The Second Sikh War (1848–9) proved just as bloody as the first. In January 1849 a terrible battle was fought at Chilianwala where the British were nearly defeated. So many British troops died that the home government felt obliged to recall the commander-in-chief, Lord Gough. Before the new commander could arrive Lord Gough took on the Sikhs again and this time defeated them decisively. In March 1849 the whole of the Punjab – 100,000 square miles of India's most fertile land – was taken under the Company's rule.

By 1850 the British had consolidated their grasp over almost the entire subcontinent. The British Raj now spread from the River Indus to Bengal, from Kashmir to Cape Comarin. What remained to be done was to integrate and organize the many different components of this vast empire.

Reform, Reorganization and Revolt

Everywhere they went the British had found things in a state of ruin and decay. Political division and constant warfare had brought about a sense of almost complete social breakdown. The landscape was littered with monuments of past glory and prosperity – palaces, towns, reservoirs – which now stood ruined and deserted. Whole regions it seemed were depopulated, their capitals in decay and their inhabitants eking out a miserable existence. This image features constantly in the minds of the British writers and travellers of the period. Spurred on by a belief in progress and in the moral, intellectual and technical superiority of the Western world, the British felt that it was their duty to reform and modernize India on western lines. Only this would enable her to develop and improve herself.

The first step was the adoption of English as the official language. For the British, this was the key to improvement and they saw English as a vital tool with which to assimilate India into the western tradition. Persian was replaced by English which henceforth became the new language of government and of education. During the government of Lord Bentinck (1828–35) an official education policy was conceived. Its purpose was to impart a knowledge of English literature and science through the medium of the English language. This, it was hoped, would lead to a downward filtration of Western knowledge and ideas. Probably the most influential advocate of this new policy was the historian Lord Macaulay (1800–59). A firm believer in the superiority of Western culture, he argued strongly and successfully against the use of Indian languages; for he felt that this would be a backward and rather pointless step. In a ringing pronouncement in 1832 he declared that 'A single shelf of a good European library is worth the whole native literature of India and Arabia'. Macaulay's aim was to create a new class of Indian who, moulded by Western culture and ideas, would lead the way in developing India:

> We must do our best to form a class who may be interpreters between us and the millions whom we govern; a class of persons Indian in blood and colour, but English in taste, in opinions, in morals and in intellect.

This attitude towards Indian languages was matched by an increasing interference in Indian customs and traditions which were regarded as backward and even barbaric. In 1829, for example, the custom of 'sati' was prohibited. A custom of great tradition and significance, sati, or suttee, called for a widow to burn herself to death in her husband's funeral pyre as a symbol of her devotion. In 1836, in an even more symbolic gesture, the guns at Fort William boomed out in honour of the first Hindu medical student who had defied religious custom by carrying out a dissection at the newly-founded Calcutta Medical College. Although these actions were hailed by educated Indians as humane and progressive, to the vast majority they seemed only the first steps in an all-out assault on Indian culture.

The policy of westernization reached its peak during the governorship of Lord Dalhousie (1848–56). Confident in the superiority of Western civilization, Dalhousie was determined to bring the benefits of British rule to India. He launched an ambitious programme of modernization which in the space of a few years was to transform the face of India completely. Previous British administrations had already begun restoring the irrigation systems and reservoirs which were so important to Indian agriculture; Dalhousie continued this process. He was responsible for building the first 450 miles of the Ganges Canal which today irrigates two million acres of the Ganges valley and provides hydro-electric power for the whole region. He also began a systematic road-building programme which laid the foundation for a new and much-improved road network. In addition, the chief centres were now linked together by the introduction of the electric telegraph and the creation of a cheap, efficient postal service. Dalhousie's most important innovation, however, was the introduction of the railways. His governorship saw the construction of 300 miles of the first railway track ever laid in India. Often described as the steel fabric which held India together, the railways are still the subcontinent's most popular and most indispensable form of travel.

In other fields too there were sweeping reforms. Dalhousie presided over the spread of English education and his term saw the foundation of a modern educational system with primary schools, high schools, colleges and universities, each leading on to the next step. Although 1857 was to be memorable in many other ways, it was also the year in which three of India's great universities – Bombay, Madras and Calcutta – were founded. Another symbol of the new progress was the Hindu Widows Act of 1856 which permitted the remarriage of widows, something previously forbidden by Hindu tradition. Like so many of Dalhousie's other reforms, although meant to be progressive its only effect was to arouse even deeper suspicion.

The most provocative of his reforms, however, lay in the field of administration. In keeping with his other ideas, Dalhousie was convinced that British administration was far superior to any Indian government. He regarded the many Indian states as enclaves of bad government which had to be swept away as soon as possible. To further his policy he evolved a new doctrine, the doctrine of lapse. Although Hindu law recognized the right of an Indian ruler to adopt his heir, the British did not. They insisted that the ruler could only be succeeded by his natural heir. If an Indian ruler did not leave behind a natural heir, the British would refuse to recognize his successor. Control of the state would then 'lapse' back to the British government, which was the supreme authority. By this method Dalhousie was able to annex huge new areas which had formerly been independent states. The most conspicuous example was Nagpur: upon the death of the Bhonsla in 1853 without a natural heir, his territories were annexed; Nagpur was extinguished and its lands absorbed into British India, thus at last linking Bombay with Calcutta.

The excuse of misgovernment was also used by the British with great effect. In 1856 the kingdom of Oudh, which had been a loyal client state, was annexed and its ruler deposed on this pretext. Dalhousie accompanied these actions by discontinuing various titles and pensions which the British had been in the habit of honouring. When the former Peshwa died, his pension of eight million rupees was stopped and his son Nana Sahib was not allowed to draw it. It was a similar story with the last Mughal emperor who was also threatened with abolition. He was only saved by the decision of his heir, who agreed to abandon the imperial title and vacate the palace on his father's death. All this was carried out in the name of administrative efficiency, on the grounds that these honours were now outdated relics which had long ceased to have any real meaning.

The Indian Mutiny, 1857–8

These policies of abolition and annexation greatly alarmed the Indian ruling classes, many of whom were already deeply uneasy about British expansion. These deep-seated feelings of fear and unease were also shared by the majority of the ordinary people. The spread of English education, the astounding technological innovations, the unprecedented social reforms, all had a deeply disturbing effect on conservative minds. Combined with the effect of the increasing missionary activity of the times, it served to give the impression that Indian religion and culture itself was in danger.

This growing unease was reflected in the ranks of the East India Company's army. It was mainly made up of Indian troops, trained and equipped on Western lines and officered by Europeans. These troops were called 'sepoys' and they had proved themselves to be the most efficient fighting force in India. Up till now their loyalty had been a key element in British success: it was sepoy troops who had defeated Tipu Sultan, had resisted the Maratha charges, and finally overcome the Sikhs. In 1830 the number of Indian troops was 187,000, by 1857 it had risen to 200,000. In contrast the wholly European element numbered only 10,000 officers and men. It was a dangerous imbalance. As one leading British administrator recognized, the sepoy army was 'a delicate and dangerous machine, which a little mismanagement may easily turn against us'. These were to prove prophetic words, for this is exactly what happened.

The Company's forces were divided into three main groups, each of them centred on one of the three presidencies – Bengal, Madras and Bombay. In Bengal there had already been several outbreaks of discontent within the ranks. These had been caused by the imposition of new military regulations which seemed to threaten the religious and social beliefs of the sepoys. The rapid changes and innovations which the sepoy saw all around him made him deeply anxious for his traditions, an anxiety which was only heightened by his suspicion of Christianity and British intentions. The British, however, did not recognize the explosive effect which these fears could have in this new climate of change. As a result very little was done to calm or alleviate the sepoy's apprehensions.

The spark finally came in 1857 with the introduction of a new rifle, the Lee-Enfield. The Enfield was issued with cartridges which had to be bitten off before they could he loaded. During the early part of the year rumours spread that these cartridges were greased with cow and pig fat. Both of these were an abomination to the sepoy, the cow being sacred to the Hindu and the pig pollution to the Muslim. These stories ignited the highly charged atmosphere and the sepoys of the Bengal army rebelled in defence of their religion. The symbolic focus of the revolt was the old, imperial capital of Delhi. In May the rebels seized the city, massacring every European they found. The old, unwilling figure of the last of the Mughals, Bahadur Shah III (r.1837–58), was dragged out of retirement and proclaimed emperor. The Mughal flag was hoisted once more over the Red Fort and the revolt was fought in his name.

The fall of Delhi was the signal for which everyone had been waiting. The Mutiny now spread all across northern and central India. There were uprisings in Oudh, Gwalior, in the holy city of Benares and at Jhansi. Some of the fiercest fighting took place in Oudh, at Lucknow and Kanpur. At Lucknow, the chief city, a small force of Europeans and loyal Indians was besieged by a huge number of rebels in the British

Residency. Although the walls and surrounding buildings have been demolished, the ruins of the Residency still stand today – a rather grim monument, pockmarked with bullet holes and spattered with memorial plaques. Kanpur, now a rather uninspiring industrial town, was the scene of even more brutal fighting. Here a small British garrison of about 1,000 eventually surrendered after a gallant struggle, only for the entire contingent, women and children included, to be butchered in cold blood. In central India one of the leaders of the rebellion was the Rani of Jhansi, Lakshmi Bai. The widow of the former ruler of Jhansi, she took up the rebel cause on behalf of her adopted son whom the British had refused to recognize as his heir. At Jhansi, in Madhya Pradesh, the brown battlements of the fort rise out of the rock and the sand. It has ten gates and its walls with their deserted towers, battlements and terraces stretch across the bare hillsides. It was here that the Rani rose in revolt, killing all the British officers and their families.

The British forces were scattered all over northern India and for a time the situation seemed quite desperate. Nevertheless, the Madras and Bombay armies remained loyal, as did the great princely states – Hyderabad, Baroda and Indore. Rajasthan also supported the British, as did the Punjab where the Sikhs stepped forward to replace an army of 36,000 restive sepoys, who were disarmed and dismissed. In all, less than a third of the subcontinent was seriously affected. The rebels themselves were divided, their actions confused and their leadership at times almost non-existent. All this gave the British the breathing space they needed and they were able to recover themselves.

In September 1857 British troops recaptured Delhi, which fell after a bitter siege. On entering the city the British troops went berserk. As *The Times* itself reported, not since the day of Nadir Shah had the city seen such brutal scenes of rape, pillage and murder. The poet Ghalib (1797–1869) mourned:

> Here is a vast ocean of blood before me, God alone knows what more I have to behold . . . Thousands of my friends are dead . . . perhaps none is left even to shed tears upon my death . . . My pen dare not write more.

Kanpur and Lucknow were also finally recaptured. Both cities were reduced to rubble and here too there were similar scenes. According to some stories Hindus were forced to eat cow's flesh, while Muslims were sewn into pigskins. By the spring of 1858 the back of the Mutiny had been broken. In central India too the rebels were forced to give way. The Rani's fierce courage held Jhansi together in the face of a bitter siege but British troops finally managed to force their way in. In the desperate hand-to-hand and door-to-door fighting which preceded the city's fall, at least 5,000 people were killed. The Rani herself was killed some time afterwards, fighting at the head of her troops dressed like a man – 'using her sword with both hands and holding the reins of her horse in her mouth'. By the end of 1858 the rebellion had been completely crushed.

'Pax Britannica', The Heyday of Empire

The Mutiny was a profound shock for the British and it brought about a radical change in their policies towards India. The most immediate outcome was that the government was finally taken out of the East India Company's hands. Control was transferred to the Crown, which meant that in future India would be governed directly by the British government, with the authority of the Cabinet of the day vested in the Secretary of State for India. In future it would be this minister, together with his representative in India, who would be responsible for Indian affairs. The British also recognized that the unease and the uncertainty caused by their policies had been a major element behind the outbreak of the rebellion. Thus they abandoned their social reforms and gave up their attempts to modernize Indian society. The new policy was to maintain the status quo; there would be no more interference with Indian customs and religion. Nor would there be any more interference with the government of the Indian princely states.

The loyalty of many of the princely states towards the British had been a key factor in ensuring the failure of the Mutiny. They were, as the British themselves recognized 'breakwaters in the storm which would otherwise have swept over us in one great wave'. It was very much in Britain's interests, therefore, to remove the uncertainties felt by the princes over previous British policies and to keep them to the British cause. The government entered into new treaties with the

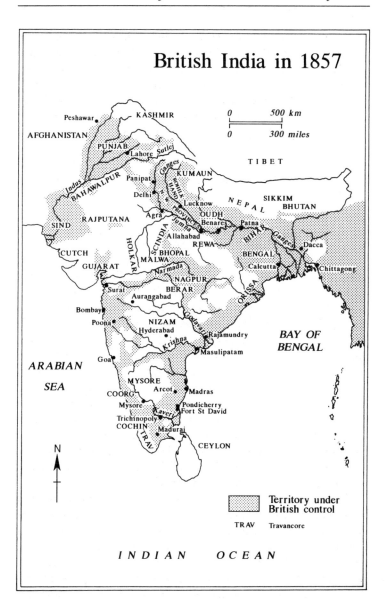

British India in 1857

Peshawar

KASHMIR

0   500 km

0   300 miles

AFGHANISTAN

PUNJAB

Lahore Sutlej

TIBET

Indus

BAHAWALPUR

Panipat

Ganges

KUMAUN

Delhi

NEPAL

SIKKIM

BHUTAN

Lucknow

N.W. PROVINCES

OUDH

SIND

RAJPUTANA

Agra

Jumna

Benares

Patna

Ganges

Dacca

CUTCH

HOLKAR

SCINDIA

Allahabad

BIHAR

Chittagong

GUJARAT

MALWA

BHOPAL

REWA

BENGAL

Calcutta

Narmada

NAGPUR

BERAR

ORISSA

Surat

Aurangabad

Bombay

Godavari

Poona

NIZAM

Hyderabad

Rajamundry

BAY OF
BENGAL

Krishna

Masulipatam

Goa

MYSORE

Arcot

Madras

ARABIAN

SEA

COORG

Mysore

Pondicherry
Fort St David

Trichinopoly

Kaveri

COCHIN

Madurai

TRAV

CEYLON

N

INDIAN   OCEAN

Territory under
British control

TRAV   Travancore

princes which assured them of their rights and promised that there
would be no more interference with the running of their states. The
political boundaries of their kingdoms were guaranteed, maintaining
the existence of 542 Indian princely states of different size and shapes.
The largest and most important were Travancore, Hyderabad, Mysore,
Baroda, Kashmir and Gwalior. Together with their smaller counterparts, all these states survived as semi-independent, self-governing units
right up to Independence in 1948; 38.5 per cent of the Indian
subcontinent was governed by these rulers – the 'Maharajahs', as they
became known collectively in the West. Renowned for their glittering
colour, exotic style and often fabulous wealth, in British eyes they were
vassal kings who epitomized the power and glory of the British empire.
British prestige was further enhanced in 1877 when Queen Victoria
was declared Empress of India. This completely transformed the
position of the governor-general, who became much more than just a
civilian official; he now became the 'Viceroy', the semi-royal representative of imperial authority.

The British were determined not to allow another such disaster to
overtake them and in the years which followed the Mutiny they
tightened their grip on power. This was particularly the case with the
army, which was completely reorganized. The proportion of Indian
troops to British troops had previously been more than five to one and
at times almost ten to one. This imbalance was corrected and the British
made sure that the Indian units would never outnumber the European
units by more than two to one. The most effective weapon, the artillery,
was kept in British hands and careful arrangements were made to station
the Indian battalions together with their European counterparts. In 1895
the separate presidency forces were dissolved and the Indian army was
welded into a single unit. Indians, however, were not allowed to
become officers; all moves to introduce Indian officers were fiercely
resisted and it was not until 1932 that they were finally enlisted.
Nevertheless, the new army proved itself a reliable fighting force and
during both world wars it served with great distinction on several fronts.
The Second World War saw a huge increase in its strength and it
expanded from nearly 200,000 to nearly 2.5 million. Although this was
later scaled down, the modern Indian army still numbers around 1.26

million, making it one of the largest armies in the world. A highly professional fighting force, the Indian army still maintains many of its old traditions and it continues to be run on British lines.

The other arms of British government, the civil service and the judicial system, were also reorganized and given a settled form. The old legal system where Indian and English courts existed side by side was abolished. In its place an entirely British legal system was instituted and high courts were established at Bombay, Madras and Calcutta. Although the British have long since gone, the system still remains in place. As many Indians will tell you, today the judiciary forms a very essential part of Indian democracy.

The Indian Civil Service (ICS), the forerunner of the vast and cumbersome giant which is modern Indian bureaucracy, was formed in 1861. A hand-picked unit, consisting of the cream of English administrative talent, it was an élite organization. Described as the 'Heaven born', its officials were regarded with something like awe by Englishmen and Indians alike. It was their business to govern and administer India; in a sense, rather like the railways, they too were the steel framework which held the country together. Like the Mauryan and Mughal bureaucracy before them, they made sure that British rule reached into every part of the subcontinent. However, like the army and the judiciary, the higher levels of the ICS were staffed almost entirely by Englishmen. One effect of the Mutiny had been to make the British deeply distrustful of Indians and they were deliberately excluded from power. Although in 1853 entry to the ICS was made available to open competition, until World War I the numbers of Indians who were admitted to the higher levels remained no more than a handful.

British Islands in an Indian Sea

The most important result of the Mutiny was the profound impact which it had on the British consciousness. The memory of the Rebellion aroused such fear and horror in the British that they withdrew from any form of social contact with Indians. This state of mind is reflected in the new towns and suburbs which they built for themselves across India. As they moved inland, military stations were set up all over the subcontinent. Instead of building forts, however, they laid out separate enclosures for their community. These little enclaves were called cantonments, which were more or less self-contained small communities. They had their own military and civilian accommodation, their own markets, hospitals, churches and jails. Everything was laid out in orderly lines, with rows of spacious bungalows along wide, tree-lined streets down which reinforcements could be rushed to the rescue. The spirit of the cantonment was that of a little British world quite separate from the rest of India.

These feelings also led to the development of 'hill stations', small European towns high up in the cool atmosphere of the hills. The most famous of these towns was Simla, in Himachal Pradesh, 7,000 feet up in the Himalayas. It was the summer capital of British India and during the hot months it was the headquarters of the Indian government, which would be moved up from the steamy heat of the plains. Here amidst the scented pine trees and deodars of the Himalayan hills, the British carved out a picturesque little country town for themselves. Dotted with timbered, gabled buildings and quaint cottages bedecked with flowers, Simla still feels more like some distant part of England than any other part of India.

With the opening of the Suez Canal in 1869, travel became much quicker and easier and increasing numbers of European wives and families began to come out to India. Hill stations mushroomed all over the subcontinent and their populations began to grow rapidly. In 1880 the permanent population of Simla numbered almost 5,000, by 1901 it had increased to 13,000. As more and more Europeans arrived in India, the British official or civilian confined himself more and more to his office, his home and his club. The Club was another institution which represented an island of Britishness in the midst of an Indian sea. Here the English would withdraw to drink, dance, play cards and meet each other. A focus for the whole European community, the Club was often one of the most spacious and elegant buildings in town. Many of these clubs – the Royal Calcutta Turf Club, the Gymkhana Club in Bombay and the Madras Club, for instance – are still in existence today, and they remain the focus of a vibrant and elegant social life.

This atmosphere of exclusivity symbolized the racial suspicion with which the English now regarded Indians. Not only did the English community want to have nothing to do with Indians, it also opposed allowing them any kind of authority. In 1883 the government of India tried to appoint Indians to the position of district judge, thus enabling them to try Europeans on criminal charges. However, this met with such a furious reaction from the European community that the government was forced to withdraw the proposal.

By the middle of the nineteenth century the British had become conscious of a clear sense of racial superiority. They saw themselves as bringing peace, justice, order and prosperity to a backward, heathen country. Their mission was to govern and to rule in the name of justice and empire. They did not seek to win friends or please those whom they ruled, merely to govern as efficiently and as fairly as they could. This was the new imperial creed. Its spirit is eloquently captured by Rudyard Kipling (1865–1936), British India's most famous writer and poet:

> Take up the White Man's burden –
> And reap his old reward:
> The blame of those ye better,
> The hate of those ye guard –
> The cry of hosts ye humour
> (Ah, slowly!) toward the light. . .

Born in Bombay, Kipling was educated in England but returned to India at the age of seventeen. An unrivalled observer of Indian people and places, many of his stories centred around British life in India and the relationship between the British and the Indians. The most popular writer of his day, Kipling's masterpieces were *The Jungle Book* (1894) and *Kim* (1901), both of which remain immensely popular to this day.

The imperial ethos reached its peak during the viceroyalty of Lord Curzon (r.1899–1905). Perhaps the most brilliant man ever to become viceroy, Curzon was convinced of Britain's destiny to rule India. At the same time he was determined to improve the efficiency and justice of British rule. In this cause he worked tirelessly to improve the administration and made himself unpopular amongst the European expatriates by vigorously punishing incidents of racial violence. Despite this, Curzon did little to hide his belief in British superiority, which he felt was essential for the good of India. It was he who was responsible for the Victoria Memorial in Calcutta, Britain's answer to the Taj Mahal. Intended by Curzon as a monument to the history of British rule in India, it took fifteen years to build. Like the Taj it was made entirely from white marble, and to quote Curzon 'a building stately, spacious, monumental and grand'.

The Impact of British Rule

Although the British no longer concerned themselves with modernizing Indian society, in other areas British rule had far-reaching effects. In less than 200 years they made an even greater impact than the Muslims had in 800. They measured and mapped, standardized and centralized, bridged and connected the subcontinent into a single workable unit. This was especially the case in communications and economic development.

The years following the Mutiny had seen a huge expansion of the railway system and by 1900 there were more than 25,000 miles of track. One of the great hubs of this network was Bombay, where in 1887 India's largest railway station, the Victoria Terminus was erected in honour of Queen Victoria's Golden Jubilee, was opened. A spectacular Gothic mass of domes, pinnacles and turrets, from the outside it seems more like a church than a station, with its rich ornamentation and tall, stained-glass windows. Rather more grimy than in its prime, the Victoria Terminus now receives as many as 900 trains and almost two million passengers every day.

Road construction too continued to develop apace. Probably the most famous of all the roads constructed by the British was the Grand Trunk Road. In an echo of Mauryan days, this ran for 1,000 miles right across the subcontinent from Calcutta to Peshawar on the borders of Afghanistan. In his great adventure story, *Kim*, Rudyard Kipling describes it: 'A stately corridor . . . it runs straight, bearing without crowding, India's traffic for fifteen hundred miles – such a river of life as nowhere existed in the world.' It is still in use today. Now a rather

The Victoria railway terminus in Bombay

alarming highway called Route 66, it is a potholed and rather battered corridor for the furious traffic of northern India.

The use of English as a single language over a variety of regional languages also greatly eased communication. The advance of English education together with the rapid spread of the electric telegraph and the printing press led to the growth of something India had never had before – a national press. In 1880 the *Indian Daily Mirror* became the first daily newspaper in English edited by Indians. By 1900 there were at least 600 newspapers in all kinds of languages. Their advent completely transformed political life, and as they developed they became a powerful medium for the expression of dissatisfaction with British rule.

The political and social impact of these new developments was huge. The press, the cheap postage service, the telegraph, the roads, and most of all the railways, all had a great unifying effect. They brought the different regions of India together, with its great cities – Calcutta, Madras, Bombay and Delhi – in close touch with each other. It made trade and commerce much easier than ever before, providing the necessary infrastructure for industrialization. Even more importantly, it helped break down age-old barriers of caste, religion and race, forging a new national identity. As the economy and society itself began to change, the old religious, political and trading centres began to be superseded, to be replaced by purely industrial towns like Ahmedabad or Kanpur, and by large metropolitan areas. As they developed, these centres attracted landless labour from the neighbouring villages, becoming in time densely-populated areas. The British themselves did little to alleviate these problems, for social engineering was no longer their concern. For all the pristine splendour of European Calcutta, outside its boundaries there lay a chaotic, stinking mass of slums. Graphically described by Kipling as that 'smokey, magnificent, many-sided city of Dreadful Night', anyone visiting today should remember that by 1900 the city was already out of control.

Although the British never had a blueprint for industrializing India, many of the developments which they pioneered helped create the infrastructure for later economic development. From 1840 to 1914 India was Britain's largest and most important trading partner. The opening of the Suez Canal in 1869 and the expansion of the railways tied her even more firmly into the international economy. India exported huge amounts of raw cotton, wheat, jute, tea and coffee, while importing equally large quantities of British-made textiles and machinery. British capital was invested in the railways and in the development of tea and coffee plantations. Although India continued to remain predominantly agricultural, this led to the adoption of a modern banking system and the founding of an industrial base, followed in turn by the establishment of textile, jute, sugar and cement factories.

These new developments threw up a new range of rich merchant families in the major cities. Bombay in particular boomed and its rising prosperity is reflected in the grand neo-Gothic buildings of the city. For most travellers to India their first port of call was the Taj Mahal Hotel, a huge edifice of crenellated towers, battlements and drawbridges looming on the waterfront. The quintessence of imperial culture, according to G.A. Mathews who stayed there in 1905, it was 'on such a scale of magnificence and luxury that at first it rather took one's breath away'. In 1926 Aldous Huxley wrote: 'The gigantic Taj combines the style of the South Kensington Natural History Museum with that of an Indian pavilion at an International Exhibition.'

Still one of the world's great hotels, the Taj was built in 1903 by the

The Taj Hotel in Bombay. One of the great hotels of the British Empire
which was unique in that it alone welcomed Indian guests

Indian industrialist J.N. Tata (1839–1904) after he had been refused
admission to a nearby British hotel because of his race. Of all the luxury
hotels in the subcontinent it was unique in that it alone welcomed
Indian guests. The British have long since vacated their great public
buildings, but both the Taj and the Tatas have survived. The Taj is one
of the most famous hotels in Asia, while the Tatas are perhaps India's
greatest industrial dynasty.

INDUSTRIAL DEVELOPMENT

Despite the wealth and the prosperity which British rule generated,
India's economic development was clearly dictated by Britain's own
interests. Her economy was regularly used to make up Britain's trading
deficit with other industrialized nations. No attempt was made to
protect Indian industry and Indian markets were flooded with cheap,
machine-made British goods. The effect of this was deeply damaging.
In Mughal times India had been renowned for its export of cotton goods

Jamsetji Tata, the founder of the Indian iron and steel industry

as well as its luxury industries – the production of muslin, silk, brocades and shawls; all these were completely destroyed. Despite its investment in certain areas, the British government's attitude to Indian industrial development was very lukewarm. British interest was largely confined to communications and the exploitation of raw materials – jute, tea, coffee – and the development of Indian industry was largely left to local industrialists like J.N. Tata and G.D. Birla (1893–1983), who gradually organized themselves on modern lines. It was Jamsetji Tata, for example, who founded India's steel industry: in 1907 the Tata Iron and Steel Company was set up at Jamshedpur in Bihar. Named after its founder, Jamshedpur was to become the single largest steelworks in the world.

The First World War, however, saw a significant change in the British attitude and the government now began actively to encourage industry. Tariff barriers were set up to safeguard Indian manufacturers and foster new developments. In this new climate Indian industry expanded hugely and by the 1920s India ranked sixth in the table of industrial nations.

'The Jewel in the Crown'

The peak of imperial power and spectacle came in 1911. Queen Victoria's grandson, George V, was recognized as King-Emperor in Delhi. Great imperial assemblies or 'durbars' had been held in 1877 and in 1903, but this was the first time a reigning English monarch had come to India. The occasion was marked by a great durbar which was a glittering spectacle of pomp, colour and feudal ritual. As the Mughal emperors had done in the past, the King of England now received the homage of all the princes and rulers of India. In a deeply symbolic moment the King-Emperor and his wife Mary, the Queen-Empress, showed themselves to their Indian subjects from the ramparts of Shah Jahan's Red Fort. Here it was announced that the imperial capital would be transferred from Calcutta to the historic site of Delhi, seat of so many past kingdoms and empires. It was George V's expressed wish that 'the new creation should be in every way worthy of this ancient and beautiful city'.

Although work began almost immediately, it was not until 1931 that the new capital was formally inaugurated. New Delhi was designed by the two leading British architects of the day, Sir Edwin Lutyens (1869–1944) and Sir Herbert Baker (1862–1946). Intended to be an official centre, it was and still is a government town. As with the British everywhere, housing was laid out in neat, symmetrical lines, strictly according to precedence and in decreasing order of grandeur. In addition to the Viceroy's palace, there were palaces for the commander-in-chief, palaces of the great princes, and sprawling bungalows for the officials. Its show place was the Kings Way (now Raj Path), a great ceremonial way two miles long. Longer and far grander than the Mall, it is almost twice as wide as the Champs Élysées. Here every Independence Day the whole scene comes vividly to life. Great processions of elephants, horsemen and infantry parade down the Raj Path in a whirl of fluttering flags and pennants, accompanied by the beat of drums. Although it is Independence Day, for a few moments memories are kindled and the Raj comes breathtakingly alive. A city of awe-inspiring size and splendour, New Delhi is indeed worthy of its forebears. As the master builder Lutyens remarked 'It is really a great event in the history of the world and of architecture.' In an even more telling aside he then added, 'It would only be possible now under a despotism.'

CHAPTER TEN

The Road to Freedom,
1850s–1948

The impact of western culture, western education and new scientific techniques gave traditional Indian life a tremendous shock. It led Indian society to re-examine and reassess its traditional beliefs and practices, fostering a new cultural awareness. As the nineteenth century progressed this new-found confidence translated itself into a growing political consciousness. Increasingly proud of their own culture and identity, Indians began to demand many more political, social and economic rights. These demands were led by the educated, westernized class which had grown up under the British. By learning English this class had absorbed new political and social ideas which helped give it a common identity and a new sense of purpose. It is in this process that the Indian nationalist movement has its origins. Today almost everyone who knows anything about India has heard of Gandhi and Nehru. Richard Attenborough's epic film *Gandhi* (1983) evokes images of a saintly little man, dressed in a piece of cotton cloth and sandals, at the head of a mass, non-violent struggle leading India inexorably towards Independence. However, this is only half the picture; the real story of Indian nationalism begins much earlier.

The Great Awakening

The road to Independence begins back in the nineteenth century with the rediscovery and reinvigoration of Indian, particularly Hindu, culture. Strangely enough, this process originated with the discoveries of many British scholars who made it their life's work to unearth the story of India's ancient past. The greatest of these scholars was Sir

William Jones (see p.34), who was responsible for translating several Sanskrit classics – amongst them Khalidasa's *Shakuntala* – into English. In doing so he laid the foundations for the study of Sanskrit learning which had become disused and long forgotten in India itself. Jones's work was taken even further by H.T. Colebrooke (1765–1837), whose scholarship in all aspects of Sanskrit literature put Sanskrit studies on a scientific footing. These writings made a great impact in Europe, where they influenced many of the leading writers, artists and thinkers of the day. The German poets, Goethe, Herder and Schiller were full of admiration for Khalidasa, especially for *Shakuntala* which they hailed as a masterpiece. Indian religions, such as Hinduism and Buddhism, also began to receive a great deal of attention. The philosopher Schopenhauer for one was greatly influenced by the discovery of the Upanishads, while the composer Wagner found himself drawn to Buddhism – *Tristan and Isolde* and *Parsifal* both have Buddhist themes.

The most celebrated Sanskrit scholar of all was the Oxford professor Friedrich Max Müller (see p.35). Renowned for his work on Indian religion and philosophy, he more than anyone else brought the glories of Indian culture to the attention of the rest of the world. His most famous work, the 51-volume *Sacred Books of the East* (1879–1904), caused a sensation in the West and announced that India had a unique spiritual message for Europe. Even today this is still how many people see India – as an ancient and deeply spiritual land, a treasure-house of knowledge and wisdom. The efforts of Max Müller and many other scholars like him had the effect of making Indian knowledge widely known and appreciated. It gave Indians an important sense of their own identity and a feeling of pride in their past. There was a new interest in Indian history, literature and art, which now began to be studied in earnest.

Ram Mohan Roy and the Revival of Hinduism

Hand in hand with these developments went a revival of Hinduism. This revival was the work of a number of religious and social movements. The first was the Brahmo Samaj, founded in 1828 by a Bengali, Ram Mohan Roy (1772–1833). A brilliant intellectual, Roy was the first Indian whose ideas were profoundly influenced by contact

Ram Mohan Roy, religious reformer and founder of Brahmo Samaj

with Western culture. Having steeped himself in Hindu learning, he went on to master Hebrew, Greek, Persian, Arabic and English and used these skills to make himself the first real modern scholar of comparative religions. Drawing on a combination of Western and Eastern learning, Roy made the first organized effort to reinvigorate Hinduism and adapt it to the new situation. A confirmed opponent of superstition and ritual, he tried to purge Hinduism of its bad traditions, condemning the caste system and attacking rituals such as animal sacrifice and the worship of idols. At the same time he defended and reasserted the positive elements and tried to promote a new sort of religion.

Ram Mohan Roy's relentless campaigning created a new spirit in Hindu society, encouraging the growth of a new social consciousness. Customs like child marriage and sati were abolished, while other taboos such as those preventing women from claiming their inheritance and widows from remarrying were also gradually undermined. Other reformers followed in his wake, determined to rid Hinduism of its superstitions and make it a social force. In 1875 another movement, the Arya Samaj, was founded by Swami Dayananda Sarasvati (1824–83). Dayananda based his teachings on the Vedas, which he regarded as the only true source of Indian religion. In keeping with this belief, he too denounced many of the practices of contemporary Hinduism and preached drastic social reform. The Arya Samaj is still an active force in Hindu life today, especially in northern India and the Punjab where it continues to exercise great appeal.

The last great reforming movement of the nineteenth century was the Ramakrishna Mission, which was based on the teachings of the mystic Ramakrishna (1836–86). It was led by his disciple, a Bengali graduate called Vivekananda (1863–1902). Following his master's example, Vivekananda turned to the living traditions of popular Hinduism for inspiration. He became particularly well known abroad where he acted as the spokesman of Hinduism in the West. He preached the virtues of Hindu civilization and proclaimed the greatness of India's history, calling on Indians to become great again by living up to the traditions of their past. After four years lecturing in England and the USA he returned to India a national hero and founded the Ramakrishna Mission which he dedicated to the task of uplifting India's past and downtrodden masses. Despite his scorn for politics, Vivekananda's teachings gave his countrymen a tremendous pride in their own culture; many of them followed his example and began to devote themselves to the needs of India's poor, opening up a new path for India's leaders whose Western outlook had previously isolated them from their own people. Gandhi was deeply influenced by Vivekananda.

The Growth of Nationalism

This growing sense of nationhood finally found its expression in 1885 with the formation of the Indian National Congress. This political organization was to become the main instrument of the independence movement, and after independence had been achieved it became India's ruling party. Today Congress is still the most important political party in India and looks likely to remain so for the foreseeable future. At first it was a very moderate organization, extremely loyal and highly anglophile in its outlook. It consisted of an élite group of highly westernized and very wealthy Indians. What these men wanted was not freedom or independence but limited reform which would give them a greater say in the way India was run. They wanted things like a larger voice in the provincial councils, greater access to the higher ranks of the civil service, and the raising of customs barriers to protect Indian-made goods. This moderation, however, was not rewarded. They were treated with disdain by the British who regarded them as a tiny minority with no claim to represent Indian opinion. British indifference to their aspirations, combined with a clear assertion of British racial supremacy, gradually antagonized and alienated them and they turned to open discontent. One famous example is the case of Surendranath Banerjee, whose career dramatizes this gradual change of heart.

Known in later life as 'Surrender Not', Surendranath Banerjee (1848–1926) was one of the first leaders of the Indian Nationalist movement. Much of his early life had been devoted to preparing for the Indian Civil Service. Defying all the conventions of his background, Banerjee travelled to London where he became one of the first Indians to sit the Civil Service examinations; here he excelled himself, obtaining the highest marks in the whole competition. Despite this he was not accepted and had to resort to the law to secure his appointment. Although he won his case and received a position in the ICS, upon returning to India he was dismissed for a very minor offence. His treatment convinced Banerjee that 'the personal wrong done to me was an illustration of the impotency of our people'. He became a confirmed opponent of the British and spent the rest of his long life campaigning for the rights of his countrymen. A fiery orator, he travelled up and down the subcontinent, rousing Indians with a greater sense of loyalty to their own country. It was Banerjee who in 1883 founded the first nationwide political organization in India, the Indian National Congress.

PARTITION OF BENGAL
The most crucial event in the early period came in 1905 with the partition of the province of Bengal. This was one of the last acts of Lord Curzon, who in order to make this large and populous province more

Lord Curzon, Viceroy of India, 1899–1905

manageable divided it into two halves – one half with a Hindu majority, the other with a Muslim majority. This move was carried out without consulting Indian opinion and without any real consideration for Indian feelings. Many Indians saw it as yet another attack on their culture and the identity of the people, especially in Bengal which was the centre of nationalist feeling. Bengal erupted in huge demonstrations; the government was openly defied and there were fierce protests and boycotts of British goods. The British retaliated by taking severe measures: peaceful pickets were beaten up and Indian political leaders deported without trial. These drastic actions failed to check the nationalist movement, which now went underground, resulting in a campaign of terror against government officials. The failure of these tactics led in 1909 to the first series of political reforms and two years later the partition of Bengal itself was revoked. These protests witnessed the birth of a new sort of nationalism. For the first time Indians had begun to realize the power of political agitation and organization. Congress too had begun to change. Before 1905 it had asked only for isolated reforms; now however its position hardened and it began to demand self-government.

THE MUSLIM LEAGUE

This period also saw the growth of a separate Muslim consciousness and a new nationalist party emerged to cater for Muslim interests. This was the Muslim League, which was founded in 1906 to look after the interests of the Muslim community. Although they numbered more than one-fifth of the total population, India's Muslims were scattered in pockets all over the country. Only in certain areas, such as Sind, northern Punjab and the eastern half of Bengal, were they in a majority. Muslims had also been slow to take advantage of education in English, so that they were poorly represented in the professions and the public service. As a result, they did not command the influence which their numbers entitled them to. They were certainly not well represented in Congress, in whose ranks there were large numbers of Brahmin Hindus. All this had the effect of making Muslim leaders increasingly uneasy and apprehensive. They began to fear that the larger community would override the interests of the smaller one and that Muslims would be left behind as a minority without any proper representation.

To combat this danger the Muslim League campaigned for Muslims to be separately represented in any forthcoming electoral reforms. In this they were successful and the British reforms of 1909 gave a special position to Muslims by creating a number of separate Muslim constituencies. The League followed this up in 1916 by reaching a special agreement with the Congress party, the Lucknow Pact. Under its terms both Congress and the Muslim League agreed to work together and campaign for self-government. In return Congress accepted the idea that there should be separate electorates for Muslims.

Expectation and Sacrifice

The First World War had a profound effect on the growth of Indian nationalism. Before it began Britain had been seen by many Indians as one of the two great superpowers along with Russia. By 1918, however, it was clear that Britain was no longer the huge imperial giant she had once seemed, merely one of several roughly equal powers. The revolutions which had overthrown the Ottoman and Chinese empires and Tsarist Russia created an atmosphere of hope and expectation. Change now seemed very possible, even in the most powerful, most despotic political structures. The air of expectation was fuelled by the huge sacrifices made by Indians in their contribution to the British war effort. Enormous loans had been raised and more than 1.2 million Indians had fought in France and the Middle East (over 60,000 were killed). There was a general feeling that India would be rewarded for her sacrifices by being granted a greater degree of self-government. 'White' colonies like Australia and Canada, for example, already enjoyed considerable freedom in their own internal affairs and Indians saw no reason why they should not be given a similar say.

The British, however, gave no sign of wanting to satisfy any of these expectations and they firmly dashed all hopes of political change. Heightened by the economic slump which followed the end of the war, there was mounting discontent all over India. The British reaction was to clamp down severely on any sign of political activity or dissent.

AMRITSAR MASSACRE

This policy of repression reached its climax in the Amritsar massacre of 1919. At Amritsar in the Punjab a British force opened fire on an unarmed crowd of Indians meeting in a walled area called Jallianwala Bagh. The enclosure allowed no room for escape and in the ensuing carnage 400 people were killed and more than 1,000 wounded. According to many accounts the firing only stopped when the British ran out of ammunition.

The massacre at Jallianwala Bagh was greeted with horror and outrage all over India. These feelings were intensified when the British, instead of punishing General Dyer, the officer in command, hailed him as a national hero. Prominent Indians, even those who had previously not been political, were appalled by such cruelty and callousness; for many of them, it shook their faith in the nature of British rule. One of these was modern India's most famous man of letters, Sir Rabindranath

Tagore (1861–1941), whose poetry had won him the Nobel Prize for Literature in 1913.

> The enormity of the measures taken up by the Government of the Punjab for quelling some local disturbances had, with a rude shock, revealed to our minds the helplessness of our position as British subjects in India.
>
> (30 May 1919).

In protest against such humiliation and degradation, Tagore and many others like him renounced the British titles and honours which had been bestowed on them. Following their example, millions of ordinary Indians abandoned their loyal support for the British Raj and began to turn towards nationalism. Their feelings were echoed in a speech made by a prominent Congress leader, Motilal Nehru (1861–1931), father of India's first prime minister and grandfather of her third. Nehru, a wealthy and successful lawyer, had previously been a very establishment figure. However the Amritsar massacre completely destroyed his confidence in the British establishment and all its promises. Speaking to the Congress Assembly of 1919, he declared that if this was how the British were capable of behaving, how could any Indian hope to trust them in future: 'then all talk of reform is a mockery'.

Gandhi and Civil Disobedience

The massacre at Jallianwala Bagh also had a profound effect on an even more influential political figure, Mohindas Karamchand Gandhi (1869–1948). Known to millions as the Mahatma, meaning simply 'Great Soul', Gandhi was the father-figure of Indian nationalism. Born into a well-to-do merchant (Bania) family, he had trained as a lawyer in London, after which he had practised in South Africa. On returning to India in 1915 Gandhi took up the cause of the Indian masses, whose poverty and suffering moved him deeply. To identify with their plight he abandoned his dapper European clothes and adopted the dress and life-style of the poorest peasant, always travelling third class wherever he went. Unlike many other such images, it is one which is largely founded on fact. Gandhi's teachings were based on a deep religious conviction: he preached self-control and a simple life-style as part of the need to develop an inner soul force which he called 'satyagraha'. At the heart of these ideas lay the Jain doctrine of Ahimsa or non-violence. According to Gandhi's creed, violence was the embodiment of hate and irrationality which must not be resorted to under any circumstances. An enemy or opponent must be met by reason and entreaty, if he became violent, this too had to be endured in good spirit. In order to achieve this strength of mind Gandhi preached and practised severe self-discipline; he took a vow of celibacy, lived frugally, and subjected himself to frequent fasting. From this core of beliefs he developed the idea of non-violence as a political weapon.

> I have simply tried in my own way to apply the eternal truths to our daily life and problems . . . I have nothing new to teach the world . . . All I have done is to try experiments in truth and non-violence on as vast a scale as I could.   (M.K. Gandhi, 1936)

Gandhi reasoned that the most effective expression of non-violence was mass civil disobedience. In this cause he perfected various tactics – the boycott, the hartal or suspension of business, and acts of non-co-operation. Non-co-operation had several different aspects: it could involve anything from hunger strikes and passive resistance to peaceful violation of the law or refusal to pay taxes. Gandhi's teachings, combined with the uniquely religious nature of his appeal, had a huge impact on the ordinary Indian population. Inspired by his example, huge numbers of ordinary people – peasants, factory workers, estate labourers – joined the Congress movement. No longer just an élite group, Congress changed utterly from what it had been before the First World War. Under Gandhi's leadership it became a mass national movement supported by men and women from all religions, all cultures and social backgrounds. It became capable of mobilizing millions in support of its policies, which were now carried forward by the strikes of factory workers, the walk-outs of tea pluckers and the tax boycotts of peasants. This massive support gave the nationalist movement a much greater potency than it had ever enjoyed before. To use Gandhi's words: 'Mass civil disobedience is like an earthquake. Where the reign of mass civil disobedience begins, there the subsisting government ceases to function.'

Gandhi's tactics bewildered the British and completely undermined the moral supremacy on which the Raj had been built. In response to British claims that they were maintaining the rule of law and order, millions of viewers across the world now saw newsreels showing the British clubbing hunger-strikers and trampling non-violent protesters underneath their horses' hooves.

When Gandhi had first begun his campaign the British had regarded him with amusement and derision. 'Dear me,' remarked the then Viceroy, Lord Chelmsford, in 1919, 'what a damned nuisance these saintly fanatics are.' By the late 1930s their perceptions had changed quite sharply. In the opinion of Lord Wavell, a much later Viceroy (1943–7), Gandhi was 'fifteen per cent charlatan, fifteen per cent saint and seventy per cent extremely astute politician'. Gandhi himself encouraged this sort of mixed reaction for he frequently seemed to operate on two very different levels: at times he was a religious figure, insisting on absolute purity and perfection; at other times, however, he was the consummate politician, careful, crafty and very practical.

In the period between the end of the First and Second World Wars, Gandhi launched three great campaigns of civil disobedience – in 1920, 1930 and 1942. The most spectacular of these was the campaign of 1930, which began with the famous salt march. With seventy-eight chosen followers Gandhi began a march to the sea, proclaiming his intention to break the British laws against the production of salt. On reaching the coast he proceeded to make salt from sea-water, defying the Salt Law. Through this dramatic action he demonstrated that British power hurt the interests of even the poorest people. In a country so well endowed with salt by nature, it seemed utterly immoral that any government should want to make money from the poor by monopolizing the manufacture of salt. His action caught the imagination of the common man and sparked off a nationwide wave of demonstrations, strikes and boycotts. The human cost of these agitations was huge: in 1930 alone 103 people were killed, 420 injured and 60,000 imprisoned. In 1942 another 60,000 Congress activists were imprisoned, many of them for the duration of the war. Despite this, each of these campaigns had their effect for they were all followed by substantial British concessions. Most of all, however, they forced the British to recognize that they could not continue to hold India in the face of such mass opposition.

Watershed

By 1935 British power was in retreat. In the Government of India Act (1935) a new constitution made the most sweeping concessions yet. Although the British still kept control at the centre, the government of the eleven provinces of British India was now handed over to elected Indian representatives. In the provincial elections, held in 1937 (when the Act came into force), the Congress enjoyed such huge support that it swept to power in seven of the states. Indians were also pressing forward in other areas – in the administration, the police and in the army, where they were gradually taking over the posts previously held by their masters and reserved exclusively for them. In 1932, after a long and bitter struggle, the army finally began recruiting Indian officers. The proportion of Indians in the higher ranks of the civil service also increased steadily; by the end of the war barely 500 of all senior civil servants and only 200 senior policemen were still British.

SPORT, SCIENCE AND LITERATURE

Indians were also beginning to make their mark on the world stage in sport, science and literature. In cricket the abilities of players like Prince Ranjitsinhji (1872–1933), his nephew Duleepsinhji and the Nawab of Pataudi seemed to suggest that Indians were already on a par with their British rulers. As one noted cricket commentator observed of Ranjitsinhji, 'Here was a black man playing cricket not as a white man but as an artist of another and superior strain.' At the 1932 Olympic Games the performance of India's gold medal-winning hockey team was so outstanding that it was voted the finest exhibition of skill in the whole contest. They were unbeaten in the Olympics from 1928 to 1960, winning six gold medals. In science there were spectacular Indian successes in physics, biochemistry and mathematics. In Calcutta Sir Chandrasekhara Raman's (1888–1970) experiments led to new advances in the theory of the diffusion of light (now called the Raman effect, after him) and won him the Nobel Prize for Physics in 1930.

Another south Indian S. Ramanujan (1887–1920), a self-taught mathematical prodigy, made a sensational impact in the world of mathematics before his premature death at the age of thirty-three. In biochemistry the work of J.C. Bose (1858–1937) brought him international renown, as did the achievements of astrophysicist M.N. Saha (1893–1956), who founded India's first Institute of Nuclear Physics.

The best-known contributors to India's international reputation came from the world of literature. In philosophy there was the remarkable philosopher-statesman S.V. Radhakrishnan (1888–1975), whose insight and vast erudition established him as a thinker of world class. Great strides were also made in history thanks to the scholarship of Sir Jagdunath Sarkar (1870–1958). Acclaimed for his work on the Mughal empire, the 18-volume *History of the Reign of Aurangzeb*, Sarkar's efforts led the way for many Indian scholars and today he is regarded as one of the father-figures of modern Indian history. The greatest inspiration of all, however, was undoubtedly Rabindranath Tagore (1861–1941). A great champion of the nationalist struggle along with Gandhi, Tagore is one of the towering Indian personalities of the early twentieth century. Almost single-handedly he pulled his native language, Bengali, on to the international stage. By making the speech of the common people the medium for his vast outpouring of poetry, prose, drama and song, he revolutionized and revitalized Bengali literature; today it is probably India's most vibrant literary tradition. His best-known work is probably *Gitanjali* ('Song Offerings', 1912), a collection of poems written after the death of his wife and three of his five children, for which he was awarded the 1913 Nobel Prize (the first Asian to be so honoured).

> Where the mind is without fear
> and the head is held high;
> Where knowledge is free,
> Where the world has not been broken up into fragments
>   by narrow domestic walls;
> Where words come from the depth of truth
> Where tireless striving stretches its arms towards perfection,
> Into the heaven of freedom, my Father,
> Let my country awake.
>
> (*Gitanjali*)

Jawaharal Nehru

As with Gandhi, Tagore was deeply influenced by the fusion of East and West, which he drew on to weave a mixture of tolerance, rationalism and universalism. To give expression to his ideals Tagore founded a university at Santiniketan in Bengal dedicated to the creative and performing arts of India. Here amidst the most idyllic surroundings Tagore's legacy still lives on. Santiniketan may be rather neglected and dilapidated now but it still possesses that air of gentle calm which pervades so much of Tagore's work.

NEHRU AND JINNAH

In 1929 Gandhi nominated Jawaharlal Nehru (1889–1964) to succeed him as the leader of the Congress movement. The son of Motilal Nehru, Jawaharlal was one of two radical younger leaders who was immensely popular in Congress and with the masses. The other was Subhas Chandra Bose (1895–1945), a Bengali who had given up the prospect of a brilliant career in the ICS to join the nationalist struggle. Although

Mohammed Ali Jinnah

both men were inspired by radical Marxist ideas, Bose advocated an even more militant policy which Gandhi feared might lead Congress down the road to violence. Nehru, moreover, was always much closer to Gandhi, unlike Bose who frequently disagreed openly and quite sharply over matters of policy. Another contender was Vallabhai Patel (1875–1950), a Gujarati farmer who was an organizer of great ability and was seen as the 'strong man' of the Congress party; he was also more powerfully supported in the provinces than either Nehru or Bose. Nevertheless Gandhi threw all his weight behind Nehru, and at the age of forty, Jawaharlal Nehru became the youngest-ever president of the Congress party.

Like his mentor, Nehru was a very dynamic figure of great personal charisma. The nature of his appeal, however, was very different. The aristocratic product of an élite western education, he combined brilliance, charm and good looks with a passionate concern for the welfare of India's masses. An author as well as a politician, Nehru produced two classic works, an *Autobiography* (1936) and *The Discovery of India* (1946), a literary history combined with personal philosophy and observation. In these works Nehru recounts how deeply moved he was by his first experience of the poverty and hardship of rural India. As he himself recognized, this encounter completely changed his whole outlook and its memory remained with him for the rest of his life.

By the 1930s the Congress party's only serious rival was the Muslim League. Led by Muhammed Ali Jinnah, a gifted Muslim lawyer who had formerly been prominent in Congress, the League had begun to develop itself into a genuine popular movement. The Muslim fear of being dominated by a Hindu majority had only been heightened by the huge success of Congress. More and more ordinary Muslims now began to join the League, which increasingly claimed the right to speak for all India's Muslims. This claim was deeply resented by Congress which saw itself as a nationwide party representing all religions and castes. The most important factor in this turn of events was Jinnah himself. An impeccable figure in his tailored Savile Row suits, he was a politician of great skill and razor-sharp intellect.

Unlike many others, however, Jinnah was not prepared to accept a minority position within India: what he wanted was a separate homeland for Muslims. The founder of Pakistan, today Jinnah is regarded as one of the father-figures of Muslim nationalism. He himself, however, always spoke in English for he never learnt to speak Urdu, the language of the Muslim masses. After Congress had swept the board in the 1935 elections, Jinnah offered to form a coalition with the new Congress ministries but Congress could not accept Jinnah's claims to speak for all Muslims. Confident of its new-found power it rejected any idea of a partnership out of hand. It was to prove a fatal mistake. From this point Jinnah devoted himself to building up Muslim fears and anxieties, emphasizing that Congress rule would mean Hindu rule.

The End of Empire: Partition and Independence

The Second World War was the final, deciding event in the story of Indian independence. At the outbreak of the war all the Congress ministers in the provinces resigned on the grounds that the Viceroy had declared war on behalf of India without consulting its political leaders. Then in 1942 Congress launched its third major campaign calling on the British to 'Quit India'. The immediate consequence was the imprisonment of the entire Congress leadership and 60,000 of its activists, many of them for the duration of the war. By these actions Congress denied itself power for that period, leaving the field clear for the Muslim League. The British, who had previously ignored Jinnah, now invited him into the government as an equal ally, and he used the opportunity to consolidate the power of the Muslim League and build it into as effective an organization as Congress. Within seven months of the declaration of war, the League had laid down its own terms for independence. These demanded the creation of a separate state – Pakistan – based on the provinces where the Muslims were in a majority.

During the war the growing estrangement between Congress and the Muslim League became complete. By 1945 a great gulf of distrust and isolation had opened up. The British, who had agreed to hand over power at the end of the war, had hoped to hand over to a single successor state. They made various attempts to break the deadlock between Congress and the League in 1945 and in 1946, but these were defeated. The breakdown of talks led Jinnah to call on his fellow Muslims for a 'Day of Direct Action' on 16 August 1946. These are his words: 'This day we say goodbye to constitutional methods. Today we have also forged a pistol and we are in a position to use it.'

August 16 led to murderous rioting between Hindus and Muslims. Calcutta became the scene of the most brutal violence; in what became known as the 'Great Calcutta Killing' 5,000 people lost their lives. The riots dealt a death-blow to Hindu–Muslim harmony and with it the idea of a united India. As Jinnah remarked, 'If not a divided India, then a destroyed India.' More violence followed as the rioting spread to the rural areas, to the Punjab and the Ganges Valley.

Faced with the prospect of anarchy the Congress leaders – Nehru and Vallabhai Patel – became convinced that some form of Pakistan was the only solution. The British too had come to the same conclusion. The new Labour government reasoned that the only way to force the two sides to come to an agreement was to set a firm date for British withdrawal. To effect this, Prime Minister Clement Attlee sent out a new Viceroy, Lord Louis Mountbatten (r. 1946–7), who was given full powers to negotiate any agreement he could to help him achieve his objective.

Mountbatten saw that the only way for the British to withdraw would be to transfer power to two governments, not one. With this in mind he pressured and finally persuaded a reluctant Congress to accept the idea of a divided India. His plan was to create two separate wings in the areas where the Muslims were the most numerous, in north-west India and eastern Bengal which together would form Jinnah's Pakistan. This meant that both Bengal and the Punjab would be divided between India and Pakistan. As for the princely states, they were to be released from their allegiance to the British Crown and urged to join one state or another. The settlement was ratified on 14 August 1947, and both India and Pakistan became independent nations within the Commonwealth. Mountbatten was asked to be the first governor-general of independent India, and in Karachi Jinnah became the first governor-general of Pakistan. In a speech to the nation on the night of 14 August Nehru, the first prime minister of independent India, ushered in the new era:

> A moment comes, which comes but rarely in history, when we step from the old to the new, when an age ends and when the soul of a nation, long suppressed finds utterance.

In Delhi huge scenes of popular rejoicing overwhelmed the formal proceedings. Here in the magnificent new capital which the British had built to be the centre of their Indian empire, the last rites of the Raj were performed. In one of the most memorable moments the Viceroy's procession of carriages was mobbed by huge happy crowds who swarmed on to the stately Kings Way, scene of so many imperial triumphs.

These happy moments were soon clouded by a bloodbath of horrifying proportions. Both Bengal and the Punjab had huge mixed populations. In Bengal there were large numbers of Hindus and Muslims living side by side, while the population of Punjab consisted of equally large numbers of Punjabi Hindus, Muslims and Sikhs. The partition of both these provinces had massive social consequences. In the Punjab there was a huge migration of peoples as Hindus and Sikhs moved eastward out of Pakistan and Muslims fled westward from India. It is estimated that at least five million refugees moved each way across the border between West Pakistan and India. In Bengal half a million Hindus migrated from their homes, matched by an equal number of Muslims. In the Punjab the migrations were accompanied by massacres of horrifying savagery as whole villages were annihilated and entire trainloads butchered. Atrocities were committed on both sides and the administration watched helplessly as Sikhs and Hindus attacked Muslims in eastern Punjab, while Muslims fell on the Sikhs and Hindus of western Punjab. The exact number of casualties remains unknown, but at least half a million people are thought to have lost their lives.

The only calming voice was Gandhi's:

> Death for me would be a glorious deliverance rather than I should be a helpless witness to the destruction of India, Hinduism, Sikhism and Islam.

His soothing influence was a vital factor in ensuring that the partition of Bengal was carried out relatively peacefully, without the bloodshed which had been seen in the Punjab. As the refugees began to pour into Delhi, feelings against the city's Muslims began to rise and it seemed that the capital too would be overwhelmed by violence. Thousands of terrified Muslims herded together into two of the most splendid monuments of the Muslim past. Here, amidst the grounds of Humayun's Tomb and the Purana Quila, 150–200,000 people lived in squalid refugee camps, waiting to be transported to Pakistan.

ASSASSINATION OF GANDHI

In response to Hindu threats of revenge, Gandhi took up residence in the Muslim quarter, in Shah Jehan's Old Delhi, and began a fast to the death. He announced that he would not give up until all violence between Hindus and Muslims in the city had ceased. Whereas the security forces had been quite unable to control the rioting, Gandhi's threat had a spectacular impact on the situation. Within a week the violence had begun to die down. Many Hindus, however, remained deeply embittered and they blamed Gandhi for siding with the Muslims. On 30 January 1948 Gandhi himself was gunned down by a Hindu extremist, enraged by his support for the Muslims. His death was a tremendous shock for the whole country. In his speech to the nation a distraught Nehru told his countrymen: 'The light has gone out of our lives and there is darkness everywhere.'

The site of Gandhi's cremation is now a national memorial. It is marked by a flower-strewn slab of black marble; on it are engraved Gandhi's last words, 'Ram, Ram', invoking Lord Rama.

CHAPTER ELEVEN

'Midnight's Children': Nehru and the New India, 1947–64

On 14 August 1947 Jawaharlal Nehru made the now famous speech which ushered in Indian independence. 'At the stroke of midnight,' he declared, 'when the world sleeps, India will awake to life and freedom.' To him and millions of his fellow countrymen, India was a nation awaking from a long sleep. As Salman Rushdie, the subcontinent's most famous novelist, writes, modern India was a nation born again at midnight. The product of the midnight hour, Rushdie christened this new generation of India 'midnight's children', the title of his first major novel.

The leader of this new generation was Nehru himself, who had emerged as the dominant political figure of his day. Although he had not been officially chosen by either the Congress movement itself or by the Congress party in Parliament, there never seems to have been any doubt that he would become India's first prime minister. In the eyes of nearly all his contemporaries Nehru simply seemed the most natural choice. Not only was he Gandhi's favoured disciple and chosen successor, he was also the son of Motilal Nehru, one of the father-figures of the Congress movement. In addition to the magic of his name, there was the tremendous charisma of his own personality. A brilliant intellectual and a gifted speaker, Nehru was the darling of the middle classes. His autobiography, which appeared in 1930, had a tremendous impact on most educated Indians who saw him as the spokesman for the new modern India. He also enjoyed huge popularity with the masses, whose affection and loyalty he continued to command for the rest of his political career.

From a very early stage Nehru had identified himself with the needs

Anand Bhavan, Allahbad. The childhood home of Nehru and Indira Gandhi

and aspirations of India's poor. His most cherished ambition was to raise their living standards and do away with the crippling poverty in which so many Indians lived. Renowned for his burning patriotism and his remarkable integrity, Nehru's ceaseless travels across the length and breadth of the country made him a familiar face in the remotest village and the smallest hamlet. After Gandhi, he was probably the best-known figure in the whole Congress movement. When he died in 1964, millions of mourners lined the roads of New Delhi on what was one of the hottest days of the year. In their eyes, as well as that of many outside observers, it was the end of an era.

The assassination of Gandhi in 1948, followed in 1950 by the death of his greatest rival Vallabhai Patel, left Nehru unchallenged at the helm of affairs. He became the father-figure of the nation, known to millions by the Brahmin title of Panditji, 'teacher', a symbol of affection and respect. His immense prestige and popularity combined with his dynamic personality made a huge impact on Indian politics. The three general elections which he fought, in 1952, 1957 and 1962, resulted in huge endorsements for both Nehru and the Congress party. Politically, socially and economically it gave him a much freer hand in moulding India's development than any British viceroy before him. Together with his many-sided interests and the tremendous energy with which he pursued them, this enabled him to influence almost every walk of Indian life.

Teen Murti House in New Delhi, today the Nehru Memorial Museum, was the prime minister's home during his years of office. A vast mansion, set in large rambling grounds, it was originally built for the British army commander-in-chief. After Independence it was occupied by Nehru who lived there for more or less the rest of his life. Although it is a museum today, Teen Murti House retains some of the atmosphere of the former occupant. Wandering through its large, comfortable rooms it is still possible to get a sense of this brilliant, mercurial personality and the way in which he lived. The study and the bedroom have been left as they were during his lifetime, his wrist-watch and a book on the bedside table. In a long corridor on the upper floor there are rows and rows of shelves stacked with his favourite books. The photos he kept of his friends are still on the topmost shelf. The gardens too have been kept more or less as they were in Nehru's day, with many rose bushes, his favourite flower, bordering the well-trimmed lawns.

Nehru's Policies

Nehru's policies were the product of his own complex personality and attitudes. A Westerner by education and extremely westernized in his outlook and in his tastes, he was inspired by India's culture and heritage. Although by birth a high-caste Brahmin, he did not regard himself as a Hindu and was deeply critical of many of the rituals and practices of Hinduism. He was especially suspicious of the stifling influence of the priests and Brahmins, which he felt was one of the principal reasons for India's decline. Unlike many Congress politicians who inclined towards Hindu orthodoxy, he was a great believer in social change and justice.

Deeply opposed to the concept of caste, he was determined to level out the inequalities in Hindu society, and to create a secular society which would not be based on religion, but where there would be equal rights for men and women of all backgrounds and religions. Hand in hand with this went Nehru's great desire to raise India's living standards and so bring her to the same material level as the West. A long-standing socialist, Nehru believed that the only way this could be done was by introducing modern technology and mechanized machinery. Capital had to be controlled in the national interest so that economic development could proceed in a planned and systematic manner. However, despite his great admiration for the Soviet Union, Nehru remained a convinced supporter of the democratic process. He was determined to achieve the Soviet Union's 'economic miracle' by democratic means, through persuasion and consent rather than by force and compulsion. Notwithstanding the huge economic and social problems facing it, Nehru's influence cemented the foundation of Indian democracy. Although the pace of its social and economic progress lagged far behind that of neighbouring giants like China or the Soviet Union, his convictions ensured that it was pursued without any of the coercion or loss of personal freedom which had characterized both other countries.

For the first two and a half years of his premiership, Nehru's ascendancy was challenged by his powerful home minister, Vallabhai Patel, who controlled the Congress party organization and next to Nehru himself was the most powerful man in the Cabinet. A very conservative figure, strongly committed to orthodox Hindu interests, Patel was deeply opposed to many of Nehru's policies. The numerous disagreements and differences between the two men rapidly increased and they were soon locked in a bitter power struggle for control of the party organization. This resulted in victory for Patel, and in 1950 his candidate, P.D. Tandon, was elected president of the Congress party. Following Patel's death soon afterwards, Nehru moved quickly to take over the party and re-establish his authority. Tandon was forced to resign and Nehru assumed the Congress presidency himself. His sweeping victory in the 1952 elections assured his position and he remained firmly in charge of both party and government until his death.

THE CONSTITUTION

On 26 January 1950 India declared itself a Republic. It adopted a new constitution based on the British parliamentary model. Under this the formal head of state was the president although the real leader of the Republic was the prime minister, who headed the majority party in the Indian parliament, the Lok Sabha (House of the People). The Lok Sabha contained 500 members elected once every five years at a general election. As in Britain, this lower house was balanced by an unelected upper house, the Rajya Sabha (Council of State). The structure of the Republic was a federal one; there were in effect two governments – a strong central government in New Delhi and a local government in each state. Every state had its own chief minister who led the largest local party and was responsible to his own state legislature. To enhance the power of the centre, New Delhi was given the authority to override the states in specific areas, and in certain cases the president was authorized to take over the state administration. As for the responsibilities of government, these were divided between the centre and the states. The central government handled defence, foreign affairs, the railways, communications and the currency. The states supervised the police, public health, education, agriculture, local government and the administration of justice.

Inspired by Nehru's ideals, the new Republic was declared a totally secular state. Although Hinduism was the religion of the vast majority, there was to be no official religion. In fact there was a complete separation between state and religion; all schools were run on secular principles and no taxes were levied to support any particular religion. Nehru and many others like him hoped that this new secular India would be able to accommodate the subcontinent's many different cultures and religious minorities.

THE PRINCELY STATES

The first problem which faced India after independence concerned the accession of the princely states. Under the agreement which Mountbatten had worked out, the 550-odd princely states were given the option of joining either India or Pakistan. Using a mixture of bribery, cajolery and the implied threat of force, Patel managed to convince nearly all these states to join India. The great state of Hyderabad, however, which had survived since Mughal times, refused to accede. The prospect of a semi-independent and potentially hostile state within the heart of India seemed quite unworkable, and on 13 September 1948 Patel sent in Indian troops to take over.

The mountainous state of Kashmir on the border between India and West Pakistan posed a more difficult problem. Although three-quarters of its population were Muslim, Kashmir was ruled over by a Hindu maharajah, Hari Singh. Faced with the choice of joining either India or Pakistan Hari Singh delayed, unable and unwilling to make up his mind. As he dithered, Pakistan launched an irregular force of Muslim tribesmen across the border. In October 1947 the tribesmen crossed into Kashmir and drove straight for Srinagar, the capital, in an attempt to seize the whole state. Rather than lose his whole kingdom, Hari Singh finally made up his mind to accede to India and appealed to New Delhi for help. Indian troops were airlifted to Srinagar, and after fierce fighting the tribal forces were driven back. Srinagar and the Vale of Kashmir were saved for India while the western part of Kashmir remained in Pakistani hands.

As for the princes, they were gradually assimilated into the rest of Indian society. In return for giving up their kingdoms, the maharajahs were guaranteed certain privileges which were written into the constitution. They were allowed to keep their titles and their estates and were granted a yearly income for their own upkeep. Although they no longer held any official position, many of them remained amongst the richest men in India. Some entered politics or diplomacy, becoming politicians or ambassadors. Others turned to the hotel industry, converting their palaces into some of the finest hotels in India.

DEMOCRACY AT WORK

The General Elections of 1951–2 confirmed India's status as the world's largest democracy. In a huge exercise 173,213,635 Indians cast their votes for 17,000 candidates contesting nearly 4,000 seats in the National and Provincial Assemblies. It was an important test for Nehru's vision of India as a secular, non-religious state. The result was a gigantic vote of confidence for Nehru and for Congress, which won 364 of the 499 seats in the Lok Sabha, while in the provincial elections it obtained a majority in twenty-two out of the twenty-six states. This huge triumph further enhanced Nehru's standing and it meant that from then on he would increasingly get his own way. The only challenge came from the Communists, whose support was confined to only three states – Andhra Pradesh, West Bengal and Kerala. In the second general elections of 1957 Congress won an even larger share of the vote from an electorate which had now increased to 183 million. Of the 500 seats in the Lok Sabha, they won 365 and held every state but one. The exception was Kerala which fell to the Communists.

Apart from the Communists, the other opposition came from the right, from parties like the Bharatiya Jan Sangh (Indian Peoples party) and the Swatantra (Freedom) party. Both appealed to Hindu social and religious prejudices, advocating a sort of Hindu chauvinism which was directly opposed to Congress' secular policies. However, neither the Jan Sangh nor the Swatantra party achieved anywhere near the same degree of success as the Communists. This was due mainly to the efforts of Nehru who used his enormous prestige to smother the growth of purely Hindu politics. As a socialist he proved so effective a performer on the political stage that for a long time the opposition had no real issues on which it could rally mass support.

Language Politics

The question of regional identity was one issue which did command mass support and it proved to be one of the few matters in which Nehru did not get his own way. Always conscious of the difficulty of holding a multi-ethnic, multi-cultural society like India together, he was very concerned by the growth of linguistic agitation in the provinces. Between 1950 and 1956 increasingly passionate demands were made for the provincial map of India to be redrawn according to the languages spoken by its different communities. Marathi speakers, Punjabi speakers, Gujaratis, Tamils, Telugus all clamoured for their own states. In addition there was growing pressure from Hindi speakers to replace English with Hindi as the official language. Nehru, however, was convinced that such reorganization would undermine the unity of the country and he

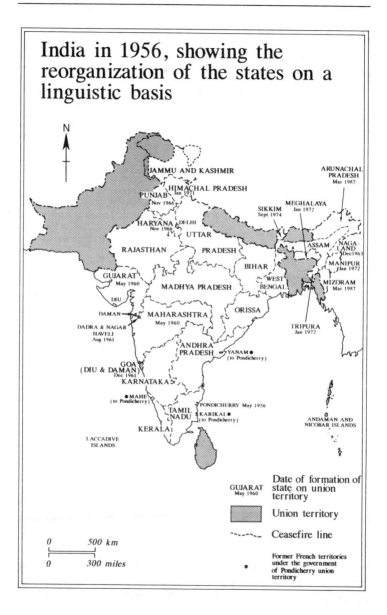

India in 1956, showing the reorganization of the states on a linguistic basis

N

JAMMU AND KASHMIR

HIMACHAL PRADESH
Jan 1971

PUNJAB
Nov 1966

HARYANA
Nov 1966

DELHI

RAJASTHAN

UTTAR
PRADESH

ARUNACHAL
PRADESH
Mar 1987

SIKKIM
Sept 1974

MEGHALAYA
Jan 1972

ASSAM

NAGA-
LAND
Dec 1963

BIHAR

MANIPUR
Jan 1972

GUJARAT
May 1960

MADHYA PRADESH

WEST
BENGAL

MIZORAM
Mar 1987

DIU

DAMAN

ORISSA

DADRA & NAGAR
HAVELI
Aug 1961

MAHARASHTRA
May 1960

TRIPURA
Jan 1972

ANDHRA
PRADESH

YANAM
(to Pondicherry)

GOA
(DIU & DAMAN)
Dec 1961

KARNATAKA

MAHE
(to Pondicherry)

TAMIL
NADU

PONDICHERRY May 1956

KARIKAL
(to Pondicherry)

ANDAMAN AND
NICOBAR ISLANDS

KERALA

LACCADIVE
ISLANDS

GUJARAT May 1960	Date of formation of state on union territory
	Union territory
- - - - -	Ceasefire line

0   500 km

0   300 miles

Former French territories
under the government
of Pondicherry union
territory

resisted for as long as he could. Although Hindi was widely spoken in northern India, English, like Sanskrit and Persian before it, remained the only lingua franca of the entire subcontinent; it was the only language in which a Tamil from South India could communicate with a Bengali from Calcutta or a Punjabi from Delhi. Nehru himself was a strong supporter of English, which he regarded as a modernizing influence as well as a crucial unifying force, and saw grave dangers in trying to impose a north Indian language like Hindi on the Dravidian cultures of the south. Finally he gave way and in 1952 he allowed the formation of the first linguistic state in India – the Telugu state of Andhra Pradesh. Although the government gradually reconciled itself to the view that the best way to keep India together was to allow its various parts a degree of cultural autonomy, Nehru continued to have reservations: 'You will observe that we have disturbed the hornets' nest and I believe most of us are likely to be badly stung.' Given the events of the recent past, it proved to be a prophetic observation.

Other changes soon followed. In 1956 the old Indian Union was radically reorganized and several new states were created on linguistic lines – Tamil Nadu for the Tamils, Kerala for the Malayalis and Karnataka for the Kannada speakers. In 1960 the Bombay presidency was divided up between Gujarati and Marathi speakers to form the states of Gujarat and Maharashtra. In 1966 the Punjab too was divided into two states – Haryana for the Hindi speakers and Punjab for the Punjabi speakers.

The Shape of Development

Nehru and Congress recognized that India's most urgent problem was poverty. They faced the enormous task of raising living standards and at the same time keeping pace with a rapidly increasing population. In 1941 India's population had numbered 389 million, by 1961 it had risen to 434 million. To combat these challenges Nehru evolved a policy of planned economic development, involving a partnership between private capital and a strong state sector. Despite its leanings towards socialism, Congress had always enjoyed the support of the great industrialists. Led by G. D. Birla and J. R. D. Tata, the giants of Indian industry had thrown all their weight behind the nationalist movement which they felt was in India's economic interests. However both Birla and Tata agreed with Nehru that, while co-ordinated economic planning was essential, the huge scale of investment needed to develop the country was beyond the capacity of the private sector. Everybody agreed that what was needed to put the Indian economy on its feet was a healthy dose of state capital. As a result the economic policy which India developed was a curious mixture of both capitalist and socialist practices. The economy was divided into public and private sectors. Established industries were left in private hands but great new public ventures, like irrigation schemes and power plants, were handled entirely by the state.

In line with Nehru's views that private industry should be controlled to work in the interests of the state, new laws were passed to regulate the activities of private companies. The most important of these were the Industries Act (1951) and the Companies Act (1956). The Industries Act gave the state considerable powers to regulate private industry; it required that anyone seeking to set up a new industry or trying to expand an old one had first to obtain a licence from the government. The Companies Act was specifically designed to curb monopolies. Well intended though they may have been, neither of these measures proved particularly effective, serving only to shackle the activities of the private sector and increase the influence of the civil servants who were now given powers of life and death over companies. Monopolies, for example, continued to grow: by 1961, 86 per cent of companies owned only 14.6 per cent of the total private capital, while a tiny minority of 1.6 per cent owned as much as 53 per cent of the capital. Something which could not be measured so easily was corruption, which reached astronomical levels as huge sums were traded to procure licences for even the smallest venture.

FIVE-YEAR PLANS

In 1950 Nehru set up a National Planning Commission to co-ordinate and plan India's economic development. It was decided that the key to improving living standards lay in the development of industry. India needed a strong self-reliant economy which could produce its own food, steel, power and other basic commodities. To put this into effect three successive Five-Year Plans were devised. The first, in 1951, placed special importance on agriculture. Targets were set for the improvement of agricultural yields and the development of irrigation. Although the British had launched the greatest irrigation projects ever seen in India, only a fraction of India's irrigation potential had yet been harnessed. The Nehru government aimed to make maximum use of the country's great rivers and it set in motion a number of huge irrigation projects, bringing an additional seven million acres under cultivation. One of the most spectacular of these was the huge Tunghabadra Dam in Andhra Pradesh and Mysore which irrigated some 1.03 million acres. Like the Tunghabadra Dam, many of these works were also designed to provide hydro-electric power and they added considerably to India's power-generating capacity. All things considered, the first plan was a great success. Food production increased by almost 25 per cent and the substantial advance in the national income was calculated at 18 per cent.

The second Five-Year Plan (1956–61) concentrated almost entirely on the development of industry. Far more ambitious in its scope, it aimed to increase the national income by a full 25 per cent. It was also bitterly controversial, spending almost three times as much as the last plan although its success was nowhere near as great as had been expected. Despite this, there were important gains on a number of fronts: food production increased once more and there were significant advances in India's industrial capacity. The generation of power, for example, almost doubled while the production of coal and iron grew by huge amounts. The Third Five-Year Plan (1961–5), which outlived Nehru, was the most ambitious of all. Involving an outlay of £8 billion, it propelled India into the ranks of the world's ten most industrialized nations.

The New India

Taken as a whole these statistics make impressive reading. Nehru's Five-Year Plans gave India the framework of a modern industrialized nation and left her nearly self-sufficient in foodstuffs. Although they did not achieve the high targets which had been projected, between 1951 and 1961 his policies succeeded in raising India's national income by as much as 42 per cent. They also had a considerable impact on the death rate, which fell by almost half during Nehru's premiership. All told, they were significant achievements for any newly-independent country.

All these advances, however, were offset by the staggering growth of India's population, which was expanding at the rate of five to six million every year. Although Nehru was well aware of the gravity of the problem, it was an issue which he completely failed to deal with. It was not until 1959 that the Indian government decided to endorse family planning, and even then it was so half-hearted that no real inroads were made at all. This perhaps was the greatest failure of Nehru's premiership, for in the long run it undermined all his greatest efforts. Indeed, it is difficult to see the gain in improving food production when the only result was a doubling in the number of mouths one had to feed. The population issue was very closely linked to another problem – illiteracy. Despite the number of universities, institutes and colleges of higher education which sprang up all over India, the Nehru government failed to make any real impact on the prevailing level of illiteracy. In 1947, 86 per cent of the population were illiterate; more than 30 years later, in 1979, almost 70 per cent of all Indians still remained unable to read and write. Overpopulation and illiteracy are both huge, complex issues, ones which the Indian government is still wrestling with today, and it is perhaps unfair to lay all the blame at Nehru's door. None the less, it is clear that in their solution lies the key to many of India's most urgent problems. Given the level of popular support he enjoyed and the amount of power which he wielded for so long, one cannot help feeling that these were issues which Nehru could and should have confronted head on.

In other areas, however, Nehru was able to effect some very far-reaching social changes. In a direct attack on the existing social system, he passed several measures which completely changed the fabric of Hindu society. Much of the work had already been carried out by Gandhi, with his personal crusades against the injustices of the Hindu caste system; however, the fabric of Hindu law still remained deeply rooted in the ancient past and its religious taboos. Although untouchability had been officially abolished by the constitution, the vast majority of untouchables, who now numbered 60 million, still had no legal remedy they could turn to. To meet this need, in 1955 the 'Untouchability Act' was passed to provide specific penalties for discrimination against them. In addition, special quotas were set aside in the government services and universities to help them overcome the handicaps which they faced.

Nehru's efforts also led to the passage of the Hindu Code Bill, arguably the most important of all his reforms. The culmination of a bitter six-year-long struggle conducted against deep-seated Congress opposition, this amounted to nothing less than a legal revolution in the position of women in India. Under both Hinduism and Islam, women in India had occupied a traditionally subordinate role. All this, however, changed with Independence, which made women equal citizens alongside men, with equal voting rights. Legally, however, their status remained very much as before and they continued to be denied many of the rights enjoyed by men. In 1955 and 1956 Nehru finally succeeded in forcing through his most important measures. The Hindu Marriage Act (1955), which gave Hindu women the right of divorce, was a landmark in Indian history; hitherto the concept of divorce had been completely unknown in Indian society. It also raised the minimum age for marriage to eighteen for males and fifteen for females, thus making it more difficult for women to be married off before they had reached a responsible age. The Hindu Succession Act (1956) which followed proved even more significant. For the first time the property rights of female children were recognized and they were given equal rights of inheritance. Although they are still ignored or bypassed in many rural parts of India, thanks to Nehru's measures Indian women now enjoy complete equality before the law.

A Place on the World Stage

It was in the realm of foreign affairs that Nehru enjoyed the greatest freedom of action, and it was here that he really put his stamp on things. Indians were keen for their newly independent nation to play a full part in international affairs and they wanted to be treated with respect by the great powers. They were content to leave Nehru to set the agenda.

With his wide vision and cosmopolitan background, he seemed the man best qualified for the job. To a large extent their trust was justified; despite her poverty and backwardness, under Nehru's direction India was to play an important and influential role in international politics. The breakdown of the wartime alliance between the USA, the USSR and Great Britain had left the world sharply divided into two mutually hostile power blocs. To help diffuse the tension between the Western powers and the Communist world, Nehru propounded the now famous policy of 'Non-Alignment'. Appealing to the smaller nations, he urged them not to commit themselves to either the USSR or the USA. The more nations remained uncommitted he said, the more careful the great powers would be before going to war. Nehru's efforts introduced a new factor into international politics, the 'Non-Aligned' Movement. Composed of a variety of nations, the Non-Aligned Movement acted as a third force in world politics, independent of both the great powers. Amidst the fear and suspicion of the Cold War it existed as a calming influence soothing the dangerous tensions between East and West. As its architect Nehru was regarded with tremendous respect throughout the Third World and his reputation greatly enhanced India's profile, giving her a new standing in world politics. Largely as a result of his efforts and those of his daughter Indira Gandhi, today India enjoys a major say in international affairs one in keeping with her position as the world's largest democracy.

RELATIONS WITH CHINA AND PAKISTAN

One area where Nehru was conspicuously less successful was in his efforts to cultivate better relations with India's great neighbours, China and Pakistan. Following the 1948 conflict, relations with Pakistan remained tense. India's and Nehru's refusal to make the slightest concession over Kashmir prevented any real understanding between the two sides. It is an issue which still separates the two countries today and arouses strong emotions in both India and Pakistan.

Despite all Nehru's best efforts, India's attempts to establish friendly relations with China proved even less successful. In 1962 a series of border disputes on India's mountainous north-eastern frontier escalated into an all-out war with China. An ill-equipped, ill-prepared Indian army proved quite unequal to the task of fighting at heights which began at 15,000 feet. Within a few days the Indian positions had been completely overrun and large numbers of Indian soldiers were captured by the Chinese, who advanced over the border with great ease and in great numbers. For a time it seemed that the north-eastern state of Assam would fall to the Chinese and there was panic in the state capital. Fortunately for India, the Chinese called off their advance and unilaterally decided to withdraw. The whole episode was a humiliating blow for Indian prestige.

For Nehru, who had worked so hard to build up good relations with China, it was especially devastating. He had thought the Chinese were his allies and had built his foreign policy around them, only to be duped and humiliated. The defeat precipitated the biggest political crisis of his premiership. An anguished and bewildered Nehru explained to a stunned Lok Sabha: 'The fact remains that we have been found lacking and there is an impression that we have approached these things in a somewhat amateurish way.'

What is clear is that neither Nehru nor his defence secretary, Krishna Menon, had expected war, despite all the evidence to the contrary. Not wanting it and not expecting it, they had left India's army hopelessly unprepared to meet the Chinese threat when it came. Although there was no question of Nehru resigning, Krishna Menon (1896–1974), the most brilliant of his ministers and his closest and most trusted colleague in the government, was forced to do so. Along with Nehru, he had been the architect of India's foreign policy, and for Nehru Menon's loss was a bitter personal blow.

NEHRU'S DEATH

Nehru's death on 27 May 1964 marked the end of an era. For seventeen and a half years he had remained in charge of India's affairs, surviving three general elections – the largest exercises in free elections anywhere in the world. By the time of his death India was well on her way to becoming an industrial power, producing her own goods and becoming increasingly self-sufficient in foodstuffs. Under his inspired stewardship, India had also begun to emerge on the international stage, becoming increasingly confident of her place in the world. Despite these advances,

India's real problems of poverty, overpopulation and illiteracy remained much the same as before: the population, for example, continued to grow apace. Under Nehru India's new democracy may have failed to achieve as much as people would have liked, but it remained a democracy nevertheless. This is Nehru's most enduring achievement – the consolidation of the democratic tradition in India.

> The greatest irony of his role in world affairs is that so many of the Asian and African leaders who fawned on him seemed to miss the point of his life. The point, most simply, was that it was possible for a country economically degraded to raise itself up, give its people rice and a roof and a book, and still maintain political freedom at home.   (Abe Rosenthal, *Profiles of Nehru*)

CHAPTER TWELVE

The End of a Dynasty: Crisis and Change, 1964–90s

To many observers the politics of modern India often appear to be nothing less than the history of the Nehru family. Since Independence the Nehrus have emerged as India's greatest political dynasty, providing the country with three of its prime ministers. Following Jawaharlal Nehru's death in 1964, he was succeeded after a short interlude by his only child, his daughter Indira Gandhi, who became one of the world's first women prime ministers. As her father had done before her, Indira Gandhi dominated Indian politics, enjoying a record three terms as premier. Less popular perhaps, and certainly more authoritarian than her father, nevertheless she proved a shrewd and highly effective political campaigner. Her assassination in 1984 appeared to leave a great void in the political scene which was filled by her only surviving son, Rajiv Gandhi. Although a comparative novice to politics, Rajiv was swept into power by a massive tide of sympathy and he was voted India's fifth Prime Minister. His murder in 1991 appeared to signal an end to his family's extraordinary dominance of Indian political life.

The rise and fall of the Nehru–Gandhi dynasty is a saga which arouses conflicting emotions and opinions amongst many Indians. In the eyes of many observers it is a tale of economic and political stagnation, characterized by political crisis, secession and increasing violence.

It is a perception which has not changed a great deal in recent times. Western newspapers are still full of ominous headlines predicting the break up of the country and its slide into chaos and anarchy. Despite all the gloomy predictions and the dire warnings, India still remains a functioning democracy and a thriving cultural and social entity. It is also a little bit too early to write off the Nehru–Gandhi family. In a country

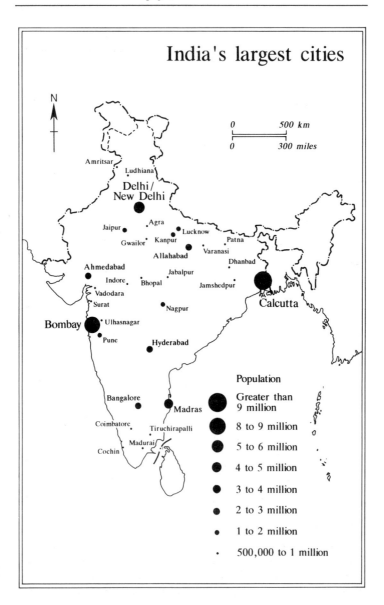

India's largest cities

where tradition still weighs so heavily, such is the charisma of the Nehru name that no one who knows anything about India can discount the possibility of another Nehru–Gandhi prime minister.

Consensus and Collective Leadership

Nehru's death cast a huge shadow across the political scene. Although he could have appointed any successor he liked, characteristically he had refused to name one. However there was no one of his stature who could aspire to fill his shoes and it was clear to everybody that the next prime minister would be a very different sort of man. The man chosen by Congress, Lal Bahadur Shastri, came from a very different background to the patrician Nehru. A lifelong Congress worker, Shastri had been a senior minister in the Nehru government and had a very different approach to politics. Quiet and unassuming, he cultivated a very low profile, far removed from the regal glamour of the Nehru era. A great believer in agreement and consensus, he placed special emphasis on collective responsibility and collective leadership as the basis of the new administration.

Although he lacked the Nehru charm, Shastri (1904–66), commanded great respect both within the Congress party and in Parliament as a whole. Yet to many others it seemed that he did not have the firmness and the direction needed to govern a country like India. These misgivings appeared to be confirmed in 1965 when Hindi was finally proclaimed as India's national language. Its imposition as the only national language was an event which Nehru had struggled to prevent, and with his tremendous authority he had managed to postpone it for the duration of his premiership. Shastri, however, was unable to resist the insistent pressure and was forced to give way. As many people had feared this measure was bitterly resented in the south where it caused widespread rioting.

In 1965 another crisis blew up over Kashmir. Ever since the 1948 war, Kashmir had remained a bone of contention between India and Pakistan. India refused to give up her position while Pakistan continued to press her claims to the whole state. In October Pakistani troops disguised as civilian volunteers infiltrated into Kashmir in another attempt to surprise India and capture the province. These incursions were followed up by Pakistani tanks and a full-scale war developed between the two countries. Contrary to all expectations, Shastri proved himself more than a match for the crisis. He quickly took control and the Pakistani forces were soon driven back. It was a complete contrast to the débâcle of 1962: this time it was the Indians who imposed their own ceasefire. Under the auspices of the Soviet Union, a peace conference was arranged at Tashkent in Central Asia; but there was no doubt about India's superiority. The whole affair erased the humiliating memory of the war with China and went a long way towards restoring national self-esteem.

Shastri's decisive handling of the crisis completely transformed his reputation. It made him a national hero almost overnight and he became hugely popular throughout the whole country. Everywhere he went enormous crowds turned up to see him. At one rally in Calcutta nearly two million people gathered just to hear him speak. This new-found popularity gave him the confidence he needed to exorcise Nehru's shadow, and all the signs suggested that he intended to put his own stamp on the government. In January 1966, however, after less than two years in office, Shastri died suddenly following a massive heart attack. Whereas Nehru's death had been expected, Shastri's came as a complete surprise, leaving the whole country in shock.

Next in line for the premiership was Morarji Desai (b. 1896), a senior Congress politician who had been minister of finance in the Nehru government. Desai had been Shastri's rival for the post of prime minister and he now seemed the most natural choice. However, he was regarded with suspicion by the rest of the Congress hierarchy. A tough, pugnacious politician, Desai was also a highly individual and rather eccentric figure who was renowned for his peculiar personal habits. Most peculiar of all was his custom of drinking a glass of his own urine every morning before breakfast. More to the point, perhaps, were his right-wing politics and his opposition to the huge state projects which had become a trademark of Congress policies.

Rather than choose Desai, the Congress leaders looked around for someone they thought would be easier to control. The person they decided on was Nehru's daughter, Indira Gandhi (1917–84). Although married to another Congress MP, Feroze Gandhi (no relation to Mahatma Gandhi), for many years Indira had lived with her father as his hostess and closest companion; in the public eye she was the person most closely associated with his legacy. Despite Nehru's disapproval Indira had progressed steadily through the Congress ranks and in 1959 had been elected president of the party. Nehru, however, had consistently refused to give her a position in the government. 'Not while I am prime minister' had always been his reply to such requests.

The Rise of Indira Gandhi

On her father's death, Indira Gandhi had been appointed minister of broadcasting in the Shastri government. By now well established within the party, after Shastri's death she was the only national figure known to the masses. A shy, self-effacing widow (her husband had died in 1960), she seemed the ideal candidate, a weak leader who could easily be moulded. It was hoped that she would be a temporary figurehead who would tide Congress through the elections of 1967. So on 19 January 1966 Indira Gandhi was chosen by the Congress party as India's first woman prime minister.

The fourth general election of 1967 saw a sharp decline in the popularity of the Congress party. Although Congress still remained the largest party in the Lok Sabha, its once commanding position shrank from 361 seats to only 283 out of 520. That year signalled the end of the massive majorities of the Nehru era; it was a clear sign that Congress was losing its hold over the Indian electorate. As if to underline this break with the past, the opposition parties, both to the left and the right, now began to do really well. The Communists made substantial gains, as did the parties of the extreme right which had been so marginalized during Nehru's day. Both the Jan Sangh and the Swatantra party more than doubled their number of seats, from 14 to 35 and 18 to 44 respectively. At the provincial level too there was widespread disillusionment with Congress rule and the government lost control of eight states.

Indira Gandhi did not prove the pliable figurehead whom the Congress party bosses had hoped for. The shy widow turned out to be

Indira Gandhi

a tough and determined politician. Within a short time she was locked
in a bitter struggle for control of the party with the very man who had
put her in power. After almost two years of infighting Mrs Gandhi
emerged as the most powerful and most popular figure in both the
government and the party. Her tactics forced a split in the party and in
1969 a large number of Congress MPs led by Morarji Desai left the
government – a defining event in Indian politics.

In 1970 Mrs Gandhi dissolved Parliament and declared elections a
year ahead of schedule. To cement her position she announced a series
of socialist policies which she knew would appeal to the masses. The
most important of these was the nationalization of India's major banks
and a concerted attack on the special status of maharajahs. Although
these privileges had been guaranteed by the constitution, Mrs Gandhi
was determined to abolish them and in 1972 she finally forced through
legislation which deprived the 500 or so former rulers of their titles,

pensions and other privileges. Despite claims that the maharajahs were an outdated feudal relic who represented a drain on the economy, in actual fact their abolition brought very little in the way of financial relief. It was really little more than a public relations exercise designed to win support for the government; its only real result was to do away with a valuable part of India's heritage. It signalled the decline and decay of hundreds of palaces, forts and stately homes all over India, not to mention the many priceless objects contained in them, for their owners could no longer afford to pay for their upkeep. What it means today is that the Maharajah of Baroda, although he may still be that to many of his former subjects, is now officially plain Mr Baroda, an ordinary citizen like every other Indian. At least this is the theory.

The 1971 elections resulted in a massive endorsement for Mrs Gandhi and her party. Under her direction, a reformed and revitalized Congress launched a vigorous campaign against poverty. Immediate action was promised to provide India's millions with the food, shelter and jobs they so desperately needed. These tactics proved a great success and the electorate moved sharply to the left. All the right-wing parties were resoundingly defeated and Congress obtained 352 seats out of 519.

1971 Indo–Pakistani War

The events of 1971 gave Mrs Gandhi her first opportunity to demonstrate her mettle on the larger stage. Ever since its inception Pakistan had been troubled by the increasing frictions between its two wings – the Punjabi-dominated West Pakistan and the overwhelmingly Bengali East Pakistan. East Pakistan felt that it was not receiving its fair share of the country's resources and for some time had been demanding a greater degree of autonomy. These demands were spearheaded by Sheikh Mujibur Rahman's Awami League. Matters came to head in the elections of 1970. The Awami League obtained an overall majority in the country but the result was rejected by West Pakistan which refused to accept a Bengali-run regime.

The Pakistani army poured troops into East Pakistan and the Awami League was brutally suppressed. The Punjabi troops of the Pakistan army set out to terrorize the local population and they launched themselves on a murderous spree of arson, rape and massacre. Within a short time there was virtual civil war in East Pakistan and a flood of desperate, terrified refugees began to stream into India. As they did so they brought with them reports of the atrocities committed by the Pakistani troops, which gradually filtered through to a horrified international community. By December 1971 9,774,140 refugees had crossed into India. The cost of providing food, shelter and medicine was a huge strain on Indian resources; there was a rising clamour for action and Mrs Gandhi soon found herself under tremendous pressure to intervene; nevertheless for the moment she held off. With great skill and foresight she first secured the support of the Soviet Union – in August 1971 India signed a 20-year Treaty of Peace, Friendship and Co-operation with the USSR. This ensured that India had the backing of a great power; in view of the United States' and China's support for Pakistan, it proved to be a wise decision. Having obtained the assurance of Soviet assistance should it be necessary, Mrs Gandhi waited for world opinion to turn decisively against Pakistan.

On 3 December 1971 the Pakistani Air Force provided India with the final excuse it needed by attacking eight Indian airfields. Mrs Gandhi was in Calcutta when the news reached her and she flew back to Delhi in an Indian air force plane, guarded all the way by squadrons of Indian fighters. War was declared immediately and Indian troops struck hard into Pakistan and Bengal. While the Indians held the Pakistani forces at bay in the west, in the east they drove the enemy back and advanced rapidly into East Pakistan. Faced with the humiliation of their ally, both the United States and China threatened to intervene. The American Secretary of State, Henry Kissinger, sent the US 7th Fleet into the Bay of Bengal as a warning to the Indians. It was here that Mrs Gandhi's strategy paid off; the threat of Russian intervention caused both the USA and China to change their minds. The Indian army closed round Dacca, the capital of East Pakistan, and on 15 December 1971 all the Pakistani forces in Bengal surrendered. On the western frontiers too, in Kashmir and Punjab, the tide of battle turned in favour of India. Enormous pressure was put on Mrs Gandhi to fight the war to its end and finish off Pakistan.

Showing great restraint and strength of character, Mrs Gandhi resisted all these pressures. She declared a unilateral ceasefire and called off the military. As she revealed afterwards:

> Naturally, as generals who had won a decisive battle, they wanted to finish the war in their way . . . They choked and spluttered, but I informed them that I was speaking with the authority of a unanimous Cabinet. Well, they saluted and said they would carry out our instructions. Now this could not have happened in many countries and I don't just mean the Third World.

Although it had overrun nearly the whole country, the Indian army was withdrawn from East Pakistan. The government was handed over to the Awami League and the new state of Bangladesh was constituted. The millions of refugees who had poured into India began to return, and by March 1972 nearly all 10 million of them had been repatriated. It was a huge triumph for India and for Mrs Gandhi. Her skill and strength of character had been a crucial factor throughout the whole crisis. Abroad it gained her and India widespread admiration and respect, whilst at home she was celebrated as the reincarnation of Durga, the Hindu goddess of war. In the eyes of many of her countrymen it was thanks to her that India had emerged as the strongest power in the region while Pakistan, her great rival, had been reduced to half its size.

'Indira Raj'

The tremendous authority which Mrs Gandhi had come to command led to the evolution of a highly personal and highly centralized style of government. She began to act in an increasingly authoritarian manner, asserting her own power over the institutions of government both at the centre and at state level. She devoted her best efforts to undermining any sign of opposition whether outside Congress or within its ranks. This was particularly apparent at state level where she set out to remove any chief minister with his own independent base and replace him with someone personally loyal to her. This autocratic style of functioning earned her government the nickname of 'Indira Raj', for it seemed that almost anything and everything had to stem from Mrs Gandhi herself. It also meant that all the attention was focused on the figure of the prime minister. This was fine so long as everything went well, for it ensured that she would obtain all the credit – as with the 1971 War. However, the moment things started to go wrong she began to be blamed for everything.

The government's pledge to eliminate poverty had created heightened expectations amongst the masses. To try and fulfil this promise Mrs Gandhi's administration launched another sweeping programme of nationalization. Many more industries were taken over (amongst them the coal mines), new land reforms were declared and harsh new taxes were levied.

The only effect of these reforms was to make the problem even worse. The land reforms were obstructed by powerful landed interests in the provinces and most of them were not implemented. The new taxes were scrupulously evaded and they served only to drive India's moneyed classes further underground. The growing dissatisfaction over the failure of the government's programme was fuelled by a spiralling rise in prices, which in India always hit the poor the hardest. The problem was intensified by an increase in the world price of oil and an enormous foreign debt (almost 2 billion dollars) which ate up almost a quarter of the country's total exports. As a result the government found itself having to restrict the import of raw materials like cooking oil, petrol, wood and even paper. By the end of 1974 the economy was in deep trouble. Industrial production had declined sharply; there were severe food shortages and galloping inflation of almost 30 per cent. All this under a regime committed to remove poverty.

The mounting discontent and dissatisfaction throughout the country was reflected in a wave of demonstrations, strikes and sit-ins. In Bombay, the industrial and financial capital of India, there were 12,089 strikes in one year alone. The most spectacular of all was the nationwide rail strike where more than one million railway workers went on strike. The government responded with very heavy-handed tactics, striking workers were threatened, beaten up and arrested; in the railway dispute alone some 60,000 railwaymen were arrested. By the end of 1974 Mrs Gandhi's government found itself deeply unpopular. In many parts of the country there were huge popular protests and violent disturbances against Congress rule. Bitter complaints were made about the corruption of the Congress regime and the authoritarian nature of Mrs Gandhi's rule. It now seemed very likely that Congress would be defeated in the next elections which were scheduled for 1976. Amidst the mounting tension the High Court declared Mrs Gandhi's election to Parliament invalid on the grounds of various electoral irregularities. It ordered her to stop voting and disqualified her from holding public office.

The offence itself was comparatively minor and at any other time it would have been dismissed as trivial. In the current atmosphere, however, its effect was explosive. There was widespread public rejoicing and many critics claimed that Mrs Gandhi had forfeited her right to govern. All the opposition parties joined forces to form a grand alliance against the government – The Janata Morcha (Peoples Front). Plans were made for a mass campaign to bring down the government and there were calls for policemen, bureaucrats and all members of the armed forces to stop taking orders from a disqualified prime minister.

The Emergency

Mrs Gandhi's response to the escalating crisis was swift and sudden. At her request the President of India declared a state of emergency on 26 June 1975. All civil rights were suspended and the whole country was placed under direct rule from Delhi. Parliament hurriedly passed new laws superseding the regulations which Mrs Gandhi had been guilty of infringing, and the forthcoming elections (March 1976) were postponed. All the opposition leaders were arrested and altogether nearly 10,000 people – students, lawyers, journalists – were jailed. Demonstrations and strikes were banned and a draconian wage freeze was imposed. To answer her critics Mrs Gandhi unveiled a 20-point programme of economic reforms, promising something to almost every major section of Indian society. At the forefront of her manifesto was a firm promise to bring down prices.

Whatever people may have thought, the emergency seemed to bring results: indeed in many quarters it was called the Silent Revolution. It eliminated strikes and as if by magic improved the performance of India's famously inefficient bureaucracy. In a sharp contrast to the past, government servants started arriving at their offices by nine in the morning and stayed for a full day's work. Industrial output grew dramatically, increasing by 6 per cent in 1975 and 10 per cent in the following year. Exports also increased sharply, so much so that by the end of 1976 India had accumulated the largest balance of payments surplus in her history.

Most important of all inflation, which had been rocketing out of control, was curbed. Within a month the price of essential foodstuffs like rice and barley had fallen by almost 5 per cent and kept on falling. Even Indian railways, one of the most notoriously eccentric and unreliable railway services anywhere in the world, appeared to be running on time. This, however, had to be seen to be believed. On every account the emergency seemed to have achieved a remarkable turnaround.

During this period the prime minister's younger son, Sanjay Gandhi (1946–80) emerged as a leading political figure. Although he did not hold an official position either in Congress or in the government, Sanjay exercised tremendous authority. This derived entirely from his close association with his mother. Lionized by the government-controlled media, who built up a personality cult around him, Sanjay was regularly seen on TV and heard even more frequently on radio. Under his direction the government launched two controversial programmes aimed at solving some of India's most chronic problems. The first was a birth-control campaign calling for the sterilization of any man with more than three children; strenuous efforts by successive administrations had failed to make any real impact on the population and it now seemed that a drastic solution was needed. The second was a slum-clearance programme aimed at the impromptu slums which seemed to spring up almost overnight in every big Indian city. Although well intended, both campaigns were prosecuted with such vigour and insensitivity that they soon became deeply unpopular amongst the masses. The birth-control project rapidly developed into one of forced sterilization, while slum dwellers were brutally uprooted from their homes. Although the emergency may have succeeded in many of its objectives, the effect of these campaigns completely destroyed any support it may have had amongst the majority of the population. In the eyes of many people in the countryside and in the poorer districts of the big cities, Mrs Gandhi's government was now regarded with fear and suspicion.

The Janata Interlude, 1977–80

In January 1977 Mrs Gandhi lifted the emergency, released all her
political opponents and announced a general election for March, barely
two months away. It was thought that the opposition would not be able
to mount an effective campaign in such a short time and Congress
expected a comfortable victory. The opposition, however, resurrected
their pre-emergency coalition and mounted a ferocious personal
campaign against Mrs Gandhi, her son Sanjay and their supporters. It
was widely felt that Mrs Gandhi had come very close to dictatorship
and the Janata leaders played on the deep unease which her policies had
fostered. They promised a return to normality and the full restoration
of all civil liberties; a vote for Janata, they said, was a vote for democracy
against dictatorship.

The result of the 1977 elections was a watershed in Indian politics.
Against all expectations the Janata party achieved a stunning victory. In
what turned out to be more or less a referendum on the emergency
itself, Indians voted heavily against Indira Gandhi and the Congress
party. Forty-three per cent of the population voted for the opposition,
giving Janata 270 out of the 493 seats contested and a substantial majority
in Parliament. After 30 years of power, Congress was displaced as India's
ruling party. In Uttar Pradesh, the largest state of all, Congress did not
win a single seat and of the 49 Congress ministers only 15 were returned
in their constituencies. Even Mrs Gandhi failed to win her own seat,
the only time in political history that a sitting prime minister had been
humiliated in such a fashion.

The new Janata government was headed by the 81-year-old Morarji
Desai. An uneasy alliance of many different interests, it consisted of a
variety of political groups which had united only to fight Mrs Gandhi.
The most powerful of these was the Hindu nationalist Jan Sangh
party, whose membership had increased tenfold since 1960. With its
slogan of 'One Country, One Nation, One Culture and the Rule of
Law', the Jan Sangh exercised a powerful appeal in both the towns and
the countryside. With a hard core of 90 MPs, it was the real winner in
these elections. Its success was a definite sign that from now on
Hindu nationalism would have an increasingly important role to play

in the Indian political scene.

However, once Mrs Gandhi had been defeated Janata's new-found unity began to evaporate. Within a short time the Janata alliance had given way to further coalitions and alignments, not to mention bitter faction fighting. Amidst a chain of scandals and continued squabbling public support gradually began to ebb away.

Although the Janata party kept its promise to restore democratic procedures, nothing was done to solve any of the electorate's other problems. The government's chronic instability led to a rapid deterioration in political and economic conditions. Prices of major foodstuffs began to rise once more and within a year inflation was climbing back to its previous levels.

In 1980 the Janata government finally collapsed under the weight of its own disunity and incompetence. In the absence of a viable alternative a disillusioned electorate turned once more to Mrs Gandhi and the Congress party. Congress seemed to offer the only chance of a stable, effective government. 'Elect a government which works', 'Government or No Government' declared the Congress posters. Although one of the calmest in recent history, the elections saw the lowest turn-out ever recorded for any Indian election. In a telling indication of just how disenchanted people had become, nearly half the electorate abstained from voting. The failure of the Janata experiment dashed the tremendous euphoria which had been built up following the end of the emergency. The optimism and expectation which had followed the defeat of Mrs Gandhi evaporated as the chance of any meaningful change in the political scene receded: Indian politics now seemed just as hopeless and cynical as ever.

Mrs Gandhi Again

Victory in the 1980 elections gave Mrs Gandhi her third term in office. The Congress party which in 1977 had seemed destined for political oblivion was returned to power with a substantial majority. A large number of the delegates were young men from the youth wing of Congress who were completely new to politics. They owed their position to Sanjay Gandhi, who had now established himself as the second most powerful figure in the government. In another striking indication of the electorate's changing mood, Sanjay, who had been so deeply unpopular during the emergency, was returned for the traditional Nehru seat of Amethi in Uttar Pradesh. In 1977 he had contested the same seat only to be heavily defeated. Although he still held no official position within the Cabinet, Sanjay had become his mother's closest adviser and confidant and he was commonly regarded as her heir-apparent. Following the uncertainty and turmoil of her election defeat in 1977, Mrs Gandhi had come to depend on him more and more; to many observers he now seemed to be the only person she really trusted.

The problems facing the new Congress administration were considerable. The economy was in decline and over the last few years there had been a steady decrease in India's GNP. In the countryside unemployment had risen rapidly while in the towns too there was a steady increase. Even more worrying was the growing unrest in the provinces, especially in the north-east border province of Assam and in India's richest and most prosperous state, Punjab. Congress too was widely discredited, no longer seen as the party of the poor and the underprivileged. It seemed no different from any other political party in its pursuit of power and office, only more effective and stable than the rest.

In June 1980 Sanjay Gandhi was killed in a plane crash. For Mrs Gandhi this was a devastating blow, depriving her of the pillar of support which she had come to rely on so much. In her desperation she turned for support to her only other child, her eldest son Rajiv, an airline pilot who had previously never had any interest in politics. Rajiv (1944–91), quietly spoken and rather self-effacing, was a well-liked character who had always steered clear of the Nehru legacy. On his flights for Indian Airways he would always introduce himself to his passengers simply as 'Captain Rajiv'. To all appearances he seemed content with his quiet family life, clear of the corruption, intrigue and self-seeking of Indian politics which he had always regarded with disdain. Finally, however, he succumbed to the pressure to follow in his brother's footsteps. In 1981 he contested Sanjay's seat at Amethi, to which he was elected in a landslide victory.

THE SIEGE OF THE GOLDEN TEMPLE

The most serious issue which confronted Indira Gandhi in her third term as prime minister was the rise of terrorist violence in the Punjab. One of the most fertile regions in the subcontinent, it enjoyed India's highest per capita income and its households earned twice as much as other peasant families in the rest of the country. A large part of the Punjab was dominated by the Sikhs who, although they numbered barely 2 per cent of India's total population, formed one of the subcontinent's most visible and most self-confident minorities. They were particularly well represented in the armed forces where they occupied nearly 10 per cent of all the higher posts in the Indian military. Many Sikhs had also risen to prominent positions in the government and in 1982 Giani Zail Singh, Indira Gandhi's home minister, was elected as India's first Sikh president.

Since Independence there had been an increasing growth in Sikh political consciousness, led by the main Sikh party, the Akali Dal. In response to growing pressure, in 1966 the Sikhs were given their own state of Punjab which was separated from the other non-Sikh regions. The Akali Dal went on to become the most important political party in the state and in 1976 ousted the Congress party in both the provincial and central elections. Mrs Gandhi, however, refused to tolerate an independent state regime and did her very best to topple the new government. To undermine the Akali Dal's popularity, Congress politicians sponsored their own Sikh fundamentalist movement led by a young militant, Jarnail Singh Bhindranwale (1947–84). Hoping completely to destabilise the Akali Dal, the government turned a blind eye as Bhindranwale attacked a number of its leaders and supporters. This strategy, however, backfired: by 1983 Bhindranwale had proved himself more extreme and more dangerous than any other Sikh leader. With a group of armed followers he established his headquarters at the Golden Temple in Amritsar.

Founded in the sixteenth century, the Golden Temple is the holiest shrine in the Sikh religion. It stands in the middle of a lake, surrounded by pavements of pure marble, and is connected with the land by a long marble causeway. The outside was covered with gold leaf, so giving the temple its name. From this peaceful, dignified setting Bhindranwale

The Golden Temple, Amritsar

launched a campaign of terror against the government. Going much further than the Akalis had ever dreamed of, he and his supporters called for an independent Sikh homeland – Khalistan. Anyone who opposed him was assassinated and by the end of 1984 he and his followers had murdered hundreds of moderate Sikhs and Hindus.

The government, which had remained curiously inactive for almost two years, was finally forced to act. In May 1984 the Indian army launched a massive operation to clear out the Golden Temple, which had been transformed into a fortress by the rebels. Nearly 70,000 troops were used to surround the area and the army was given strict instructions to use the minimum of force so as not to damage the temple too much. The initial assaults, however, failed completely; Bhindranwale's men had amassed a huge quantity of heavy weapons which they used to devastating effect. In the first attack alone, nearly 100 Indian soldiers were killed as they charged up the narrow causeway. Finally the army brought in tanks and artillery and battered down the defences. In the process one of India's most sacred shrines was reduced to a pile of rubble. Operation Blue Star, as it was called, had cost the lives of 200–300 Indian soldiers and almost 1,000 rebels.

The political consequences of the siege were even more devastating. It left the Sikhs of the Punjab in a deep state of shock; the sanctity of their shrine had been violated and they felt deeply humiliated by what they saw as an outrage to their religion. Many amongst them held Indira Gandhi herself personally responsible. This mounting sense of anger found its outlet a few months later when, on the morning of 31 October, as she walked to work Mrs Gandhi was assassinated by two of her most trusted bodyguards, both of them Sikhs.

Rajiv Gandhi: Next in Line

In the days following Mrs Gandhi's murder, New Delhi exploded into a frenzy of rioting. Law and order seemed to have completely evaporated as anti-Sikh mobs roamed the city seeking revenge. Sikh families were attacked and their homes and businesses burnt and looted. Mrs Gandhi's death left a gaping hole in the administration. She had centred power around herself to such an extent that no one seemed to have the will or the courage to take her place. The only candidate was the inexperienced figure of Rajiv Gandhi, who was hurriedly sworn in by panic-stricken Congress officials. At the age of 40, after a political career of scarcely four years, Rajiv Gandhi became India's youngest-ever prime minister. As the anti-Sikh fury gradually subsided the army was finally called out to restore order. In the intervening chaos, however, more than 1,000 Sikhs were murdered and more than 50,000 made homeless. It was hardly a promising start to a new era.

Rajiv's comparative youth and dignified demeanour combined with his mother's memory to win him tremendous sympathy throughout the whole country. This was the crucial factor in the elections of 1984. Rajiv and the Congress administration recorded an overwhelming victory at the polls. It was not for Congress that Indians really voted but for the youthful figure of Rajiv Gandhi. He seemed to personify a 'New Deal', a break with the corruption, the disappointments and the excesses of the past. At the same time he represented a continuing link with India's most public family and her greatest political dynasty. With India facing one of the worst crises in recent history this link seemed to offer the best chance of stability and security.

There was widespread agreement that the new prime minister would have to undertake major reforms if he was to get the economy moving again. In the last two years of Mrs Gandhi's administration the economic growth rate had fallen to barely 2.5 per cent. Despite plentiful agricultural harvests, productivity was sluggish and every initiative had become bogged down in a welter of red tape. With an overwhelming majority in Parliament and almost total authority over his party, Rajiv found himself in a unique position to restructure the economic and administrative system.

In accordance with his promise he began to dismantle some of the socialist controls which had been imposed by his mother and grandfather. He initiated a campaign of partial liberalization, sharply reducing the previously high levels of taxation and the strangling power of the bureaucracy. However the basic structure of official control over who could import, who could produce, what could be produced and where they could be produced remained more or less the same. Rajiv's political inexperience and inability to provide strong leadership meant that the majority of his reforms drowned in the usual sea of Indian red tape. But there were signs that things were beginning to change. There was a boom on the Bombay stock market and a flourishing computer industry grew up throughout the country.

Nevertheless Rajiv's perceived ineffectiveness brought back a familiar sense of disenchantment. The tremendous support which the new regime had enjoyed gradually began to decline and there were a number of defections from the government. Its position was further undermined by damaging accusations of corruption. The attempt to relax controls had been accompanied by a startling rise in the level of corruption; many people in the private sector and within the government scrambled to take advantage, including a number of Rajiv's close associates. The biggest scandal of all involved the secret and illegal payment of millions of dollars by Bofors, a Swedish arms manufacturer, to people allegedly close to the prime minister. The resulting scandal smeared even Rajiv himself and seriously discredited his government.

By 1989 Congress had lost so much support that it failed to muster enough seats in the general elections to form another government. It was succeeded by the Janata Dal coalition, led by Rajiv's former finance and defence minister V.P. Singh, heir to a small princely state in Uttar Pradesh. The new government was supported by the Bharatha Janata party (BJP). Formerly the Jan Sangh party, the BJP now enjoyed immense popular support although it still retained its militant Hindu outlook. Alongside the gradual decline of Congress, the rapid rise of the BJP represents one of the most significant changes in the Indian political landscape. Between 1984–1991 it has spectacularly increased its share of the national vote, climbing from 7 per cent in 1984 to 20 per cent in 1991. Today the BJP dominates the Hindi heartland of northern and central India, where its potent Hindu nationalism is seen as a powerful force for change and reform. Only time can tell whether its appeal will spread across the rest of the country.

The other great change in India's recent history stems from the assassination in 1991 of Rajiv Gandhi, and with it the removal of the Nehru–Gandhi dynasty from the political scene. For the Congress party which had for so long relied on the magic of the Nehru name to deliver victory it was the end of an era. It signalled a complete change of direction: if Congress was to survive it would have to refashion its organization, its policies and even its identity. Interestingly enough this is already beginning to happen. The new Congress administration which was returned to power in 1991 had to undertake several major social and economic reforms. Congress, previously the party of government control and regulation, now found itself committed to deregulation and decentralization.

India at Fifty

14 August 1997 marked the fiftieth anniversary of Indian Independence. The world's largest democracy and still one of the poorest countries in the world, India is now passing through a time of painful transition. The old certainties have gone, yet many of the old evils remain, bedevilled now by new, more urgent problems. Political corruption on an

unimaginable scale, increasingly criminal and violent politics, rising caste conflict, separatism and militant communalism – these are some of the spectres which India will have to face in the new century. What solutions there are seem far too drastic and far too painful, nor do they necessarily promise to cure the disease.

One thing however, is certain. For most of its fifty years India has been ruled by one party, Congress. This chapter has now come to an end and we are in a new chapter. The last three General Elections – 1989, 1991 and 1996 – show that Indian politics is now divided three ways, making a majority government almost impossible. Instead of the monolithic blocks of the past, we now have three groups, the Congress, the militant Hindu politics of the BJP and the United Front coalition, a loose collection of ideologically and politically very distinct elements, united only in their anti-BJP stand. The inability of any of these three groups to form a stable government suggests that this will be the shape of things to come. In future the real issue will not be who will form the next government, but who will form the single largest group within it.

In 1947 when India achieved independence Jawaharlal Nehru had spoken of India's 'tryst with destiny'. During the next fifty years he predicted India would make great strides towards redeeming this pledge and he foresaw a vastly improved standard of living for all her citizens. Nehru's dream has yet to be realized but significant progress has been made. One of the most telling indications of this lies in the dramatic way life expectancy has improved since independence. In 1930, for example, the life expectancy of the average Indian was only 32 years; by 1978, however, most Indians could expect to live to the age of 52. By 1995, life expectancy at birth reached 62.

Despite the all too apparent poverty and backwardness, in many other respects modern India is extremely advanced. Today's India is almost entirely self-sufficient. In 1956 all its manufactured goods and vital foodstuffs had to be imported; for many years India had to depend on huge shipments of grain from abroad. By the late 1970s, however, India had become a net exporter of grain. Since independence, India has also become one of the world's fifteen most powerful industrial nations. In addition to her own consumer goods, India produces her own cars, computers and even her own aircraft, some of which are sold abroad. She also has a film industry which is the largest in the world, churning out almost 1,000 films every year. These are watched by millions of people all over Asia and in some of the most unlikely places around the world such as Africa, the Far East and even the USA.

India's progress has been especially striking in the fields of atomic energy and space technology. In April 1975 the first Indian satellite was launched into space from a Russian rocket; appropriately enough it was named after Aryabhata, the great fifth-century mathematician and astronomer. In mid-1980 India launched its own satellite into orbit, becoming one of a select group of only seven countries to do so. India's atomic energy programme has also reached maturity: there are now five atomic power stations and the level of development places India among the first ten countries in the world. In 1974 the Indians exploded their first nuclear device in the Thar desert in Rajasthan. Until 1998 India voluntarily restricted its nuclear technology to purely peaceful purposes. However, in May 1998 the government carried out a nuclear test which was met with worldwide condemnation. The Pakistan government swiftly followed with a nuclear test of their own, raising fears of a new arms race. Both countries have subsequently announced a moratorium on any future tests.

On 14 August 1947 speaking of India's 'tryst with destiny', Nehru envisaged, 'the ending of poverty and ignorance and inequality of opportunity.'

Democracy, secularism and economic progress lay at the heart of this vision – all these conditions had to be fulfilled if India was to achieve the objectives which had been set for her. Fifty years later there is now no doubt that the maintenance of democracy and the preservation of freedom of speech has been India's greatest success. In this respect she has done better than most countries in the post-colonial world, the press has remained free, civil rights have stayed in place and the army has remained in barracks. Nehru's dream of a secular India however, is under threat, crumbling under the pressure of Hindu nationalism in northern India and Muslim extremism in Kashmir. Almost every year brings some new threat to the united non-religious state that he cherished so dearly.

The economic development that Nehru envisaged was state planned and officially regulated. Today this model has become quite unworkable and is being dismantled as fast as possible. The economy had become so controlled and over-regulated that India, which in the 1940s, 1950s and 1960s had been more industrialized than any of her South East Asian neighbours (except Japan), found herself being overtaken and left far behind in the 1970s. Economic reform and liberalization when it came in 1991 was both vitally necessary and long overdue. However, this is not to say that India's economy has not developed, it has and today it is growing at 6–7 per cent every year. Nevertheless, despite all the spectacular achievements in industry, atomic energy and space technology, very little has been done to alleviate mass poverty and improve the condition of the poor. More than half of India's population still lives below the poverty line.

Now fifty years old, modern India is still no nearer 'ending . . . poverty, ignorance and inequality'. It is here that her greatest failure lies. Educational progress for example, has been unbelievably slow and incredibly unequal. While her great neighbour China is getting close to universal literacy, half the Indian population remain illiterate. Today India is the only country in the world approaching the twenty-first century with the bulk of her people still unable to read or write. Even more ominous is the country's staggering population growth. Every year 18 million people are being added to an already huge population, by 2050 India will have 1.4–1.5 billion people. The resources that do exist are gradually being depleted all the time and the country's infrastructure is inexorably and inevitably being overwhelmed. It is this failure to control these enormous numbers which accounts for everything else – the chaotic, overcrowded cities, the lack of primary health care, the dearth of pure drinking water and adequate sanitation. Instead of the great public sector and social programmes of the 1950s and 1960s, India should have concentrated her efforts on more basic, fundamental measures, like primary education and population control. This would have resulted in far fewer numbers, more civic sense, better hygiene and a better quality of life for all.

What is clear is that India at fifty has begun a period from which she can only emerge very different from the way she is now. How long this transition will take, what form and what direction it will follow only time can tell. When Nehru died in 1964, four lines of poetry by Robert Frost were found on his table:

> The woods are lovely, dark and deep,
> But I have promises to keep,
> And miles to go before I sleep,
> And miles to go before I sleep.

Today these lines seem as appropriate for India at fifty as they must have seemed to Nehru.

India faces the next fifty years with many of its problems – poverty, illiteracy, and communal violence – still endemic. Funds to alleviate these crises are even scarcer after India's costly decision to test a nuclear weapon at Pokhara in May 1998, which was quickly followed by Pakistan's own nuclear tests. India's government, led by the Hindu nationalist BJP, claimed that going nuclear would make India a world power. But the international response was not one of new respect or admiration, and the harsh sanctions imposed by the US and others did little to improve India's positioning.

Having abandoned the tenets of Gandhi, India faces its next fifty years struggling to find its way through the challenges of globalization and economic liberalization, an exploding population born into unmitigated poverty, and an uncertain leadership caught between the assertion of Hindu nationalism and the threat of communal violence that could wreak havoc on India's secular identity.

Chronology of Major Events

BC

2500	Indus Valley civilization; Mohenjo-Daro and Harappa
1500	Migration of the Aryans into India; origins of Hinduism
570–450	Spread of Buddhism and Jainism
563–483	Siddhartha Gautama, the Buddha
543–334	Kingdom of Magadha
540–468	Mahavira, founder of Jainism
c.500	*Mahabharata* and *Ramayana*
327	Invasion of Alexander the Great
324–184	Mauryan empire
269–232	Reign of Asoka
78 BC–AD 248	Kushan kingdom

AD

320–499	The Gupta empire
375–415	Reign of Chandragupta II
405–11	Visit of Fa-hsien
476	Birth of Aryabhata, the astronomer
606–47	Reign of Harsha Vardhana, king of Kanauj
712	Arab conquest of Sind
997–1030	Mahmud of Ghazni raids north India
1191–2	Battles of Tarain; overthrow of Rajput power
1206–1526	The Delhi sultanate
1336	Kingdom of Vijayanagar founded
1346	Bahmani sultanate founded in the Deccan
1398	Timur sacks Delhi
1440–1518	Life of Kabir
1469–1538	Guru Nanak and the rise of Sikhism
1482	Bahmani sultanate collapses, breaking up into 5 independent states
1498	Arrival of the Portuguese
1526	First battle of Panipat; beginning of the Mughal empire

1530	Death of Babur
1530–56	Reign of Humayun
1556–1605	Reign of Akbar
1565	Battle of Talikota; fall of Vijayanagar
1571–86	Building of Fatehpur Sikri
1600	Formation of the East India Company in London
1605–27	Reign of Jahangir
1628–57	Reign of Shah Jahan
1631	Building of the Taj Mahal begins
1639	Foundation of Fort St George in Madras
1658	Aurangzeb deposes Shah Jahan
1659	Rise of Shivaji; the beginnings of Maratha power
1686–7	Bijapur and Golconda conquered by Aurangzeb
1688	East India Company receives Bombay from Portugal
1707	Death of Aurangzeb
1739	Nadir Shah sacks Delhi
1748–61	Anglo–French wars
1756	Fall of Calcutta; 'Black Hole'
1757	Battle of Plassey; beginning of British supremacy in Bengal
1761	Third battle of Panipat; Maratha power destroyed by Afghans
1774–85	Warren Hastings first governor-general of India
1782–1819	Maratha wars
1828	Lord Bentinck governor-general; new policy of reform and modernization; Brahmo Samaj founded by Ram Mohan Roy
1839–48	Sikh wars
1848–56	Lord Dalhousie governor-general; peak of westernization
1857–8	Outbreak of the Indian Mutiny
1858	Government of India transferred from East India Company to the Crown
1861	Indian Civil Service (ICS) founded
1869	Opening of Suez Canal
1875	Arya Samaj founded by Swami Dayananda Sarasvati
1877	Queen Victoria proclaimed Empress of India
1885	First session of Indian National Congress
1899–1905	Lord Curzon viceroy
1900	Ramakrishna Mission founded by Vivekananda
1901	Coronation Durbar for Edward VII in Delhi
1905	Partition of Bengal
1906	Formation of the Muslim League
1911	George V holds Delhi Durbar; capital transferred to Delhi from Calcutta

1913	Rabindranath Tagore awarded Nobel Prize for Literature
1914–18	First World War
1915	Mahatma Gandhi returns to India
1919	Amritsar massacre
1921	Opening of the Victoria Memorial in Calcutta
1929–30	Nehru president of Congress
1930	Gandhi's salt march
1931	Inauguration of New Delhi
1935	Government of India Act creates a central legislature; provincial government handed over to elected Indian representatives; Burma separated from India
1937	Government of India Act comes into force in April; first elections
1939–45	Second World War
1942	Congress leaders imprisoned
1945	British prime minister Attlee agrees to Indian independence
1946	'Great Calcutta killing'
1947	Lord Mountbatten viceroy; Partition; India becomes independent; new Muslim state of Pakistan created; Jawaharlal Nehru first Indian prime minster; fighting in Kashmir
1948	Assassination of Gandhi
1950	India becomes a republic within the British Commonwealth
1961	India annexes Goa
1962	Border clashes with China
1964	Death of Nehru; Shastri prime minister
1965	War with Pakistan over Kashmir
1966	Death of Shastri; Indira Gandhi becomes prime minister
1971	Indo-Pakistan war; East Pakistan becomes Republic of Bangladesh
1975	State of emergency declared
1977	Morarji Desai becomes prime minister
1980	Indira Gandhi prime minister again; Sanjay Gandhi killed in plane crash
1984	Storming of Golden Temple at Amritsar; Indira Gandhi assassinated; Rajiv Gandhi becomes prime minister; Bhopal gas leak kills over 2,000
1989	V.P. Singh becomes prime minister
1991	Rajiv Gandhi assassinated; P.V. Narasimha Rao prime minister
1997	Fiftieth Anniversary of Independence
1998	Hindu nationalist Bharatiya Janata Party (BJP) comes to power: India test nuclear bomb at Pokhara.

Governors-General and Viceroys

Governors of Bengal

Robert Lord Clive *1765–1767*
Henry Verelst *1767–1769*
John Cartier *1769–1773*

Governors-General of Bengal

Warren Hastings *1774–1785*
Sir John Macpherson *1785–1786*
Lord Cornwallis *1786–1793*
Sir John Shore *1793–1796*
Lord Cornwallis *1796–1798*
Sir Alured Clarke *1798*
Lord Wellesley *1798–1805*
Lord Cornwallis *1805*
Sir George Barlow *1805–1807*
Lord Minto *1807–1813*
Lord Hastings *1813–1823*
Hon. John Adam *1823*
Lord Amherst *1823–1828*
Lord Butterworth Bailey *1828*
Lord William Bentinck *1828–1835*

Governors-General of India (from 1833)

Lord Metcalf *1835–1836*
Lord Auckland *1836–1842*
Lord Ellenborogh *1842–1844*

Sir Henry Hardinge *1844–1848*
Lord Dalhousie *1848–1856*
Lord Canning *1856–1862*

Viceroys (from 1858)

Lord Elgin *1862–1864*
Sir John Lawrence *1864–1869*
Lord Mayo *1869–1872*
Lord Northbrook *1872–1876*
Lord Lytton *1876–1880*
Lord Ripon *1880–1884*
Lord Dufferin *1884–1888*
Lord Lansdowne *1888–1894*
Lord Elgin *1894–1899*
Lord Curzon *1899–1905*
Lord Minto *1905–1910*
Lord Hardinge *1910–1916*
Lord Chelmsford *1916–1921*
Lord Reading *1921–1926*
Lord Irwin *1926–1931*
Lord Willingdon *1931–1936*
Lord Linlithgow *1936–1943*
Lord Wavell *1943–1947*
Lord Mountbatten *1947–1948*

Heads of State since Independence

Governors-General

Lord Mountbatten *1947–1948*
C. Rajagopalachari *1948–1950*

Presidents

Rajendra Prasad *1950–1962*
S. Radhakrishnan *1962–1967*
Zakir Hussain *1967–1969*
V. V. Giri *1969–1974*
Fakhruddin Ali Ahmed *1974–1977*
Neelam Sanjiva Reddy *1977–1982*
Giani Zail Singh *1982–1987*
R. Venkataraman *1987–1992*
Shankar Dayal Sharma *1992–1997*
K. R. Narayanan *1997–*

Prime Ministers

Jawaharlal Nehru (Congress) *1947–1964*
Lal Bahadur Shastri (Congress) *1964–1966*
Indira Gandhi (Congress) *1966–1977*
Morarji Desai (Janata) *1977–1979*
Charan Singh (Janata) *1979–1980*
Indira Gandhi (Congress I) *1980–1984*
Rajiv Gandhi (Congress I) *1984–1989*
V. P. Singh (Janata) *1989–1990*
Chandra Shekhar (Janata) *1990–1991*
P. V. Narasimha Rao (Congress I) *1991–1996*
Atal Behari Vajpayee (BJP) *1996*
H. D. Deve Gowda (United Front) *1996–1997*
I. K. Gujral (United Front) *1997–1998*
Atal Behari Vajpayee (BJP) *1998–*

Historical Gazetteer

Numbers in bold refer to main text

Abu (Rajasthan) The Jain temples of Mt Abu are located at Dilwara, a hill station rising some 3,000 feet above the surrounding plains. Four temples, arranged in a cross, comprise an important pilgrimage site of great beauty, surpassed only by the Taj Mahal. In addition to its attractive landscape Abu had a strategic value for the chiefs of the Paramara, the local Rajput clan, who used it as their headquarters from the 12th to the 13th centuries. Near the water tank called 'Gomukh' (cow's head) is a 14th-century shrine dedicated to Vaishishtha, a Vedic bard and one of the chief protagonists in the Rig Veda. A few miles away is the plateau of Guru Sikhar, about 5,700 feet high, which contains a small but important Jain shrine. **94**

Agra (Uttar Pradesh) Spread conveniently around the most beautiful building in the world, the Taj Mahal, the city of Agra houses some of the greatest architectural masterpieces. Most are confined within the awesome walls of the Red Fort which dominates the whole city. Once the imperial capital of the Mughals, it bore witness to countless dramas, and many emperors and empresses are buried here.

In addition to the main attractions, there are several other buildings which should not be missed, including the Diwan-i-Khas, the Diwan-i-Am, the Jehangiri Mahal, the Khas Mahal, the Nagina Mosque and the Mina Masjid, the emperor's private mosque. Dotted with gardens and fountains mimicking the Islamic paradise, the city represents the zenith of Mughal authority and achievement. **103, 110, 115, 128, 130–2, 135, 139, 160**

Ahmedabad (Gujarat) Today Ahmedabad is a large industrial centre and the chief city of the state of Gujarat. The old city, however, dates back to the first half of the 15th century when it was the capital of the sultans of Gujarat. Founded in 1411, it remained the focus of an independent state for almost 150 years, and during the 17th century it was renowned as one of the greatest cities in India. The object of any visit should be the old part of the town, whose narrow streets are full of interesting buildings and historic monuments. **102, 119, 127**

Ahmednagar (Maharashtra) Founded in 1494, Ahmednagar was the capital of the Nizam Shahi dynasty. The first sultan was Ahmad Nizam Shah, who established a powerful state which lasted until the middle of the 17th century, when it was conquered by the Mughals. Along with its Fort (1559), the city has a number of impressive and very well-preserved buildings, foremost amongst them being the Tomb of Nizam Shah himself, the Qasim Mosque (1500–8), and the elegantly carved Damadi Mosque (1567–8). **107, 128–130**

Ajanta (Maharashtra) The Ajanta Caves form a complex of some 27 Buddhist and Hindu temples carved out over a period of 600 years. The earliest dates back to the 2nd century AD but the majority belong to the 5th century. These later constructions, *chaitya* halls and monasteries, contain commanding sculptures and vivacious frescos in the Gupta tradition. **86**

Amaravati (Andhra Pradesh) Founded sometime in the 3rd–2nd centuries BC, Amaravati flourished under the Satavahanas (1st–4th centuries AD) when the Great Stupa was built. All that is visible of what was one of the greatest of all Buddhist monuments is a ruined earthen mound surrounded by a circular pathway. **73**

Amritsar (Punjab) The holy city of Amritsar was founded in 1579 by Ram Das, the fourth Guru of the Sikhs. The principal monuments in the city are all closely associated with Sikhism and many of them belong to the reign of Ranjit Singh, the Sikh ruler of the Punjab. Pride of place goes to the Golden Temple, the Sikh holy shrine, which in recent years has witnessed some of the bloodiest scenes in modern Indian history. Also near by is the garden of Jallianwala Bagh, the scene of the notorious Amritsar massacre. **188–9, 232**

Ayodhya (Uttar Pradesh) Celebrated in the *Ramayana* as the capital of Rama and one of the holiest places of Hinduism. The opening chapters of the *Ramayana* recount the magnificence of the city and the glories of its monarch. Its best-known site is the Rama Janan Bhumi, reputed to be the birthplace of Rama. Until very recently this site was occupied by a mosque, the Babri Mosque; in 1992 it was pulled down by Hindu extremists. **45–6, 49**

Barabar (Bihar) The Barabar Caves are a group of seven Jain temples cut out of solid granite. The earliest date from the middle of 3rd century BC and one of them is dedicated to the Emperor Asoka himself. **67–8**

Baroda (Gujarat) Renamed Vadodara, this city was formerly the capital of the Gaekwads of Baroda. The Gaekwads erected a number of interesting and rather splendid buildings and there is a great deal for the visitor to see – the Museum and Art Gallery (1894), the Maharaja Fateh Singh Museum, which contains a number of European masters as well as Chinese and Japanese exhibits, the Makarpura Palace, an Italian Renaissance-style extravaganza set in some beautiful gardens, and the extraordinary Lakshmi Vilas Palace which should not be missed. **145, 167, 170, 223**

Benares (Uttar Pradesh) Also called Varanasi, Benares is the most sacred of all Hindu cities. Known to Hindus as Kashi, the City of Light, and located on a bend of the River Ganges, it has attracted pilgrims from all over the Hindu world for over 2,500 years. The founders of Buddhism and Jainism, and the poets Kabir and Tulsi Das, are all associated with Benares. No temple predates the 17th century, due partly to renovation by the Hindus and partly to the depredations of the Muslims. As befits a holy city it is crammed with temples, the most important being the Vishvanatha Temple dedicated to Shiva, the presiding deity of Benares. The present construction, rebuilt many times over the centuries, belongs to a rather modern style (18th century), with clustered, pointed spires and columns, the beams and walls being decorated with Hindu iconography.

The primacy of Benares as a holy city is founded on the purifying power of the waters of the Ganges and this is amply demonstrated by the crush of pilgrims on the stepped banks (ghats) which form the city's river frontage. The river is deified as the Goddess Ganga who sprang from the matted tresses of Shiva the Ascetic to nourish the Earth; its waters have the power to cleanse the soul of sin and liberate it from the laws of Karma. The 11 main ghats, by means of which the devout reach the holy waters, commemorate important aspects of Hinduism. Yama, the Lord of the Underworld, grants audience at the Mir Ghat, where the dead are cremated and their ashes consigned to the waters of Mother Ganga. The Dashashvamedha Ghat is popular among early-morning bathers and is revered as the site where Divodasa, chief of the

Aryans of the Rig Veda, received a signal favour from the God Brahma. **105, 136, 166**

Bhaja (Maharashtra)   The rock-cut monasteries of Bhaja are some of the earliest examples of Buddhist art in the Deccan. There are at least 20 caves, all of which date from the 2nd century BC. **71–2**

Bharhut (Madhya Pradesh)   Location of a famous 2nd-century BC stupa whose artefacts have been removed to the Indian Museum in Calcutta and the Allahabad Museum. **71**

Bhubaneshwar (Orissa)   The complex of Hindu temples of Bhubaneshwar dates mainly from the 7th–11th centuries and is the most important example of the architectural style native to Orissa. The climax of the whole enterprise is the Lingaraja Temple, stylistically the most evolved, dominated by a curvilinear towered sanctuary and ornamented with numerous foliated arches and lions rampant. All the main phases of the Orissan style are represented: the sandstone sculptures of the early phase are among the finest examples of Hindu art; in the middle phase the Orissan craftsman exercised his ingenuity in filling the innumerable niches with graceful figures; while in the last he occupied himself with more abstract architectural features. Everywhere the Hindu genius for the delicately poised human form is celebrated. **94**

Bidar (Karnataka)   About 80 miles north-west of Hyderabad, Bidar, once the capital of the Bahmani dynasty, is a fascinating medieval town with a number of striking monuments. The most remarkable is its Fort: built between 1426–32, it is one of the greatest works of military architecture in southern India. Even though Bidar is not on the regular tourist track it is well worth the visit just to see the fort alone. **107**

Bijapur (Karnataka)   Once the centre of one of the most powerful Muslim kingdoms in southern India, Bijapur was established in 1490 by Yusuf Adil Shah, who founded the Adil Shahi dynasty. This lasted until the end of the 17th century when the city was finally conquered by Aurangzeb. The Adil Shahi sultans erected a whole host of remarkable public buildings, many of which are still standing today. The largest and most conspicuous is the Gol Gumbaz (1659), intended as the architectural masterpiece of the dynasty. Together with the all-encompassing city walls (6¼ miles in circumference) it forms one of the unmissable sights of Bijapur. It is worth bearing in mind that the modern city is only the central core of what was once a much larger settlement, with a perimeter of almost 30 miles. **107, 129, 130, 137–8**

Bodhgaya (Bihar)   One of the holiest of all Buddhist sites, Bodhgaya is the scene of the Buddha's enlightenment. The principlal monument is the Mahabodhi Temple, which dates back to the 7th century when its proportions were described by the Chinese traveller Hsieun Tang. It is surrounded by votive stupas and shrines, and near by there is an excellent archaeological museum containing several important pieces from the Shunga and Gupta periods. **50–1**

Bombay (Maharashtra)   has the largest collection of Victorian Gothic buildings outside England, mostly constructed from the local honey-coloured stone. These include many of the buildings vital to the city's life – the Town Hall (1820–3), the Secretariat (1874), the Council Hall (1870–6) and Elphinstone College (1890). The Five Parsee Towers of Silence is one of the few non-British-influenced buildings in the city; here the Parsees expose their dead to the elements and the vultures, a rather incongruous sight in this most sophisticated of all India's cities. **11, 148–9, 226**

Calcutta (West Bengal)   Founded by the British in 1690, the great city of Calcutta remained pre-eminent until the construction of New Delhi in the early part of the 20th century. In its heyday a city of palaces, it has a fine and distinctly British architectural heritage, and boasts a number of imitations of well-known European buildings. St John's Church and St Andrew's Kirk are modelled on St Martin-in-the-Fields in London, the High Court on the Cloth Hall at Ypres, and the East Indian Railway Offices on the Palazzo Farnese in Rome. The General Post Office (1864–8) now stands on the site of the Black Hole of Calcutta. Among these grand, crumbling piles is the Marble Palace containing several paintings by Rubens and Joshua Reynolds. **11, 148–9, 152, 158, 174, 176**

Chitorgarh (Rajasthan)   Situated on top of a rocky hill, the hill-fort of Chitor is approached by a winding ascent, defended at intervals by seven massive gateways. Supposedly founded

Rashtrapati Bhawan, Presidential palace in New Delhi.
Formerly the Viceroy's palace

in 728 by the Rajput rulers of Mewar, it is the scene of some of the bloodiest and most historic sieges in Indian history. Located within the defences on the very top of the hill are the remains of several palaces and buildings; most of these date from the 15th and 16th centuries and are classic examples of Rajput architecture. **118–19**

Delhi (Federal Territory of Delhi) The pre-eminent city of India, it has served as a capital since legendary times when the Pandava king Yudhishthira founded Indraprastha in the wilderness. It is believed that the earliest settlements were on the site of the Purana Quila. After a period of neglect it re-emerged as an important city under the Rajputs (*c.* 1060) when the citadel of Lalkot was built. Thereafter with the coming of the Muslims Delhi's importance never waned.

According to tradition there are seven cities of Delhi which have grown up along the Yamuna river. The second city of Siri was founded by the Khalji sultans in 1304, while the third at Tughluqabad (1321–5) was established by their successors, the Tughluqs, who also founded the fourth of Jahanpanath and the fifth of Firuzabad. The sixth, Shergarh, was founded around the Purana Quila and on the ruins of Firuzabad. In 1638 the construction of Shahjahanabad constituted the last phase of Delhi's development before the British, who built New Delhi. All its great monuments before the British belong to one or the other of Delhi's traditional cities.

The eighth and most important city is New Delhi. Conceived in 1911, it was inaugurated in 1931 and became the new capital. It is a catalogue of imperial achievement, from the All India War Memorial in the east to the President's House in the west, from Connaught Place in the north to the National Museum in the south. Since the days of empire this whole area has been consecrated solely to the functions of government, ceremony and diplomacy. **10, 102, 132–4, 144, 156, 166, 179, 199**

Ellora (Maharashtra) contains a number of Buddhist, Jain and Hindu cave temples which stretch for more than 1½ miles along a rocky escarpment and date from the late Gupta times to the 9th century AD. The most eye-catching works belong to the 7th to 9th centuries. The 7th-century Hindu group of temples is the most artistically developed of the whole complex; stylistic details point to a period when the Deccan was in a state of transition from Buddhism to orthodox Hinduism. **86**

Fatehpur Sikri (Uttar Pradesh) The ruined royal city is the crystallization of the Muslim architectural enterprise in India, its imperial vision proclaimed by pink sandstone edifices. Somewhat like a butterfly, it flourished for a brief moment during the reign of Akbar, enriched by Persian genius then abandoned. Its buildings, striking monuments every one, are too numerous to mention and any visitor is advised to spend at least a few days savouring the atmosphere of this extraordinary city.**122–3**

Goa (Federal Territory of Goa) Once the headquarters of Portugal's colonial empire, Goa is a territory of 1,429 square miles with a coastline of 65 miles along the shores of the Arabian Sea. Its historic centre is the old colonial city of Old Goa, which once rivalled Lisbon in its size and splendour. Although most of it is now in ruins, it remains a very picturesque site and is graced by several Portuguese buildings of the 16th, 17th and 18th centuries. **147**

Golconda (Andhra Pradesh) was the capital of a powerful and prosperous kingdom which came into being during the early 16th century. Its actual history dates back at least as far as the 13th century, when it was described by Marco Polo, amongst others, as a flourishing commercial centre. Most of the city's monuments however, belong to the 16th and 17th centuries when Golconda was ruled by the Qutb Shahi dynasty (1512–1687). The principal sights are the Fort itself together with all its attached buildings, and the Royal Tombs which form one of the most complete and interesting collections of Islamic tombs in the whole of India. **107**

Gwalior (Madhya Pradesh) Gwalior's most famous attraction is its great hill fortress. Supposedly constructed around 510, for most of the medieval period it was retained by a succession of Rajput dynasties. In 1232 Iltumish, Sultan of Delhi, seized the Fort, and it remained in Muslim hands until 1398 when it was recaptured by another Rajput dynasty. In 1516 it finally fell to Ibrahim Lodhi and after his death passed into the hands of the Mughal emperors. In 1755 Gwalior was seized by the Marathas and became the home of the Scindia dynasty. Contained within the Fort are several palaces, the most spectacular and historic of them the Man Mandir (1486–1516), one of the most interesting examples of Hindu architecture in India. Another sight worth seeing is the opulent 19th-century Jai Vilas Palace, home of the later Scindias; its magnificent Durbar Hall contains the largest carpet in the world, while hanging from the roof are two of the largest chandeliers. **146, 160**

Hyderabad (Andhra Pradesh) Once the seat of the fabulously wealthy Nizams, it is now the 5th-largest city in India. It was founded in 1591 by the Sultan of Golconda who allegedly named it after one of his mistresses. Since then the city has accumulated an interesting collection of palaces, mosques, libraries, colleges and museums which bear witness to its colourful and varied history. Amongst these are the elegant creations of the Qutb Shahi sultans, the vast palaces of successive Nizams and the buildings of the British. One of the most attractive parts of the town is the area occupied by the British Residency, which contains one of the finest Georgian houses in the subcontinent. **142–3, 153, 159, 206**

Indore (Madhya Pradesh) Founded around 1760, Indore was the capital of the Holkar dynasty. Although it is now an important commercial town, it still possesses several charming buildings, most of them put up during the 19th century by the ruling dynasty – the Old Palace (1811–34), the Gopal Temple (1832) and the New Palace (1894). **146**

Jaipur (Rajasthan) The model of a city of the fabulous east, Jaipur was founded in 1727 after its ruler had driven the Mughals from his realm. Since 1037 the ancient capital of the Rajputs had been the citadel of Amber. It is located at the head of a gorge whose summit is dominated by the giant Jaigarh Fort *c.* 1600. Built of pink sandstone, of outstanding architectural value, Jaipur celebrates a prophecy that its founder would be the greatest of his line. It is laid down to a strict geometrical plan, a fusion of European and Indian ideas attributed to the Rajah's celebrated architect Vidyhar Bhattacharya. To the northeast of the city is the Tiger Fort, and Jaipur itself is encompassed by huge defensive walls. The Sarhad or City Palace, displaying consummate confidence, is set in a pleasure ground appointed with fountains and flowering plants, covering the whole of the northern part of the city. Amongst Jaipur's many sights is the Rambagh Palace (*c.* 1920), designed by an Englishman, now a luxury hotel which contains an unexpected Chinese room filled with rich tapestries. **161**

Jhansi (Uttar Pradesh) The great stronghold was founded in the early 17th century. Most of it, however, dates from the middle of the 18th century when the Fort was seized and strengthened by a Maratha general. During the Indian Mutiny Jhansi was the scene of bloody fighting and it was the home of one of the leaders of the Mutiny, the Rani of Jhansi. **167, 168**

Jodhpur (Rajasthan) Founded in 1459, Jodhpur was the capital of the Rajput state of Marwar. The site dominates the whole of the Thar desert. The old city was enclosed within massive walls nearly 6 miles long and contains many excellent examples of Rajput architecture. In former times the seat of the rulers was the Meherangarh Fort, set 400 feet above the surrounding plain; it is approached by a hazardous climb, and along the route is the Jaswant Thada, the cremation grounds of the monarchs. The new city is almost a Victorian exhibit, with surprising edifices of

Victorian baroque which would not be out of place in Manchester or Liverpool. The most striking of these is the Umaid Bhavan Palace (1929–44), now a hotel of over 300 rooms.**102**

Kalinjar (Madhya Pradesh), an ancient hill shrine and fortress on the last spur of the Vindhya range, has been occupied by successive invaders of India since antiquity – it is mentioned by Ptolemy who knew it as Kanagora. The fortress is situated on a small plateau with the city at its foot; to the north is the vast expanse of the Gangetic Plain. The city itself was probably founded in the 7th century AD, while the plateau has fragments dating back to the 4th century. The history of this site constitutes a series of snap shots of the turbulent state of the peninsula at various times. Some of the greatest Muslim generals – Mahmud of Ghazni (1023), Qutb-ud-Din (1202), Humayun (1530), Sher Shah (1545) – besieged it, the last being killed in the attempt. During the Mutiny a small British garrison held it unaided and its fortifications were finally dismantled in 1866.

The only approach is from the north and is defended by seven gates carrying inscriptions in Persian or Sanskrit glorifying previous owners. All its occupants have left some memento of their sojourn – there are remains of Hindu temples, Muslim tombs and British monuments. Features characteristic of Indian civic planning, such as water tanks, are also found, the most impressive being the Bhairan Kund, cut into the solid rock, with a carving of a colossal figure above it. Here also are reminders of the Rajput wars between the Chandellas and Chauhans in 1193. **115, 118**

Kanauj (Uttar Pradesh) The centre of Harsha Vardhana's empire in the 6th century, Kanauj was one of the capital cities of India until it was completely destroyed by Muslim raids. The only remains of any real interest are to be found in the Archaeological Museum, which has a number of sculptures collected from the site. **89, 93**

Kanpur (Uttar Pradesh) Called Cawnpore by the British, Kanpur became notorious during the Indian Mutiny when the British garrison was besieged and all its members massacred. The event is marked by a number of memorial tablets and monuments which are situated in and around All Soul's Memorial Church (1862). **167**

Kapilavastu (Uttar Pradesh), the birthplace of the Buddha, has been identified with the modern town of Piprahwa. Recent excavations here have yielded a casket which is thought to have contained the relics of the Buddha himself. **49**

Khajuraho (Madhya Pradesh) served as the capital of the Chandellas, a Rajput clan which attained prominence in the 9th century. What remains is a complex of water tanks, and Hindu and Jain temples attesting to the ingenuity of local architects. These edifices are adorned with sculptures of such graceful perfection that they are counted among the masterpieces of Indian art. **94**

Konarak (Orissa) The great ruined temple of Surya, the Sun God, at

Konarak is used only once a year – in spring, when the birth of the God is celebrated; it is otherwise abandoned. Built to commemorate the victory of King Narasimha (of the Eastern Ganga dynasty, *c.* 1238–64) over the Muslims, the masterpieces of Hindu sacred art which once adorned its walls are now in the Indian Museum in Calcutta and the National Museum in Delhi. Yet enough remains *in situ* to recall its prime – finely modelled human figures, elephants, lions and mythical beasts rampant. **94**

Kurukshetra (Haryana) Celebrated in the epic *Mahabharata* as the legendary battlefield of the Pandavas and the Kauvravas. **44**

Lauriya Nandangarh (Orissa) Site of a 3rd-century BC sandstone column erected by the Mauryan emperor Asoka. **59**

Lucknow (Uttar Pradesh) Although it is fairly dilapidated today, Lucknow remains a very interesting place to visit. It is filled with Islamic and British monuments and buildings, mostly belonging to the late 18th and 19th centuries. The most important of these are the Kaisarbagh Palace (1848–50), the Great Imambara (*c.* 1780), one of the largest vaulted halls in the world, and of course the remains of the British Residency complex. **142–3, 166–7**

Madras (Tamil Nadu) The starting point for any tour is the original British settlement of Fort St George. From here Madras developed into one of the major cities of India, which until the emergence of Calcutta remained the focus of British influence in the subcontinent. The earliest ex-

ample of large-scale English town-planning in India, Madras has a fine legacy of colonial architecture. Its buildings display a wide range of influences, from the elegant classical style of the 18th century to a much more mixed Anglo-Indian style which became fashionable in the late 19th century. **147–9**

Mathura (Uttar Pradesh) Situated on the right bank of the Yamuna river, Mathura is one of Hinduism's seven holy cities, being the birthplace of Krishna, adored as an earthly incarnation of Vishnu. He is a central character in the *Mahabharata* where he oversees the mutual destruction of the lawless Aryan tribes. As the author of the Bhagavad Gita he holds an unparalleled position in Hindu worship. The whole region resonates with Krishna-lore, although no monument from his time has survived. Pilgrimage is done during the rainy season when episodes from his eventful and rather colourful life are re-enacted, both for worship, and for entertainment.

During Kushan and Gupta times Mathura was an important cultural and artistic centre and it remained a prominent city until the beginning of the 13th century when it was plundered by the Muslims. Architecturally there is very little to see as hardly anything has been preserved *in situ*. The Government Museum houses an important collection of Kushan and Gupta antiquities. **75, 85–6, 95**

Murshidabad (West Bengal) Once a leading centre of Islamic culture, since its days of glory in the 18th century Murshidabad has steadily declined in importance. It is now a small town, distinguished only by its fine architectural heritage. **143**

Mysore (Karnataka) Modern Mysore was founded in 1793 by Tipu Sultan. An elegant and spacious city, it is regarded as one of the most beautiful in India. Under the Hindu rajas who succeeded Tipu, Mysore was endowed with some splendid buildings, notably the exotic Amber Vilas Palace (1897) and the Lalitha Mahal Palace (1930), now a delightful luxury hotel. **153–4, 159**

Nagpur (Maharashtra) dates back to the 18th century, when it became the seat of the Bhonslas, a Maratha dynasty who conquered the surrounding country. Very little remains of the Palace of the Bhonslas, but their fort still dominates the town. **146, 160–1, 164–5**

Nalanda (Bihar) The monastic site of Nalanda was one of India's great centres of Buddhist learning. The remains date from the Gupta period (5th century AD) and the university is thought to have reached a peak in the 7th century – accounts of the university and its intellectual life have been left by Chinese monks who studied there. By the 12th century Buddhism was in decline and as Muslim power increased during the 13th century Nalanda was abandoned. All the sculptures discovered here are exhibited in the Archaeological Museum; this contains a variety of Buddhist sculptures, miniature shrines and architectural models. **88, 89, 97**

Panipat (Haryana) Three of the most crucial battles of modern Indian history were fought at Panipat, which is situated on the old course of the Yamuna river, 53 miles north of Delhi. **104, 110, 117, 146**

Pataliputra (Bihar) The importance of Pataliputra (Patna) dates back to the 5th/6th centuries BC when it was one of the centres of the kingdom of Magadha. From the 4th century BC it was capital of the Mauryan empire and it remained an imperial city to the end of the Gupta period. **54–6, 62–4, 66–7, 72, 76–7**

Plassey (West Bengal) The site of Colonel Robert Clive's famous victory on 23 June 1757 over the forces of the Nawab of Bengal. Owing to erosion there is very little left of the actual site itself but the spot is marked by a number of monuments. **152–3**

Pondicherry (Tamil Nadu) was bought by the French from the sultans of Bijapur in 1672. Since then it has remained the centre of French influence in India. Its story is an interesting one and it is well described in the Pondicherry Museum, whose collection documents the history of French India. **149, 151**

Pune (Maharashtra) Located in the Western Ghats at an altitude of 1,905 feet, from 1750 onwards Poona (now Pune) was the home of the Peshwas and the capital of the Maratha empire. In 1817 it was taken over by the British and developed into a hill station, eventually becoming the summer capital of the government of Bombay. As a result most of its buildings are of British rather than Maratha origin. **145**

Puri (Orissa) The presiding deity at Puri is Vishnu in the form of Jaganatha, the Lord of the World, and as such he almost ranks in sanctity with Benaras. The festival of Jaganatha, celebrated during June and July, is an especially important one for Hindus, when images of the god are paraded through the town in chariots. The sight of Jaganatha, in a 16-wheeled chariot towering 46 feet in height, frees the believer from sin. Fanatics were known to seek self-immolation beneath its wheels – thus the fearful and ruthless wheels of Jaganatha, anglicized as 'juggernaut' by unbelievers, entered the English language. Ironically, the god embodies the principle of cosmic preservation. The dominant feature of the temple, modelled on the Lingaraja Temple at Bhubaneshwar, is a curvilinear, highly-ornamented towered sanctuary, its deep niches filled with finely modelled figures.

The image of Jaganatha is unique in that it has a flat face with large glowing eyes, possibly indicating a non-Aryan origin. It was originally connected with funerary rites but subsequently adopted as the divinity of the local kings. The worship of Jaganatha has remained a royal cult and the rajah of Puri holds himself the servant of this God. **68, 94**

Ranthambor (Rajasthan)   Situated in the middle of a forested tiger reserve, the Madhopur Game Reserve, the fort of Ranthambor stands on a great rock 700 feet high. It was built in 944 by a Rajput king of the Chauhan dynasty, although only the walls and bastions dating from the 13th century have survived. These are a spectacular sight and consist of lines of encircling walls, each defended by huge gate-ways and approached only through heavily fortified defiles. **118**

Sanchi (Madhya Pradesh)   Although it has no obvious connection with the Buddha, Sanchi is one of the great Buddhist sites. It has a number of Buddhist temples, monasteries and stupas dating from the 3rd century BC to the 6th–7th centuries AD. The most notable is the stupa erected during the Shunga era: this a solid brick dome 150 feet in diameter, crowned with a triple stone umbrella. Around it is a paved processional way encircled by a stone balustrade, with four vast gateways facing the cardinal points: three of these carry vivid sculptures of elephants, human beings and other subjects depicting scenes from the Buddhist legends. **73**

Sarnath (Uttar Pradesh) is renowned as the place where the Buddha preached the sermon which marks the birth of Buddhism. An important archaeological site, it has a history of continuous occupation from the 3rd century BC to the 12th century AD. Its most imposing monument is the 5th-century Dhamekh Stupa which is believed to denote the place of the sermon. In addition to a wealth of other pieces the Archaeological Museum also contains the famous 'Lion Capital' of Asoka. **50–1, 69, 85–6**

Sasaram (Bihar) is famous for its tombs, chief amongst them being the Tomb of Sher Shah, a red-stone mausoleum which is located on the western edge of the town. Constructed between 1540 and 1545, this is an eccentric building whose five storeys rise to some 150 feet. Due to an architectural error the first stage has a different alignment to the succeeding stages. **115**

Seringapatam (Karnataka) is an island in the River Cauvery which came to prominence in 1610 when the first independent ruler of Mysore moved his capital there. In 1761 the Hindu dynasty was ousted by Haidar Ali, a Muslim general, and for the next 40 years Seringapatam was the capital of Haidar and his son Tipu Sultan. Most of the 18th-century buildings and monuments are connected with either Haidar or Tipu, and several of them are closely associated with the fierce struggle they waged against the British. After Tipu Sultan's death in 1799, the capital was removed to Mysore and most of the later constructions are the work of British soldiers and officials. **154**

Sikandra (Uttar Pradesh), 5½ miles from Agra, is the location of the Mausoleum of Akbar. The tomb itself is set inside a large garden, enclosed on all sides by high, battlemented walls which are pierced by four great gateways. **126–7**

Simla (Himachal Pradesh) Approached by one of the world's most remarkable railways, the Kalka to Simla Narrow Gauge Railway, the town is perched at an altitude of 7,084 feet. From 1833–1947 Simla acted as the summer capital of British India, and nearly all its major buildings are the products of the British Raj. Many of these works are attractions in their own right, such as the imposing and rather curious Vice-Regal Lodge (1888) where the treaty leading to Indian independence was signed. **172**

Sravana Belgola (Karnataka) Re-garded as one of the most famous Jain religious sites in southern India, it is associated with the Mauryan emperor Chandragupta. Most of the shrines and temples here, however, are of much later origin dating from the 10th to the 12th centuries AD. **56**

Srinagar (Jammu and Kashmir), 5,227 feet above sea level, is the capital of the state of Kashmir. Its name means beautiful city and during the summer it is one of the most popular holiday resorts in India. Many of the visitors who come here stay in houseboats along the shores of Lake Dal, which runs along the borders of the town. This site was also much favoured by the Mughal emperors, who laid out several beautiful gardens in the vicinity. Many of these – the Shalimar Gardens (1616), the Nishat Bagh (1632) – are still in existence today and are some of the loveliest gardens anywhere in the world. **206**

Talikota (Karnataka) is the site of the battlefield where on 23 January 1565 the armies of the empire of Vijayanagar were annihilated by the combined forces of the Muslim sultans of the Deccan. Today there exists a small town of the same name which is some 30 miles from the scene of the battle. **107**

Trichinopoly (Tamil Nadu) Little now remains of the great fortress which once dominated Trichinopoly. However, the town has been an important religious centre since the 7th century and is the home of several Hindu temples. **149**

Udaipur (Rajasthan) The celebrated city of Udaipur was founded after the sack of Chitorgarh (1567) and named after its founder, the most exalted of the Rajputs. The old city, planned around three lakes and with every comfort in mind, was nevertheless strongly fortified, with five gates punctuating its walls. Later bastions made it impregnable. Its charming streets lead away from these gates and are dotted with shrines. Most noteworthy of its buildings are the Jagdish Temple (1640) and the City Palace of The Maharana (1567) along the shore of the Pichola lake, built in a hybrid style and whose walls are a continuation of those of the city. The city's palaces, such as the Manak Mahal, the Moti Mahal and Chini-Ki-Chitra Mahal, decorated with exotic glass and tile works, bear testimony to the independent greatness of its monarchs. Several of Udaipur's palaces have been converted to hotels, of which Lake Palace Hotel is the most famous. **127**

Vijayanagar (Andhra Pradesh) Originally a religious settlement centred at Hampi on the Tungabhadra river, Vijayanagar was transformed into an impressive imperial capital under the patronage of its rulers. It enjoyed renown throughout Asia and Europe for its civic splendour, not-withstanding stout fortifications and a constant feud against the Muslims, with whom its kings contended for the control of the Deccan (14th–16th centuries). At the final defeat of its army and the cold-blooded murder of its last king, the city was abandoned and later destroyed.

Its situation had been consecrated since antiquity as the place where Rama met Hanuman and planned the famous campaign to Ceylon. In addition it possessed a strategic value, protected by hills and the river to the north against the advance of its enemies, and flat ground to the south whence the city could be provisioned from its hinterland. Thus all its important constructions were to the south of the river. The fragments which remain suggest formidable granite walls that encompassed the principal administrative and religious buildings. The suburbs were protected by a system of concentric fortifications. **102, 106–7**

Wandiwash (Tamil Nadu) Now re-named Vandivasu, this was the scene of the battle fought on 21 January 1760 between the English and the French. The English won a resounding victory which brought to an end French influence in India. **151**

Further Reading

ACKERLEY, A.J. *Hindu Holiday. An Indian Journal* (Harmondsworth, 1983)

AKBAR, M.J. *Nehru. The Making of India* (London, 1988)

ALLCHIN, B. and R. *The Birth of Indian Civilization: India and Pakistan before 500 BC* (Harmondsworth, 1968)

ALLEN, C. and DWIVEDI S. *Lives of the Indian Princes* (London, 1984)

BABUR, *Memoirs*, trans. A.S. Beveridge, 2 vols. (London, 1922)

BASHAM, A.L. *The Wonder that was India* (New York, 1967)

BERNIER, FRANÇOIS *Travels in the Moghul Empire*, trans. A.C. Constable (London, 1934)

FORSTER, E.M. *A Passage to India* (Harmondsworth, 1962); *The Hill of Devi* (Harmondsworth, 1965)

GUPTA, P. *India. The Challenge of Change* (London, 1989)

HARLE, J.C. *The Art and Architecture of the Indian Sub-Continent* (Harmondsworth, 1986)

HIRO, D. *Inside India Today* (London, 1976)

KIPLING, RUDYARD *The Jungle Book* (London, 1961); *Kim* (London, 1961); *Plain Tales from the Hills* (London, 1964)

NAIPAUL, V.S. *India. A Million Mutinies Now* (London, 1990)

NARAYAN, R.K. *The Man-Eater of Malgudi* (London, 1961); *Bachelor of Arts* (London, 1965); *The Vendor of Sweets* (Harmondsworth, 1963)

NEHRU, J. *The Discovery of India* (Calcutta, 1946)

NEWBY, E. *Slowly Down the Ganges* (London, 1966)

O'FLAHERTY, W. *Hindu Myths* (Harmondsworth, 1975)

PRAWER-JHABVALA, R. *An Experience of India* (London, 1971); *Like Birds and Like Fishes and Other Stories* (London, 1963)

RUSHDIE, S. *Midnight's Children* (London, 1981)

SINGHAL, D.P. *History of the Indian People* (London, 1983)

Index

OF RELATED INTEREST

Spectrum Guide to India

compiled and edited by Camerapix

From the Himalayas to the beaches of Trivandrum, from the deserts of Rajasthan to the jungles of Assam, India has beckoned, bewitched and bewildered for a millennia.

Land of the Hindu gods and of the Buddha, of mystics and militants, of Mughals and Sikhs, here are spectacles — landscapes and cultures, wilderness and wildlife — that fascinate and enchant.

Now *Spectrum Guide to India*, with more than 200 full-color pictures, tells you all you need to know — and more — about this ancient land and modern nation with its great architecture and its superb settings: from which maharaja's expalace to stay at, to where to buy a railway ticket, how to get a curry in Madras, and what to do during the *holi* festival.

With a detailed guide to investment in one of the world's great marketplaces, it is as comprehensive as India is colorful; as specific as India is contradictory.

❀

Travel • 5¼" x 8¼" • 364 pages
ISBN 1-56656-268-6 • paperback • $22.95 (in Canada, $30.00)
plus $4.00 shipping and handling • MA residents add 5% sales tax

Over 130 recipies featuring the best of Tamilian home cooking

A Taste of Madras
A South Indian Cookbook
by Rani Kingman

"Highly recommended: a must for cooks of Indian cuisine."

—The Bookwatch

"The food of southern India is a delight... this book is both a good introduction for those wanting to get their tongues wet and a nice addition to the cookbook library of those who've already had the pleasure of digging into masala dosais."

—The Asian Foodbookery

Washed by three seas, Madras lies along the Malabar and Coromandel coasts of South India. It is a land of surf, spice and magic, a land of coconut and tamarind, turmeric and chili, with a wealth of fish and seafood.

Rani Kingman, in the first book of its kind specifically devoted to the distinctive flavors of Tamilian cooking, shares with us her favorite recipes from Tamil Nadu—where she grew up watching her mother, aunts and grandmother at work in their kitchen—and tells us something of its rich and ancient culture, of everyday life and legend.

In addition to its extensive coverage of vegetarian dishes, this book includes chapters on fish and seafood, meat dishes, rice, breads and pancakes, sauces, pickles and relishes, savory snacks, sweets and deserts.

Beautifully illustrated with full-color photographs of the food and of the landscapes and ways of life of the people of South India, *A Taste of Madras* is an excellent introduction to this unique and healthy cuisine.

Isabel Rani Kingman was born and raised in Madras, where she studied English literature at college. She now lives in England and gives adult education classes and demonstrations in Indian cooking.

Cookbook • 8¼" x 10¼" • 160 pages • full color photos throughout
ISBN 1-56656-195-7 • hardback • $29.95 (in Canada, $41.95)
ISBN 1-56656-196-5 • paperback • $17.95 (in Canada, $24.95)
plus $4.00 shipping and handling • MA residents add 5% sales tax

Interlink's Bestselling Travel Publications

The Traveller's History Series

The Traveller's History series is designed for travellers who want more historical background on the country they are visiting than can be found in a tour guide. Each volume offers a complete and authoritative history of the country from the earliest times up to the present day. A Gazetteer cross-referenced to the main text pinpoints the historical importance of sights and towns.

Illustrated with maps and line drawings, this literate and lively series makes ideal before-you-go reading, and is just as handy tucked into suitcase or backpack.

A Traveller's History of Australia	$14.95 pb
A Traveller's History of the Caribbean	$14.95 pb
A Traveller's History of China	$14.95 pb
A Traveller's History of England	$14.95 pb
A Traveller's History of France	$14.95 pb
A Traveller's History of Greece	$14.95 pb
A Traveller's History of India	$14.95 pb
A Traveller's History of Ireland	$14.95 pb
A Traveller's History of Italy	$14.95 pb
A Traveller's History of Japan	$14.95 pb
A Traveller's History of London	$14.95 pb
A Traveller's History of North Africa	$14.95 pb
A Traveller's History of Paris	$14.95 pb
A Traveller's History of Russia	$14.95 pb
A Traveller's History of Scotland	$14.95 pb
A Traveller's History of Spain	$14.95 pb
A Traveller's History of Turkey	$14.95 pb

The Traveller's Wine Guides

Illustrated with specially commissioned photographs (wine usually seems to be made in attractive surroundings) as well as maps, the books in this series describe the wine-producing regions of each country. The authors recommend itineraries, list wineries, describe the local cuisines, suggest wine bars and restaurants, and provide a mass of practical information — much of which is not readily available elsewhere.

A Traveller's Wine Guide to France	$17.95 pb
A Traveller's Wine Guide to Germany	$17.95 pb
A Traveller's Wine Guide to Italy	$17.95 pb
A Traveller's Wine Guide to Spain	$17.95 pb

The Independent Walker Series

This unique series is designed for visitors who enjoy walking and getting off the beaten track. In addition to their value as general guides, each volume is peerless as a walker's guide, allowing travellers to see all of the great sites, enjoy the incomparable beauty of the countryside, and maintain a high level of physical fitness while travelling through the popular tourist destinations.

Each guide includes:

• Practical information on thirty-five extraordinary short walks (all planned as day hikes and are between 2 and 9 miles), including: how to get there, where to stay, trail distance, walking time, difficulty rating, explicit trail directions and a vivid general description of the trail and local sights.

• Numerous itineraries: The Grand Tour which embraces all thirty-five walks; regional itineraries; and thematic itineraries.

• One planning map for the itineraries and thirty-five detailed trail maps.

• Trail notes broken down into an easy-to-follow checklist format.

• A "Walks-at-a-Glance" section which provides capsule summaries of all the walks.

• Black and white photographs.

• Before-you-go helpful hints.

The Independent Walker's Guide to France	$14.95 pb
The Independent Walker's Guide to Great Britain	$14.95 pb
The Independent Walker's Guide to Italy	$14.95 pb
The Independent Walker's Guide to Ireland	$14.95 pb
American Walks in London	$14.95 pb

The Spectrum Guides

Each title in the series includes over 200 full-color photographs and provides a comprehensive and detailed description of the country together with all the essential data that tourists, business visitors or students are likely to require.

Spectrum Guide to India	$22.95 pb
Spectrum Guide to Jordan	$22.95 pb
Spectrum Guide to Mauritius	$19.95 pb
Spectrum Guide to Maldives	$22.95 pb
Spectrum Guide to Pakistan	$22.95 pb
Spectrum Guide to Tanzania	$22.95 pb
Spectrum Guide to Uganda	$19.95 pb
Spectrum Guide to the United Arab Emirates	$21.95 pb

The *In Focus* Guides

This new series of country guides is designed for travellers and students who want to understand the wider picture and build up an overall knowledge of a country. Each *In Focus* guide is a lively and thought-provoking introduction to the country's people, politics and culture.

Belize in Focus	$12.95 pb
Brazil in Focus	$12.95 pb
Chile in Focus	$12.95 pb
Cuba in Focus	$12.95 pb
Costa Rica in Focus	$12.95 pb
The Dominican Republic in Focus	$12.95 pb
Eastern Caribbean in Focus	$12.95 pb
Ecuador in Focus	$12.95 pb
Guatemala in Focus	$12.95 pb
Nicaragua in Focus	$12.95 pb
Peru in Focus	$12.95 pb

Available at good bookstores everywhere.
We encourage you to support your local bookseller.

To order or request our complete catalog, please call us at **1-800-238-LINK** or write to: **Interlink Publishing** 46 Crosby Street, Northampton, MA 01060 E-mail: interpg@aol.com • Website: www.interlinkbooks.com